IMPERIALISM, ART AND RESTITUTION

This book is about the repatriation, or not, of great works of art and antiquity taken during the Age of Imperialism and held today by European and American museums. The Elgin Marbles are the most famous example, but there are thousands of others. The nations of origin, supported by UNESCO, want these cultural treasures returned, while the museums unsurprisingly prefer to keep them. Public interest in the outcome runs high. In this volume prominent museum and government officials and leading scholars consider the ultimate disposition of the Elgin Marbles in the British Museum, the bust of Nefertiti in Berlin, and American Indian artifacts and human remains in American museums.

John Henry Merryman is the Sweitzer Professor of Law, Emeritus, and Affiliated Professor in the Department of Art, Emeritus, as Stanford University.

D1570538

IMPERIALISM, ART AND RESTITUTION

Edited by

JOHN HENRY MERRYMAN
Stanford University

CAMBRIDGE UNIVERSITY PRESS
Cambridge, New York, Melbourne, Madrid, Cape Town, Singapore,
São Paulo, Delhi, Dubai, Tokyo

Cambridge University Press
32 Avenue of the Americas, New York, NY 10013-2473, USA

www.cambridge.org
Information on this title: www.cambridge.org/9780521123877

First published 2006
This digitally printed version 2009

A catalog record for this publication is available from the British Library

ISBN 978-0-521-85929-5 Hardback
ISBN 978-0-521-12387-7 Paperback

CONTENTS

CONTRIBUTORS

Willard L. Boyd, Rawlings–Miller Professor of Law and President Emeritus University of Iowa and The Field Museum of Chicago, **Willard-boyd@uiowa.edu**

Michael F. Brown, Lambert Professor of Anthropology and Latin American Studies, Williams College, **Michael. F. Brown@williams.edu**

Margaret M. Bruchac, Abenaki, Repatriation Research Liaison for the Five College Repatriation Committee in the Connecticut Valley of Massachusetts, and Ph.D. candidate in anthropology at the University of Massachusetts Amherst

James Cuno, President and Director, The Art Institute of Chicago, **jcuno@artic. edu**

John O. Haley, Wiley B. Rutledge Professor of Law and Director, The Whitney R. Harris Institute for Global Legal Studies, School of Law, Washington University in St. Louis, **johaley@wulaw.wustl.edu**

Talat Halman, Turkey's First Minister of Culture, **turkedeb@bilkent.edu.tr**

John Henry Merryman, Sweitzer Professor of Law, Emeritus, and Affiliated Professor in the Department of Art, Emeritus, Stanford University, **merry@stanford.edu**

Kurt G. Siehr, M. C. L. (Ann Arbor), Dr. iur. (Hamburg), Ph.D. (Zürich), **kssiehr@compuserve.com** or **kurt.siehr@rwi.unizh.ch**

William St Clair, Fellow of Trinity College, Cambridge, **ws214@hermes.cam. ac.uk**

David Hurst Thomas, Curator, Division of Anthropology, American Museum of Natural History, **thomasd@amnh.org**

Stephen K. Urice, Director, Project for Cultural Heritage Law and Policy, Philadelphia Museum of Art, and Lecturer-in-Law at the University of Pennsylvania Law School, **urice@heritagepolicy.org**

FOREWORD

The articles collected in this volume were first presented at a conference held at the Washington University School of Law on March 26–27, 2004. The conference was the fourth in a series of annual symposia organized and sponsored by the Whitney R. Harris Institute for Global Legal Studies. The complete proceedings, including the original presentation of each article in this volume with the discussion that followed, remain available in the Institute's electronic archive of all of its principal conferences at http://law.wustl.edu/igls(Conferences/2003–2004/ ImperialismArtRestitutionConf04.html.

The topic and title of the conference – Imperialism, Art and Restitution – originated with John Henry Merryman. His intellectual vision and organizing acumen made the event possible. Without his efforts neither the conference nor this volume could have been realized. Others also share credit. First and foremost are those who participated in the symposium as principal presenters, whose contributions are collected here, as well as the moderators and discussants: Michael Cosmopoulos (University of Missouri-St. Louis), Steven Gunn (Washington University), Michael Kelly (Creighton University), Serena Stier and Pamela Trimpe (University of Iowa), Susan Rotoff and Sarantis Symeonoglou (Washington University), Frederike Seligman and Mark Weil (Washington University).

A special note of appreciation needs to be extended to the Washington University School of Art, which with the support of its Dean, Jeffrey Pike, cosponsored the event. Others whose guidance, support and various forms of assistance require mention here include Joel Seligman, currently President of the University of Rochester, whose leadership and enthusiasm have been vital to the life of the Harris Institute since its founding during his tenure as Dean of the School of Law. Whitney and Anna Harris were active participants and from inception enthusiastic supporters of the conference.

Robert Archibald, President of the Missouri Historical Society, provided useful advice. No program of this magnitude could have been successful, however, without the energy and dedication of Linda McClain, the Harris Institute's especially able conference coordinator.

I would like to extend a final word of appreciation to the editors of Cambridge University Press, who by making this volume possible have given permanence to the presentations in St. Louis, thereby enabling the ideas and intellectual contributions of the authors to reach a broader audience in both place and time.

John O. Haley

INTRODUCTION

John Henry Merryman[1]

This book is about the return, or not, of great works of art and antiquity that were taken from their sites during the Age of Imperialism[2] and are found today in Western museums. That this topic is alive and hotly contested today reminds us that old art grievances do not die; they rankle and smolder and, from time to time, conflagrate.

The Elgin Marbles[3] are the most famous example, but there are thousands of others. The Louvre and other French museums are filled with paintings and sculptures "acquired" by Napoleon's forces during his Northern and Italian campaigns and with extensive antiquities collections (including a metope, a frieze slab and assorted fragments from the Parthenon and the Code of Hammurabi). The British Museum contains much more of antiquity than the Elgin Marbles: metopes from Selinunte, great collections of Babylonian and Assyrian antiquities, Benin bronzes, and so on and on. The Nefertiti bust from Egypt, the Pergamon Altar from Turkey and the Ishtar Gate from Mesopotamia in the State Museums in Berlin; the Rosetta Stone

---

[1] My thanks to Thomas Ehrlich, and Robert Hallman, Jody Maxmin, Nora Niedzelski-Eichner, and Allen Weiner for their advice and criticisms.

[2] "Age of Imperialism" is a conventional concept without sharp edges. In this book, with its emphasis on art, the Age of Imperialism extends from the Roman sack of Veii in 396 B.C., through Napoléon's Northern, Italian and Egyptian campaigns and the U.S. suppression of American Indian cultures to the fall of the Third Reich at the end of World War II. As this is written the world is still struggling to deal effectively with the consequences of the Nazis' enormous art-looting program, which created a major set of new grievances, many of which, despite international conferences, interested scholarship, national legislation and private litigation, remain uncorrected.

[3] I use *Elgin Marbles* to refer to the works taken from the Acropolis of Athens by Lord Elgin and now held by the British Museum, in order to distinguish them from the rest of the Parthenon Marbles, nearly all of which remain in Athens.

from Egypt in the British Museum; Schliemann's Trojan and Mycenean treasures, formerly in Berlin and now in the Pushkin Museum in Moscow; the art and antiquities in the Staatlichen Kunstsammlungen in Munich; the extensive collections in the Metropolitan, Brooklyn, Boston and Cleveland museums, the Art Institute of Chicago and the Asian Art Museum of San Francisco; relics of the great cultures of South and Southeast Asia; vast collections of art from the peoples of Africa, the Pacific Islands and the Americas in many of the same museums – the list is very long.

The museums presently holding such objects strongly prefer to keep them, while nations of origin typically want them returned. Since the end of World War II, much of the public discourse on the question has strongly favored the source nations. A Director of United Nations Educational Scientific, and Cultural Organization (UNESCO) has published an impassioned appeal for return.[4] A result-oriented UNESCO committee, the Intergovernmental Committee for Promoting the Return of Cultural Property to Its Countries of Origin or Its Restitution in Case of Illicit Appropriation (UNESCOICPRCP-CORCIA, for short), provides a forum for the introduction of requests for return and for mediation of differences.[5]

During the same post–World War II period, the museums' side of the discourse has been scarcely audible, and the question whether there might be good reasons why museums should retain cultural objects, rather than return them to states of origin, has received comparatively little attention in public discussions about displaced art and antiquities.[6] In 2003, however, a joint statement released by eighteen major museums in the United States

[4]   Amadou-Mahtar M'Bow, "A Plea for the Return of Irreplaceable Cultural Heritage to Those Who Created It," 31 *Museum*, 58 (1979).
[5]   The committee meets biennially. An examination of its recent reports indicates that only two cases have been formally brought to the committee: one a 1984 request by Greece for the return of the Elgin Marbles from the United Kingdom and the other a 1986 request by Turkey for return of the Boguzkoy Sphinx from the Federal Republic of Germany. Both requests have been discussion agenda items at subsequent committee meetings, but there is little evidence of action occurring between meetings. The related International Fund for the Return of Cultural Property to Its Countries of Origin or Its Restitution in Case of Illicit Appropriation, which relies on voluntary contributions by member nations, appears to remain unfunded.
[6]   For example, in a book-length treatment of the topic by Jeanette Greenfield, *The Return of Cultural Treasures* (2d ed. Cambridge, 1996), the author discusses return of a wide variety of displaced objects without any significant consideration of retention as an alternative for any of them. See also the symposium on "Return and Restitution of Cultural Property," in 31, no. 1, of *Museum*, published by UNESCO, which displays a similar bias.

and Europe entered the discourse and made consideration of museums' claims for retention less easy to ignore.[7]

A major difficulty in discussing proposals for return is that the topic lacks definition and structure. A history of art imperialism has yet to be written. The bases for retention or return of artworks have yet to be clarified and refined. There is little agreement on the terms of discourse. Much of the debate is carried on at a level of abstraction and generality that washes over important factual and logical distinctions. No thoughtful person would seriously argue that everything should be returned or that everything should be retained, but there is little agreement on the criteria for deciding whether a particular object presently in the collection of a certain museum should be returned or kept, or whether some other disposition of the object is desirable. The dialog is accordingly more often one of assertions than reasons. This book is an effort to move the discussion to a more fruitful level. We begin with history.

ART IMPERIALISM: A ROUGH MAP

This is a brief and sketchy history of art imperialism and some of the forms it has taken, specifically aggression, opportunism, *partage* and accretion. Of these, aggression has the longest and richest history.

Aggression

The Greek myth of Jason and the Golden Fleece illustrates the aggressive acquisition paradigm. As readers will recall, King Pelias of Iolcus sent Jason and the Argonauts to Colchis, the realm of King Aeetes, to seize the Golden Fleece. By a combination of force and artifice, Jason and his band of heroes invaded Colchis, found the Golden Fleece, overcame its guardians and seized

---

[7]   *Declaration on the Importance and Value of Universal Museums*, signed by the Directors of The Art Institute of Chicago; Bavarian State Museum, Munich (Alte Pinakothek Neue Pinakothek); State Museums, Berlin; Cleveland Museum of Art; J. Paul Getty Museum, Los Angeles; Solomon R. Guggenheim Museum, New York; Los Angeles County Museum of Art; Louvre Museum, Paris; The Metropolitan Museum of Art, New York; The Museum of Fine Arts, Boston; The Museum of Modern Art, New York; Opificio delle Pietre Dure, Florence; Philadelphia Museum of Art; Prado Museum, Madrid; Rijksmuseum, Amsterdam; State Hermitage Museum, St. Petersburg; Thyssen-Bornemisza Museum, Madrid; Whitney Museum of American Art, New York, www.clevelandart.org/museum/info/CMA206_Mar7_03.pdf (last viewed May 25, 05).

and made off with it. This was an early example of aggressive acquisition of cultural property.

Aggressive art imperialism became institutionalized under the Romans, beginning with the looting of cultural property by Roman forces in the sack of Veii, "the richest and most powerful city of the Etruscan nation," in 396 B.C.[8] After the victory over Pyrrhus in 275 B.C., according to Florus,[9] "if you looked at the [victory] procession you would have seen richly adorned statues of gold and charming Tarentine painted panels." Pliny records the reproach of Metrodoros of Skepsis that "the people of Colsinii were conquered for the sake of two thousand statues."[10] Plutarch wrote that after the defeat of Mithridates, the Roman procession of L. Lucullus paraded "a large gold statue of Mithridates himself, six feet high, a long shield set with stones, twenty loads of silver vessels.[11] Pollitt records many other examples. They suggest that among the many factors that determined the Roman course of empire, the prospect of rich art loot was a significant consideration. The art was desired for itself but also for its role in political triumphalism: the practice of prominently displaying loot on the return to Rome in order to stimulate public admiration for the generals and their legions and public approval and support for the imperial enterprise. Many of these triumphal objects were displayed in the Roman Forum, which became the world's first great outdoor art museum.

The same pattern was followed in the Eastern Empire. The Hippodrome of Constantinople was ornamented with antiquities, including many that were the spoils of military victories:

Of the antiquities brought to the Hippodrome, images of victory were by far the most common. Within this general category, some monuments may be viewed as generic victory dedications, others as commemorative of military triumphs, and still others as exemplars for Hippodrome competitors. . . . *spolia* had the potential for enormous symbolic import. . . . In the case of works of art, the more ephemeral issues of civic pride and cultural identity were often at stake. This was the case, for example, with the Lysippan Herakles. From the moment of its creation, the colossal bronze was synonymous with Tarentum, becoming both the focus and the emblem of the city's pride. Its removal to Rome in the aftermath of the city's conquest was,

[8]   Livy, V, 22, 3–8, in J. J. Pollitt, *The Art of Rome c. 753* B.C.–337 A.D. (1966). This event is famous as an early example of Roman art imperialism. It also provides an irresistible opportunity (suggested by the Stanford Classics Professor Jody Maxmin) to speculate that the lamentation of the sacked Veiites might have taken the form "oy Veii."
[9]   Florus, *Epitomae* I, 13, 26–27, in Pollitt 23.
[10] Pliny, *N. H.* XXXIV, 34, in Pollitt 25.
[11] Plutarch, *Life of Lucullus*, 37, Pollitt 64.

therefore, no idle act of plunder. Fabius Maximus, the general in charge of the campaign, must have been aware that the transport of the beloved Herakles to Rome would cap the city's sense of humiliation and degradation. It was tantamount to dragging the city away in chains. Conversely, at Rome, the display of the Herakles would have proclaimed the reality of Roman expansion and the force of her dominion.[12]

The Roman style of aggressive art acquisition was revived during the Crusades. "In Venice, as in Byzantium, the parade of booty was a potent vehicle of political triumphalism."[13] The cathedral of San Marco was greatly enriched by spoils from the Fourth Crusade:

The Venetians had played a key role in the complex series of events that diverted the Fourth Crusade from its original goal in the Holy Land and that culminated in the conquest of Constantinople. Their reward was commensurate.... The resplendent adornment of the façades of the church of the city's patron saint was conceived as a triumphant declaration of the Serenissima's new status as a great power in the Mediterranean world. The link between the new decoration and the conquest of 1204 is direct and concrete, for the façades incorporate numerous spoils carried off from Constantinople. It is widely assumed that this is the manner in which many of the columns, revetment panels, and works of sculpture were acquired.... Of course, the most celebrated of all the prizes brought back from Constantinople is the team of four gilded horses.[14]

There are obvious parallels between the Golden Fleece myth, aggressive Roman art looting and its equivalent in the Crusades and Napoléon's exactions of works of art for the Musée Français (later to become the Louvre) during his first Italian Campaign in 1796–99. The planning for that extended plundering enterprise began in Paris, where "as early as October 16, 1794, the Commission temporaire des arts had appointed a subcommittee of four members to compile full information concerning works of art and science to be found in countries which the republican armies were expected to invade."[15]

---

[12]   Sarah Guberti Bassett, "The Antiquities in the Hippodrome of Constantinople," *Dumbarton Oaks Papers* no. 49, p. 89 (1991).

[13]   Anthony Cutler, "From Loot to Scholarship: Changing Modes in the Italian Response to Byzantine Artifacts," *Dumbarton Oaks Papers* no. 49, p. 238 (1995).

[14]   Michael Jacoff, *The Horses of San Marco & the Quadriga of the Lord* 3–5 (1993).

[15]   Cecil Gould, *Trophy of Conquest* 41 (1965). For fuller accounts of the art confiscations of the Italian Campaign see Gould at pp. 13 ff. and Wilhelm Treue, *Art Plunder: The Fate of Works of Art in War, Revolution and Peace,* 147 ff. (Basil Creighton trans. 1960).

Accompanied by commissioners armed with these lists, Napoléon exacted huge concessions of works of art from the Italians, formalizing many of them as "reparations" in the terms of armistice treaties imposed on the losers. Thus the Duke of Modena surrendered forty-nine pictures; Parma another forty-seven; Milan twenty-five; Venice its famous bronze horses, the lion from St. Mark's, sixteen pictures and other treasures; and so it went. The list is long, and at one time Napoléon boasted, "We have stripped Italy of everything of artistic worth, with the exception of a few objects in Turin and Naples!"[16]

Although waging aggressive war and appropriating the victim's art treasures did not violate then-prevailing international law, the French plunder of Italian art excited strong feelings. Poets declaimed and intellectuals argued. Some emphasized the benefit to a larger public of mounting and publicly displaying so great a concentration of important works of art that had formerly been widely dispersed, often among private holders, and visible only to the few. Many French defended their behavior on a variety of grounds: compensation for the blood and toil of French soldiers; the cultural superiority of France, which made it only right that great art be taken and kept there; if France did not "give a home" to Italian cultural treasures they would be acquired by England or the tsar through purchase; they had been ceded to France in treaties and they were now legally French; and so on. Others referred to the French actions as those of "a band of practiced robbers" and "hordes of thieves."[17]

The British Punitive Expedition against Benin in 1897 provides another well-known example of colonialist aggression linked with plunder of art objects, in this case the famous Benin bronzes, a collection of more than a thousand brass plaques from the royal palace of the Kingdom of Benin.

---

[16]   Quoted in Treue, *Art Plunder*, p. 151.

[17]   For a discussion of the varying reactions, see Wilhelm Treue, *Art Plunder: The Fate of Works of Art in War and Unrest* (Basil Creighton trans. 1960) at 175 ff. Among the French intellectuals who opposed the plunder of Italy's art was Quatremère de Quincy, whose published protest took the form of letters addressed to Miranda, one of Napoléon's generals: Antoine Crysostome Quatremère de Quincy, *Lettres au général Miranda sur le déplacement des monuments de l'art de l'Italie* (Paris, 1796). Reproduced with an introduction and notes by Édouard Pommier (Paris, 1989). There is no evidence that Quatremère de Quincy's plea had any restraining effect on the French forces in Italy, but it may have influenced the decision of an English judge in an 1813 prize case, *The Marquis de Somerueles*, Stewart's Vice-Admiralty Reports 482 (1813). For an account of the case see Merryman, "Note on *The Marquis de Somerueles*," 5 *International Journal of Cultural Property*, 321 (1996).

They were seized by a British force and given to the British Foreign Office. Around two hundred of these were then passed on to the British Museum, while the remainder were divided among a variety of collections.[18]

Systematic art looting on a much larger scale was carried out by the Third Reich in World War II. They began with the wholesale appropriation and sale or destruction of so-called degenerate or depraved art within Germany itself. (Their working definition of degenerate art – *entartete Kunst* – was broad enough to include works by many of the best contemporary artists, works by Jewish artists, and works in Jewish collections.)[19] As the German armies invaded and occupied other nations this policy was extended, first to the property of Jews and then indiscriminately to privately and publicly held works that Nazi party officials, principally Hitler and Göring, directed to be seized and transported to Germany. Hitler's stated purpose was to establish a major art museum in Linz, Austria, to honor his mother. Göring was interested in building his own already imposing collection of valuable works.

The German art-looting operation was placed in the hands of a "special unit" (Einsatzstab) directed by another high Nazi official, Alfred Rosenberg. The Einsatzstab Reichsleiter Rosenberg, which was separate from the German military and uninhibited by the military's policy against art looting, was ruthless, voracious and efficient. The quantity of material taken and shipped to Germany was enormous. Rosenberg produced an illustrated catalog of thirty-nine volumes, with about twenty-five hundred photographs of works seized. If the entire body of loot had been photographed and cataloged it would have run to about three hundred volumes.[20]

The international law of war, which had not prohibited aggressive military art-looting campaigns like that of Napoléon in Italy in the late eighteenth century or the British Punitive Expedition in Benin in 1897, had radically changed by the time of the Nazis' enterprise. Their seizure of works of art in the occupied countries violated an international law prohibition on the confiscation of private property by aggressive occupying powers. This was, by 1939, a customary international law norm that had been formalized

[18] Nigeria, which includes the area of the Kingdom of Benin, bought back about 50 bronzes from the British Museum between the 1950s and 1970s and has repeatedly called for the return of the remainder.
[19] For discussions of the "degenerate art" episode see Stephanie Barron, *"Degenerate Art": The Fate of the Avant-Garde in Nazi Germany* (New York, 1991); Jonathan Petropoulos, *Art as Politics in the Third Reich* (Chapel Hill, N.C., 1996), pp. 51 ff.
[20] The story is told at length by Lynn H. Nicholas in *The Rape of Europa* (1994).

in Art. 46 of the 1907 Hague Convention (Hague IV) on the Laws of War and in the Kellogg-Briand Pact of 1928,[21] to both of which Germany was a party.

At Nuremberg, the German wars of aggression were characterized as "crimes against peace" and art seizures in the occupied countries as "war crimes." Rosenberg was charged at Nuremberg with "the looting and destruction of works of art." He was found guilty of this "war crime," as well as "crimes against peace" and "crimes against humanity," and was hanged. Rosenberg's fate symbolizes the end of an era – a very long era – during which aggressive art looting was often deplored but was not considered a violation of international law.

Opportunism

The Elgin Marbles were acquired not by aggression but by what might be called opportunism. In preparing for his assignment as Minister to the Sub-lime Porte, Elgin originally intended only to take back to Britain drawings and molds of Classical Greek antiquities, and he enlisted artists and tech-nicians to go to Athens to carry out this plan. The possibility of actually acquiring such works themselves arose after he arrived in Constantinople. The British defeat of Napoléon's forces in Egypt was a significant contribut-ing cause. The story is told in William St Clair's excellent book[22] and is sup-plemented in his chapter in this volume. The debate about the legality and morality of the removals continues, and there are more or less respectable arguments on all sides.[23] The separate question of whether the Marbles

---

21   The Treaty Providing for the Renunciation of War as an Instrument of National Policy of August 27, 1928, generally referred to as the Kellogg-Briand Pact, was proposed in 1927 by Aristide Briand, foreign minister of France, as a treaty between the United States and France outlawing war between the two countries. Frank B. Kellogg, the United States Secretary of State, responded with a proposal for a general pact against war. After negotiations it was signed in Paris on August 27, 1928, by eleven states – the United States of America, Australia, Canada, Czechoslovakia, Germany, United Kingdom, India, Irish Free State, Italy, New Zealand, and South Africa. Four states added their support before it was proclaimed – Poland (in March), Belgium (in March), France (in March), and Japan (in April). Sixty-two nations ultimately signed the pact, indicating a substantial international consensus that aggressive war violated international common law.

22   William St Clair, *Lord Elgin and the Marbles*, 80ff (3rd ed., 1998).

23   My position on the legality and morality of Elgin's actions in acquiring the Marbles is set out in Merryman, "Thinking about the Elgin Marbles," 83 *Mich. L. Rev.* 1880 (1985), reprinted in John Henry Merryman, *Thinking about the Elgin Marbles: Critical Essays on Cultural Property, Art and Law* 24 (2000) (cited herein as *Critical Essays*).

should today be returned from the British Museum in London to Athens is the topic of Chapters 4 and 5, by Mr. St Clair and the writer.

Partage

The University of Chicago's Oriental Institute Museum is the most important center for the study of the ancient Near East in the United States. Its Near East collection includes 120,000 objects, most of which were excavated by the University of Chicago in the early decades of the last century. The works were acquired under an arrangement known as *partage*, by which a foreign archaeological team and the source nation would equally divide any objects found during excavations. *Partage* was long a standard practice in international archaeology, providing a significant flow of artifacts to European and American museums.

Since the midtwentieth century, as one consequence of the growth of cultural nationalism in source nations, the practice of *partage* has declined. According to Oriental Museum Director, Karen Wilson; "Very little has been added to the collection since Iraqi laws put an end to '*partage*' around 1970 and nothing of significance has been added in the last 15 years."[24] Dr. Cuno makes a plea for the resumption of partage in Chapter 1. The portrait bust of Queen Nefertiti in Berlin was acquired by *partage* by a privately financed German excavation team working in Egypt in 1912. The case is discussed in Chapters 6 and 7 by Professor Siehr and Dr. Urice.

Accretion

In the long (since 1533) and sometimes dishonorable history of America's relations with American Indian nations they have been variously treated as sovereigns whose relations with the colonists were governed by treaties, as belligerent outlaws, as pagan savages whose religion and customs should be repressed, as dependent beneficiaries of a federal trust, as anomalous foreigners who should be assimilated to white society, and currently as U.S. citizens who, by law, are entitled to large areas of self-government and cultural self-determination.

During much of that history quantities of American Indian art and artifacts, including ceremonial and religious objects, gradually but with seeming inevitability left their Indian homes and found their ways into private and

[24] Kaufman, "The Largest U.S. Collection of Antiquities Is Back on Show," *The Art Newspaper*, June 14, 2005, http://www.theartnewspaper.com/news/article.asp?idart=11378 (last viewed June 14, 2005).

museum collections. Some were acquired from their holders as ceremonial gifts or by barter or purchase on fair terms, but others were acquired in a variety of less respectable ways. Accretion of this kind has occurred elsewhere. A similar process of erosion of the store of cultural objects in the hands of colonialized peoples and accretion of such objects in the hands of the imperial powers can be observed in the histories of colonial regimes in other parts of the world and is evidenced by the collections in private and museum collections in the capitals of former empires.

With the enactment of the 1991 Native American Graves Protection and Repatriation Act (NAGPRA) the accretion of Native artifacts in non-Native museums and private collections was abruptly reversed. Hundreds of U.S. museums were required to inventory their holdings of American Indian objects and, on proper request, to return them. Thus began what may be the greatest art restitution project in history. The experience under NAGPRA reveals that the decision to return works of art to the cultures that produced them creates its own interesting problems and legitimate concerns, which are discussed by Professors Brown, Bruchac, and Thomas in Chapters 8 and 9.

PRINCIPLES

How do we, and how should we, think about questions of return? What kinds of principles should guide decisions about claims from source nations for the restitution of works of art and other cultural objects acquired during the Age of Imperialism? In the literature on restitution, one can identify appeals and recourse to principles of nationalism, legality, morality, preservation, truth and access. That list is quite possibly incomplete, and some readers may have identified others, but it includes the principles that most commonly appear in the literature concerning restitution.

Nationalism

One way of thinking about works of art and antiquities is as parts of a national cultural "patrimony" or "heritage."[25] This implies the attribution of national character to cultural objects, independently of their location or ownership,

---

[25] See Merryman, "Two Ways of Thinking about Cultural Property," 80 *American Journal of International Law* 831 (1986), reprinted in *Critical Essays* 66; id., "The Retention of Cultural Property," 21 *U.C. Davis Law Review* 477 (1988), reprinted in *Critical Essays* 122.

and legitimizes demands for their "repatriation." Source nations and their supporters frequently invoke cultural nationalism, and several UNESCO instruments give it significant legal support. A common argument for return of the Elgin Marbles to Athens, made most effectively by the dramatic actress Melina Mercouri when she was the Greek Minister of Culture, is that they belong in Greece because they are Greek.

Legality

If one thinks of cultural objects as property it is reasonable to apply property law and argue that art illegally taken or withheld from its owner should be returned. Thus art wrongly seized by the Nazis in occupied countries clearly should be returned to its legal owners. It is, however, a general principle of property law that transactions legal at the time remain legal if the law subsequently changes. As we have seen above, until the twentieth century aggressive art looting did not violate international law. If art looting in earlier centuries by the French and the Romans, among others, was legal under the then-applicable international law, it cannot now be legally claimed that the loot they acquired and still hold should be legally treated as stolen property, subject to recovery by the offended state.

Morality

Even though it may have been legal, aggressive art acquisition has long been deplored. In the words of Polybius of Athens, writing before 146 B.C.:

One may perhaps have some reason for amassing gold and silver; in fact, it would be impossible to attain universal dominion without appropriating these resources from other peoples, in order to weaken them. In the case of every other form of wealth, however, it is more glorious to leave it where it was, together with the envy it inspired, and to base our nation's glory, not on the abundance and beauty of its paintings and statues, but on its sober customs and noble sentiments. Moreover, I hope that future conquerors will learn from these thoughts not to plunder the cities subjugated by them, and not to make the misfortunes of other peoples the adornments of their own country.[26]

[26] Polybius, *History of the Roman Republic*, book IX, ch. 3, *The Spoils of Syracuse* (before 146 B.C.). The English text of this quotation is taken from Charles de Visscher, "International Protection of Works of Art and Historic Monuments," 1 U.S. Dept. Of State, *Documents & State Papers* No. 15 (1949), which itself is a translation (translator unidentified) of the passage in De Visscher's original French article.

And, as we have seen above, Napoléon's Italian art-looting campaign aroused objections in Europe, even among French intellectuals. Lord Elgin's removal of sculptures from the Acropolis was famously and effectively decried by Byron in his poetry and correspondence.[27]

It seems reasonable to argue that the moral quality of an action should be judged by the ethical standards applicable at the time and place of the action. The difficulty may lie in establishing what those ethical standards were. Quatremère de Quincy's opposition to the French seizures of Italian art was clear and his arguments were influential, but his was hardly the prevailing opinion; many French and some Italians disagreed with him.[28] The moral climate in Athens at the end of the eighteenth century is even less easily established. Athens was at that time a remote corner of the Ottoman Empire in which Eastern public and private morality prevailed and public office was a franchise. Reasonable people can differ about the proper interpretation of historical evidence for one or another view of the prevailing ethical standards in those times and places.

Cultural Property Internationalism

Another group of principles is less commonly found in discussions of return. Their basis lies in "cultural property internationalism": the idea that everyone has an interest in the preservation and enjoyment of cultural property wherever it is situated, from whatever cultural or geographic source it derives.[29] In the frequently quoted words of the 1954 Hague Convention, cultural property is "the cultural heritage of all mankind." Cultural property internationalism is the premise on which UNESCO's cultural property competence stands. It also underlies three additional principles that clearly are applicable to the restitution dialog: preservation, truth and access.[30]

[27]   The reactions to Elgin's actions in Greece are described in William St Clair, *Lord Elgin and the Marbles* 180ff. (3rd ed., 1998).

[28]   See 16, supra.

[29]   For fuller discussions of cultural property internationalism see Merryman, "Cultural Property Internationalism," 12 *International Journal of Cultural Property* 11 (2005), and Merryman, "Two Ways of Thinking about Cultural Property, supra n. 25.

[30]   Preservation (of cultural objects from destruction and damage), truth (the information and insight that can be derived from the study of objects and contexts) and accessibility (to scholars and the public for study and enjoyment). These principles can also be thought of as "object-oriented" and thus distinguished from the "nation-oriented" principles of nationalism, legality and morality. For a discussion see Merryman, "The Nation and the Object," 3 *International Journal of Cultural Property* 61 (1994), in *Critical Essays* 158.

THE PLAY OF PRINCIPLES

As readers know, and as the contents of this book demonstrate, art and antiquity world actors frequently differ in the relative importance they attach to these (and possibly other) principles. Any reasoned discussion of the proper disposition of a work of art or other cultural object necessarily involves choices among competing principles. Being human, interested parties are likely to give greater weight and partisan shades of meaning to the principles they favor.

The play of principles is accordingly various and unpredictable, with limited utility as a predictor of outcomes. Indeed, the principles may often seem, in practice, to be mere rhetorical devices, loaded terms employed in "discourses" and "narratives," bricks in the construction of arguments. Still, over time, each principle develops a growing core of shared understanding, and hence of agreed meaning.

In their application to concrete cases even agreed principles sometimes conflict and sometimes support each other. A demand for the return of a Buddhist sculpture to Afghanistan might satisfy the nationalist principle but, while the Taliban continue to exist, could cause concern for the sculpture's preservation. French retention of Italian paintings appropriated by Napoléon, or British retention of the Benin bronzes, while arguably legal, may seem to offend morality. Retention of a great work of antiquity in a "universal" museum may maximize its accessibility to scholars and to an international public while it frustrates nationalist and ownership claims of the nation of origin and limits the object's accessibility to that nation's people.

It sometimes appears that every case is fact-specific. The Elgin Marbles, the Nefertiti bust, the Rosetta Stone, the Code of Hammurabi – each of these has a character and history that seem to defy generalization. Each is likely to be treated as the object of a "case" that has to be decided on the basis of its own unique record. At other times it may seem important to minimize specific differences and historical variations and, as in NAGPRA, to dictate a broad program of return in which individual characteristics of objects are suppressed in favor of one or a few generalizations, with the details left to be worked out in practice. This book provides readers with the opportunity to consider both approaches.

As this is written, Egypt has announced a campaign for the return of objects taken during the Age of Imperialism and held today in London, Berlin,

Paris, Hildesheim, and Boston.[31] The restitution of works of art seized by
the Nazis has entered a new phase with the decision of the U.S. Supreme
Court in *Republic of Austria v. Altmann*.[32] Italy has returned the Axum
Obelisk to Ethiopia. Greece continues to seek return of the Elgin Marbles. UNESCO's Intergovernmental Committee for Promoting the Return
of Cultural Property to Its Countries of Origin or Its Restitution in Case of
Illicit Appropriation, lurks in Paris and, once awakened, may, or may not,
turn out to have been a sleeping giant. The massive program of return of
American Indian cultural objects under NAGPRA continues. Eighteen of
the greatest Western museums have produced the *Declaration on the Importance and Value of Universal Museums*, in which they strongly state their case
for retention, rather than repatriation.

It appears that strong forces are at work in the art and cultural property
world. Great changes are (or perhaps are not) under way. Read on.

---

[31] Maggie Michael, "Egypt Seeks Help in Getting Back Artifacts: Egypt Asks UNESCO
for Help in Securing Return of Rosetta Stone, Other Precious Artifacts," *The Associated Press*, July 13, 2005.

[32] *Republic of Austria v. Altmann*, 541 U.S. 677 (2004). Altmann claims six important
paintings by Gustav Klimt that were seized by the Nazis and are presently in the
Austrian National Museum in Vienna. She brought an action against Austria in the
federal district court in Los Angeles. The U.S. Supreme Court held that under a
provision of the Foreign Sovereign Immunities Act Altmann's case could proceed in
Los Angeles.

1   VIEW FROM THE UNIVERSAL MUSEUM

James Cuno

Like land trusts or centers for the preservation of endangered species, museums are entrusted with the responsibility of preserving things – in the case of museums, objects of human cultural and artistic manufacture – for all of time. And as with land trusts and centers for the preservation of endangered species, the museum's responsibility is a moral one. To preserve the cultural

I interpret *universal museum* to have same meaning as "encyclopaedic museum": a museum that aspires to building, presenting, and studying a collection of objects representative of the world's many cultures. During discussion at the Imperialism, Art and Restitution conference questions were raised about the origin and implication of the term *universal museum*. Most recently, the term was used by a group of museum directors who signed the "Declaration on the Importance and Value of Universal Museums" (eighteen museums in Europe and North America were represented by their directors, who wrote and signed the declaration in the autumn of 2003 on behalf of their museum). The declaration addressed the current movement for repatriation of objects long in museums back to the countries where they originated (the Parthenon Marbles are just one case). It included the following sentences "Calls to repatriate objects that have belonged to museum collections for many years have become an important issue for museums. Although each case has to be judged individually, we should acknowledge that museums serve not just the citizens of one nation but also the people of every nation. Museums are agents in the development of culture, whose mission is to foster knowledge by a continuous process of interpretation. Each object contributes to that process. To narrow the focus of museums whose collections are diverse and multifaceted would therefore be a disservice to all visitors."

The British Museum was not among the eighteen signatories to the declaration. Its director, Neil MacGregor, nevertheless issued a statement, which was posted on the museum's Web site as a kind of preface to the declaration. MacGregor's statement reads: "This declaration is an unprecedented statement of common value and purpose issued by the directors of some of the world's leading museums and galleries. The diminishing of collections such as these would be a great loss to the world's cultural heritage."

See www.thebritishmuseum.ac.uk/newsroom/current2003/universalmuseums.html for both the declaration and MacGregor's statement.

and artistic diversity of humankind is good, and to reduce it by the elimination of a species of cultural and artistic manufacture through negligence or
choice is bad. In the United States, the museum is given such responsibility
as a matter of trust.

The origins of such trust lay with the founding of the British Museum.
On his death in 1753, the physician and collector Sir Hans Sloane offered to
the British nation his collection of natural and artificial things.[1] As did his
French contemporaries, the *enclyopédistes* Denis Diderot and Jean le Rond
D'Alembert, Sloane held that access to the full diversity of human industry

Equally, during discussion at the conference, questions were raised about the ideological implications of the term. Some suggested it raised the specter of a kind of monotheism,
like the "universal church," and noted that only museums in Europe and North America
(i.e., in "collecting" and not "source" nations) participated. As do all such issues around
the collecting of antiquities and cultural property these days, the issue has become a
political one. Geoffrey Lewis, chair of the International Council of Museums (ICOM)
Ethics Committee, wrote an editorial opinion for *ICOM News* (no 1 2004) on this subject.
He noted, "The concept of universality is embodied at the origin of museums. As we
know them today, museums originated in the eighteenth century encyclopaedic movement of the so-called European Enlightenment.... The real purpose of the declaration
was, however, to establish a higher degree of immunity from claims for the repatriation
of objects from the collections of these museums. The presumption that a museum with
universally defined objectives may be considered exempt from such demands is specious.
The Declaration is a statement of self-interest, made by a group representing some of
the world's richest museums; they do not, as they imply, speak for the 'international
museum community'. The debate today is not about the desirability of 'universal museums' but about the ability of a people to present their cultural heritage in their own
territory."

One can disagree with Lewis's statements. To my mind, the declaration does not imply
that it speaks for the "international museum community." The only such mention of
such a community is in its opening line: "The international museum community shares
the conviction that illegal traffic in archaeological, artistic, and ethnic objects must be
firmly discouraged." Surely Lewis agrees with this statement. Equally, it must be the case
that the statement that the debate today is "about the ability of a people to present their
cultural heritage in their own territory" is a statement of self-interest by "source" nations
and those who support their claims as represented by Lewis's statement.

Lewis's statement, and other statements by Peter-Klaus Schuster, General Director,
State Museums of Berlin (in favor of the concept "universal museum"), and George
Abungu, Heritage Consultant and Former Director General of the National Museums
of Kenya (opposed), can be found together with a statement by Neil MacGregor on the
ICOM Web site (www.icom.org) under "publications."

[1] Quoted in Kim Sloan, " 'Aimed at *Universality and Belonging* to the Nation': The
     Enlightenment and the British Museum," in Kim Sloan, ed., *Enlightenment: Dis-
     covering the World in the Eighteenth Century* (London: The British Museum Press,
     2003): 14.

and natural creation would promote the polymathic ideal of discovering and understanding the whole of human knowledge and thus improve and advance the condition of our species and the world we inhabit. Drawing on the English common-law device of the trust, Sloane's collection and the responsibility for its preservation and advancement were given by Parliament to trustees, who in turn held it in trust " not only for the Inspection and Entertainment of the learned and the curious, but for the general use and benefit of the Public," and on the principle that "free Access to the said general Repository, and to the Collections therein contained, shall be given to all studious and curious persons."[2]

Public museums in the United States are similarly held in trust. Their trustees and members of professional staff are obliged to preserve and advance their collections for the benefit of the public. They are expected to disseminate learning and improve taste by encouraging refined and discriminating judgments between what is true and what is false. A prerequisite for this is access to objects representative of the world's diverse cultures. The principle that underlay the formation of the British Museum – that its collections are a force for understanding, tolerance, and the dissipation of ignorance, superstition, and prejudice[3] – underlies the purpose of U.S. museums. Any policy that inhibits the collecting – and through collecting the *preserving* – of antique works of art and cultural objects puts at risk the potential for good that collecting represents and calls into question whether such policies are the result of judicious, scholarly caution or matters of political expediency.

Since the United Nations Educational, Scientific, and Cultural Organization (UNESCO) adopted the Convention on the Means of Prohibiting and Preventing the Illicit Import, Export, and Transfer of Ownership of Cultural Property in 1970, the legality and morality of U.S. museums' collecting antiquities have been hotly debated. Too often, archaeological artifacts (antiquities, henceforth) have been confused with cultural property; the latter by definition is not limited to artifacts of antique origin and may include even ceremonies, songs, language, and other forms of cultural expression. Archaeological artifacts are scientific fact. They are what they are: things

---

[2]   From Parliament's British Museum Act of June 7, 1753, as quoted in Marjorie L. Caygill, "From Private Collection to Public Museum: The Sloane Collection at Chelsea and the British Museum in Montagu House," in R. G. W. Anderson, et al., eds., *Enlightening the British: Knowledge, Discovery and the Museum in the Eighteenth Century* (London: The British Museum Press, 2003): 19.

[3]   Keith Thomas, "Afterword," in Anderson, et al., eds., *Enlightening the British*, 186.

of ancient human manufacture. Cultural property is a political construct: what one political entity claims to be important to its identity, whether that be a modern nation or a religious or ethnic group. By including antiquities within the political construction "cultural property," national, retentionist cultural policies often claim all antiquities found beneath or on the soil of the lands within their borders as cultural property and of importance to their national identity and their citizens' collective and individual identities. This is the case, for example, for Iraqis, who are said to derive their identity in part from ancient objects found in the ground within their national borders, whether they be of Assyrian or Arab origin; or for Afghans, whether the ancient works are of Buddhist, Islamic, or Hindu origin; for Italians, whether they are of Greek, Roman, or Etruscan origin; or for Greeks, whether they were made under Athenian, Byzantine, or Ottoman rule.

Such nationalist interpretations of antiquities as cultural property, and such retentionist policies that restrict the international trade in antiquities, are counter to the principles on which museums in Britain and the United States were founded and to which they are still held accountable. The legislation passed by the U.S. Congress in 1983 implementing the UNESCO convention sought to preserve the right of U.S. museums to acquire antiquities under certain circumstances and for the benefit of U.S. citizens.[4]

Recent actions by the U.S. Department of State and the U.S. courts have further restricted the circumstances within which U.S. museums can acquire antiquities. These actions have been taken to enforce foreign nations' retentionist cultural policies and have been taken at the expense of the Enlightenment principles on which public museums in the United States were founded.

I should be clear. I am convinced of the values of the Enlightenment museum – call it the "Universal" museum, if you like – just as I am convinced of the humanist values of such recent scholars as Edward Said, who in his preface to the 2003 edition of his groundbreaking work *Orientalism* wrote that of "those of us who by force of circumstance actually live the pluri-cultural life as it entails Islam and the West" – but the same is true of those of us who live the pluricultural life as it entails any combination of cultures – "I think it is incumbent upon us to complicate and/or dismantle the reductive formulae and the abstract but potent kind of thought that leads the mind away from concrete human history and experience and into

<hr/>

[4] See James Cuno, "U.S. Art Museums and Cultural Property," *Conn. J. Int L.* (2002): 189–96.

the realms of ideological fiction, metaphysical confrontation and collective passion.... Our role is to widen the field of discussion, not set limits in accord with the prevailing authority."[5] Museums have an important role to play in this regard. Those that include works of art from multiple periods and cultures have the opportunity and obligation to present their visitors with experiences that encourage looking for connections between apparently disparate works and cultures rather than reaffirming distinctions that often are, as Said notes, the result of ideological fictions.

As Patrick Geary wrote in *The Myth of Nations: The Medieval Origins of Europe*, which explores the role the academic discipline of history has played in defining nations and substantiating their nationalist claims:

Modern history was born in the nineteenth century, conceived and developed as an instrument of European nationalism. As a tool of nationalist ideology, the history of Europe's nations was a great success, but it has turned our understanding of the past into a toxic waste dump, filled with the poison of ethnic nationalism, and the poison has seeped deep into popular consciousness. Clearing up this waste is the most daunting challenge facing historians today.[6]

And facing museums, too, I would propose. At their best, museums do not affirm but complicate and challenge the easy and dangerous reliance on such simplistic definitions. They expand rather than narrow our view of the world and the history of its – and our *common* – artistic patrimony. And as Neil MacGregor, director of the British Museum, wrote recently: "All great works of art are surely the common inheritance of humanity.... This is a truth that it is surely more important to proclaim now than ever before. In a world increasingly fractured by ethnic and religious identities, it is essential that there are places where the great creations of all civilizations can be seen together, and where the visitor can focus on what unites rather than what divides us."[7] And as Said said, "Rather than the manufactured clash of civilizations, we need to concentrate on the slow working together of cultures that overlap, borrow from each other, and live together in far more interesting ways than any abridged or inauthentic mode of understanding can allow. But for that kind of wider perception we need time and patient and

5 Edward W. Said, *Orientalism*, (London: Penguin Books, 2003): xvii–xviii.
6 Patrick Geary, *The Myth of Nations: The Medieval Origins of Europe* (Princeton: Princeton University Press, 2002).
7 Neil MacGregor, "Oi, Hands Off Our Marbles," *The Sunday Times*, Jan. 18, 2004, section 5, p. 7.

sceptical inquiry, supported by faith in communities of interpretation that are difficult to sustain in a world demanding instant action and reaction."[8]

Museums are, or should be, instruments for encouraging our skeptical inquiry into the simplistic notions of cultural identities. And national policies and laws should respect this all-important contribution by the world's museums by encouraging a licit trade in antiquities and cultural property. Increasingly, in my view, such policies and laws are doing just the opposite.

Historically, the United States government takes an internationalist position with regard to culture.[9] It presumes that exposing our citizens to works of art from the world's many cultures is in their best interest and promotes cultural understanding. For similar reasons, the United States has made few laws restricting the export of our cultural property, limiting such laws to the protection of historically, architecturally, or archaeologically significant objects on land that *is owned, controlled, or acquired* by the federal government. Even the Native American Graves Protection and Repatriation Act "vests title to cultural objects discovered on tribal lands in the individual descendant or tribe on whose tribal land the object was discovered, not in the U.S. government. Native American cultural objects found on federal land become the property not of the government but of the tribe which has the 'closest affiliation' with the object."[10]

Our government believes that citizens of other countries benefit from exposure to American works of art just as we benefit from exposure to works of art from other cultures. This is why I so forcefully disagree with the recent decision by the United States government to fund a special exhibition of American art to tour around the United States. At this time especially, when the United States is in military, political, and ideological conflict with

8   Said, *Orientalism*, xxii.
9   Compare Irvin Molotsky, "Donations May be Sought to Send U.S. Arts Abroad," *New York Times*, Nov. 29, 2000, E3 (reporting on a conference on culture and diplomacy convened at the White House by President William Clinton and Secretary of State Madeleine Albright. The purpose of the conference was to promote the establishment of an endowment in the State Department for the distribution of American culture abroad), with John Henry Merryman, "Two Ways of Thinking about Cultural Property," 80 *Am. J. Intl L.* 831, 831–32 (1986), and John Henry Merryman, "Thinking about the Elgin Marbles," 83 *Mich. L. Rev.* 1881, 1911–21 (1985) (on the "internationalist" viewpoint on cultural property issues).
10 Brief of Amici Curiae American Association of Museums et al., at 14, *United States v. Steinhardt*, 184 F.3d 131 (2d Cir. 1999) (No. 97–6319).

high-profile elements in the Islamic world, when much of that world – its glorious past and present, its historic and current internal political and religious conflicts – is almost totally unknown, and certainly too-little understood, by almost all Americans, the Bush administration should be funding and touring across the United States exhibitions of Islamic art, not American art. We Americans do not need to celebrate more our identity as Americans. We need much more to know better and come to appreciate more fully the beauty, sophistication, subtleties, and complexities of the art and culture of that part of the world in which our government, in our name, is engaged in military conflict.[11]

Efforts to restrict the international trade in cultural property have been the subject of much debate over the past thirty years. In 1970, UNESCO adopted the Convention on the Means of Prohibiting and Preventing the Illicit Import, Export, and Transfer of Ownership of Cultural Property.[12] Only in 1983 did the U.S. Congress pass legislation implementing the convention and committing U.S. museums to its principles. In debating the terms of our enacting the UNESCO convention, Congress was concerned that it might lead other countries to enact trade restrictions unilaterally. Congress wanted to make sure that U.S. interests in the international exchange of cultural property were maintained and that any restrictions on such trade were the result of multilateral and not unilateral action.[13]

The 1983 legislation provides for a federal government review of requests from countries for U.S. import restrictions on cultural property. Such

---

[11] The touring exhibition will be part of the initiative *American Masterpieces: Three Centuries of Artistic Genius*, announced on January 29, 2004, by Mrs. Laura Bush. The cost of the exhibition and accompanying education program is projected to be $15 million and would be paid for out of a requested increase of $18 million to the budget of the National Endowment for the Arts. The press release announcing the exhibition reads in part: "This ambitious three-year program will combine arts presentations with education programming to introduce Americans to the best of their cultural and artistic legacy. *American Masterpieces* will sponsor presentations of the great American works across all forms, and will reach large and small communities in all 50 states." See the press release: www.nea.gov/national/masterpieces/Press/AmericanMasterpieces1.html

[12] See 1 UNESCO, *The Protection of Movable Cultural Property: Compendium of Legislative Texts* 357–63 (1984).

[13] See Paul M. Bator, *The International Trade in Art* 94–108 (1983) for an account of the UNESCO convention's legislative history, from drafting sessions to final approval.

reviews are conducted by the President's Cultural Property Advisory Committee, which makes recommendations to the State Department, which in turn makes decisions with regard to the requests and may enter into a cultural property agreement with the requesting parties. The Cultural Property Advisory Committee is meant to be representative of U.S. interests in this matter, from archaeologists, to museums, collectors, art dealers, and other interested citizens.[14]

The Cultural Property Advisory Committee (CPAC) reviews each request and bases its recommendations on four determinations: first, that the cultural patrimony of the requesting country is in jeopardy from pillage of archaeological or ethnological materials; second, that the requesting country has taken measures for the protection of its cultural patrimony; third, that import controls by the United States with respect to designated objects or classes of objects would be of substantial benefit in deterring such pillage; and fourth, that the establishment of such import controls in the particular circumstances is consistent with the general interest of the international community in the interchange of cultural property among nations for scientific, cultural, and educational purposes.

These are very serious considerations. They are intended to allow for the international exchange of cultural property within very specific terms: when a requesting country's cultural patrimony is not in jeopardy from pillage and when import restrictions are in keeping with the interests of the international exchange of cultural property. Any recommendation to establish import controls is to be an emergency measure of only limited duration: it is meant to be a desperate action taken in a moment of crisis.

When acquiring antiquities, U.S. museums respect these principles and acknowledge that, in political terms, antiquities are considered cultural property, something I still think needs to be debated and decoupled: antiquities from cultural property. In any case, U.S. museums acknowledge other countries' interests in their cultural property and abhor the loss to knowledge that results from the pillaging of archaeological sites. Equally,

---

14 See "Proceedings of the Panel on the U.S. Enabling Legislation of the UNESCO Convention on the Means of Prohibiting and Preventing the Illicit Import, Export and Transfer of Ownership of Cultural Property," 4 *Syracuse J. Intl L. & Com.* 97–139 (1976), for the text of the legislation, and of an Association of American Law Schools' panel discussion on the enabling legislation as proposed in the U.S. House of Representatives Bill H.R. 14171, 94th Congress, 2nd Session (1976). The text of the 1983 implementing legislation regarding 19 U.S.C. 2600 can be found on http://exchanges.state.gov/education/culprop//97–446.html

and in keeping with the 1983 legislation, U.S. museums are opposed to the illicit trade in antiquities.

U.S museums practice "due diligence" when acquiring antiquities. This means, as set forth in Article 4 of the 1995 International Institute for the Unification of Private Law (UNIDROIT) Convention (of which the United States is not yet a signatory), that museums consider "the circumstances of the acquisition, including the character of the parties, the prices paid, whether the possessor consulted any reasonably accessible register of stolen cultural objects, and any relevant information and documentation which it could reasonably have obtained, and whether the possessor consulted accessible agencies or took any step that any reasonable person would have taken in the circumstances."[15]

Certain parties believe that museums should go further and not acquire antiquities without clear evidence of their archaeological circumstances (their *provenience*) and positive proof of their legal export from their country or origin. Unfortunately, there are instances when such documentation and evidence are not known at the time of acquisition. What should an art museum do then?

U.S. law permits museums to acquire antiquities unaccompanied by such evidence. Professional practice allows the same after due diligence has been performed. Museums are then obliged to preserve, exhibit, and further study the works of art in question once acquired. Such further study may uncover evidence that a work of art was taken illegally from an archaeological site or important monument and/or was illegally exported and that it belongs to another party, perhaps in its country of origin. This may result in the return of that work of art to its country of origin, something more likely to occur when a work of art is held openly in a museum's collection than when it is held in a private collection.

More and more, countries are seeking bilateral agreements with the United States that forbid the import of cultural property unless accompanied by a valid export license. Universal prohibition of import without a valid export license (or "embargo") was proposed in the original draft of the UNESCO convention ("Secretariat Draft") but was defeated.[16] In the words of Paul Bator, then Professor and Associate Dean of the Harvard Law School

---

[15] Final Act of the Diplomatic Conference for the Adoption of the Draft UNIDROIT Convention on the International Return of Stolen or Illegally Exported Cultural Objects, June 24, 1994, art. 4, 52, *UNIDROIT Proceedings and Papers* (Int l. Inst. for the Unification of Private Law).

[16] Bator, supra n. 4, at 52.

and a principal author of the U.S. legislation, "Prohibiting imports in this manner is a 'blank check' rule; it says to other countries, we will enforce your export laws *whatever* their content, without any judgment of our own whether these export rules are consistent with our substantive interests or those of the international community generally, and without any judgment of our own as to what material, political, and psychological resources should be devoted to the enforcement of the rules regulating the traffic in art"[17] The "blank check" rule is based on the presumption that responsibility for the ineffectiveness of export controls lies with art-importing countries rather than with art-exporting nations or "source countries."[18]

This could mean, however, that one could legally import into the United States cultural property, which may have been illegally exported from its country of origin. To this Bator replied:

> The fundamental general rule is clear: The fact that an art object has been illegally exported does not in itself bar it from lawful importation into the United States; illegal export does not itself render the importer (or one who took from him) in any way actionable in a U.S. court; the possession of an art object cannot be lawfully disturbed in the United States solely because it was illegally exported from another country.[19]

Still, it is against the law to import or subsequently gain possession of stolen art (National Stolen Property Act). How then should we regard foreign laws that claim all antiquities as state property and the illicit exportation of such theft (this is the case, for example, in Mexico, Guatemala, Ecuador, and Costa Rica; in Italy, private individuals can own cultural property but cannot export it)? Case law is building on this question and is far too subtle and complicated for a nonlawyer like me to understand fully. It is enough for my purposes, however, to note simply that the 1977 case of *U.S. v. McClain*[20] was different in fact and decision from the recent case of *U.S. v. Frederick Schultz.*

In the former case, the court ruled "that 'our basic standards of due process and notice preclude us from characterizing the artifacts as stolen' if they were in fact exported before 1972.'"[21] In the *Schultz* case, the court ruled in favor of the 1983 Egyptian Law 117, which declares "all antiquities are considered to be public property.... It is impermissible to own, possess

---

[17]   Id.
[18]   Id.
[19]   Id., 11.
[20]   545 F. 2d 988 (5th Cir. 1977).
[21]   Id. at 74.

or dispose of antiquities except pursuant to the conditions set forth in this law and its implementing regulations."[22] In other words, as I read it, precedent is building in favor of U.S. law's enforcing foreign retentionist cultural property – of which antiquities are all too often and too promiscuously, in my opinion, considered a part – with theft.[23]

Of course, foreign countries do not have to wait for U.S. legal precedent to build on this question. They can, as some already have done, enter into a bilateral agreement with the United States that achieves the same end.

In 2001, the President's Cultural Property Advisory Committee recommended that the United States enter into a memorandum of understanding with the government of Italy that restricts the import of stone sculpture, metal sculpture, metal vessels, metal ornaments, weapons/armor, inscribed/decorated sheet metal, ceramic sculpture, glass architectural elements and sculpture, and wall paintings dating from approximately the ninth century B.C. to approximately the fourth century A.D.; that is, virtually every kind of object produced in or imported to the land we now call Italy over twelve hundred years of recorded human history. It is hard to accept that *all* of these objects are worthy of restriction because they are important archaeologically or as cultural property, unless, of course, one believes that every found old object is by definition of archaeological value, or that every found old object is culturally important to the people who now reside within the political boundaries of the land in which it was found. And this is more or less what the U.S.-Italy memorandum of understanding does: it subsumes archaeological artefacts under the category of cultural property and it assumes that everything – or almost everything – found in Italy, or *likely* to have been found in Italy (since it will almost always be a judgment call on this point and not a matter of fact), whether it was produced there or imported there, is cultural property and thus crucial to the national identity and self-esteem of the Italian people.

---

[22] *United States of America v. Frederick Schultz*, Docket No. 02–13575 (2nd Cir 2003).

[23] As I write this, months since I delivered it as a paper, the Italian government has indicted Marion True, curator of antiquities at the J. Paul Getty Museum, on criminal charges involving the acquisition of antiquities. Captain Massimiliano Quagliarella, commander of Italy's Carabinieri that oversees archaeological theft, was quoted in the *Los Angeles Times* as saying: "We want this case to be a big deterrent. . . . It is important to stop the phenomenon of illegal excavations and illegal exportation by eliminating the demand and thus eliminating the offer" (Tracy Wilkinson and Suzanne Muchnic, "Indictment Targets Getty's Acquisitions," LATIMES.com, May 20, 2005) Ms. True is accused of criminal conspiracy to receive stolen goods and illicit receipt of archaeological items.

For example, the memorandum states that (1) "the value of cultural property, whether archaeological or ethnological in nature, is immeasurable... [and that] such items often constitute the very essence of a society and convey important information concerning a people's origin, history, and traditional setting"; (2) "these materials are of cultural significance because they derive from cultures that developed autonomously in the region of present day Italy... [and] the pillage of these materials from their context has prevented the fullest possible understanding of Italian cultural history by systematically destroying the archaeological record"; and (3) "the cultural patrimony represented by these materials is a source of identity and esteem for the modern Italian nation." In other words, as the memorandum would have it, the destruction of the archaeological record in modern day Italy is problematic not because the world has lost vital information about humanity, about the way our human ancestors lived and ornamented their lives thousands of years ago, but because without it "the fullest possible understanding of Italian cultural history" is not possible and because the lost materials are "a source of identity and esteem for the modern Italian nation." This line of reasoning runs counter to the intention of our 1983 legislation. It devalues the international exchange of archaeological artiefacts and cultural property for the benefit of the world's peoples and privileges instead the retention of cultural property (of which it determines archaeological artifacts to be but a part) by modern nation states for the benefit of local peoples.

Since delivering this paper, the government of the People's Republic of China has requested of the U.S. government import restrictions on objects including but not limited to all metal, ceramic, stone, painting and calligraphy, textiles, lacquer, bone, ivory, and horn objects from the Paleolithic period to the Qing dynasty, or nearly 2 million years of human artistic production.[24]

The request states that the pillaging and smuggling of cultural artifacts (it does not distinguish between archaeological and cultural artifacts) is rampant and destructive to Chinese and world heritage. In so doing it assumes

---

[24] See Randy Kennedy, "China's Request for Art-Import Ban Stirs Debate," *New York Times*, Apr. 1, 2005, E31. The Chinese government's request occurs at the same time as the declared intention by the China Cultural Relics Recovery Programme, funded by the China Foundation for the Development of Folklore Culture, to claim back to China from around the world what it has declared to be Chinese cultural relics. Xie Chensheng, a "senior cultural heritage preservation expert," has been quoted as saying that "the spiritual wealth [of such relics] can be shared (by the whole world), but not the ownership.... Ownership of the scattered treasures should lie with the Chinese people" ("China to Reclaim Looted, Stolen Relics," www.chinaview.cn, April 13, 2005).

that all such material was pillaged from and caused damage to archaeological sites, resulting in the loss of knowledge. The latter may not be the case, as such material, particularly easily transportable material like textiles, ceramics, painting and calligraphy, was often made for the market and has circulated in the trade since at least the Han dynasty more than two thousand years ago.

Equally, it presumes that restricting imports of such material to the United States will stop or at least significantly reduce such pillaging and smuggling. This will not be the case so long as there are markets for such material elsewhere in the world, including within the People's Republic of China. The booming trade within China for the material covered by the request is well known and has been reported widely in the world's press. Mr. Xu, an eel tycoon, is reported to be negotiating with the Ningbo government to exhibit his collection of Chinese artifacts worth an estimated 12 million Great Britain Pounds (GBP). Chen Lihua, chair of the real estate company Fu Wah International Group, has built a private museum to house her collection of furniture. The Beijing Huaye Real Estate property developer is reportedly planning to open a museum for its collection. Perhaps the best known is the Poly Museum, which opened a few years ago and has ties to the Chinese military. These domestic collections are having an effect. They are diminishing the export of Chinese cultural artifacts abroad, reversing the trend of the past century, which saw much of this material going to public and private collections in Europe and North America. But they are not diminishing the alleged pillaging and smuggling. As long as there is a market for such material somewhere, and certainly as long that market is within the borders of China, restricting the import of such material into the United States will not have the effect desired by the Chinese government's request.

The request will have one effect: it will reduce the opportunities U.S. citizens have to study carefully and frequently the art and cultural production of China, one of the world's oldest, largest, and soon once again richest and most powerful cultural, economic, and political forces. To restrict the international trade in such material is to promote nationalist retentionist cultural policies. As noted above, these hold that whatever one country claims to be its vital cultural patrimony should by rights remain within the borders of that country (a modern political entity). The irony of this with regard to China is obvious. Over millennia, "China" has increased and decreased in territorial size and enlarged and reduced the number of ethnic groups that "China" comprises. China today is very different from the "China" of most of the periods covered by the Chinese government's request. For thousands of years, China has been a particularly potent example of what anthropologists call "hybridity," or the ways that peoples in a developing society grab ideas, objects, and technologies from a more developed society and reshape them to suit their local needs.

Hybridity acknowledges the political construction of identity.[25] What is "Chinese" is what the current Chinese government claims it to be. For students and scholars, identity is much more complicated and dynamic. Edward Said has written, "every domain is linked to every other one, and . . . nothing that goes on in our world has ever been isolated and pure of any outside influence."[26] This is obvious in art museums. A nineteenth-century chair from Kenya's Swahili culture now in the Art Institute of Chicago betrays stylistic influences from India and Mamluk Egypt, as well as from Portugal or Spain, all of which were available to Swahili artists through centuries of participation in overland and maritime trade. And images of chairs like it can be found in a seventeenth-century Ethiopian Christian manuscript, also in the Art Institute, as thrones on which the Virgin sits in one illumination, King David in another, and Saint Ildephonsus of Toledo in still another. In fact, it is the power of art museums to make evident – to present as *evidence* – the interrelatedness of the world's cultures. The Isfahan Cope in the Victoria and Albert Museum is a beautiful example of a Christian vestment woven in the manner of "Islamic" textiles for a Christian, perhaps Armenian community living in the capital city of the Safavid court under Muslim rule in the early years of the seventeenth century.

Art museums in the United States and Britain are public trusts working to acquire, preserve, and present the world's artistic legacy for the public's benefit for all of time. Universal museums like the British Museum do this by emphasizing the hybridity of human culture: they offer a rich comparative context for considering the particular contributions of any one culture.

The favoring of restricting free trade in antiquities argues against the facts of hybridity and against the benefits of the universal museum. It is an argument made on two counts: that antiquities are also cultural property and thus the inalienable property of the government and people of the modern nation in which they are thought or known to have originated; and that the free trade in antiquities only encourages looting and pillaging of archaeological site and results in the loss of the knowledge derived from them.

[25]   See Michael F. Brown, *Who Owns Native Culture?* (Cambridge, MA: Harvard University Press, 2003): 5.
[26]   Said, *Orientalism*, xvii.

The latter is a serious charge. Museums abhor looting and the destruction of archaeological evidence and are opposed to the illicit trade in antiquities. But when an antiquity is offered to a museum for acquisition, the looting, if indeed there was any, has already occurred. The museum now must decide whether or not to introduce the object into its public collection, where it can be preserved, studied, enjoyed, and where its whereabouts can be made widely known. Museums are havens for objects that are already, and for whatever reason, already alienated from their original context. Museums do not alienate objects. They keep, preserve, research, and share them with the public, holding them in public trust for future generations and all of time. They transfer objects from the private to the public domain and do so in order to protect the world's cultural heritage and encourage appreciation and understanding of the world's many cultures and our common artistic heritage.

Some parties hold that works of art about whose original circumstances we do not know – whose archaeological find spot we do not know – have little value and need not then be preserved through acquisition by a museum.[27] The loss of that object, should it be damaged through movement in private ownership or lost from public view, is thus of little consequence. This is the argument against museums' acquiring unprovenienced and unprovenanced antiquities: to acquire them only encourages looting and the destruction of archaeological sites, and the loss of the so-alienated object is no loss at all since such objects are meaningless.

To be sure, as works of art, objects have value as documents of their use by a certain culture, of that culture's interest in specific decorative motifs and iconography, and/or of that culture's ability to manufacture and work the materials of which the objects are made. But even if we cannot know the specific culture that produced the objects in question, we can examine the objects for their manufacture, form, style, iconography, and ornamentation and place them in the larger context of all we know about such objects. A piece of Roman glass (identified by comparison to glass excavated from a Roman site) with a very peculiar decorative motif, or of a different size, color, or shape, tells us something about the range of Roman glass types we did not know before even if we do not know where that specific piece of glass originated. Similarly, an object with an inscription may tell us something very important about its culture even if we have no knowledge of the circumstances in which it might have been found.

---

[27] Ricardo J. Elia, "Chopping away Culture: Museums Routinely Accept Artifacts Stripped of Context by Looters," *Boston Globe*, Dec. 21, 1997, D1.

Works of ancient art have many meanings, some of them historical, others aesthetic and philosophical. How for example can one inquire into the question of beauty without examples of beauty? By definition, works of art manifest beauty. To great benefit, they can be studied for this reason alone. But works of art need not be studied to have value in our culture. They can provide pleasure, inspiration, even spiritual or emotional renewal. And, in their great variety, identifiable as Korean, Mexican, Mali, Greek, English, or Native American, they can remind us that the world is a very large and great place of which we, our culture, are an important part.

It is for all of these reasons, and on the terms that I have described, that U.S. museums acquire works of art. Acquiring, preserving, and exhibiting works of ancient art are a very great responsibility, something museums undertake with the greatest of care, always in our public's best interest, and always within the context of our nation's high regard for the international exchange of cultural property and of our profession's insistence on best practices. Whether a work of art should be repatriated or not and on what terms depend, in our country, on the U.S. court's interpretation of U.S. law and on the current state of relations between congressional intent and U.S. Customs actions, and on the state of U.S. foreign policy, more, it seems, a matter for the Department of State than for Congress, which wrote and passed the original cultural property legislation.

Recently, U.S. museums and the public they serve, as well as the fate of the ancient works of art that U.S. museums might be offered for acquisition, have suffered a serious setback.

I mentioned earlier the recent case of *U.S. v. Frederick Schultz.* As you will recall, this resulted from the arrest in 2001 of a New York antiquities dealer, Frederick Schultz, who was subsequently indicted on one count of conspiring to receive stolen Egyptian antiquities that had been transported in interstate and foreign commerce in violation of U.S. law (18 U.S.C. #371), with the underlying substantive offense a violation of the National Stolen Property Act (NSPA) (18 U.S.C. # 2315). Among Schultz's defenses was the claim that the NSPA does not apply to an object removed in violation of a national patrimony law, since such an object was not "stolen" in the commonly used sense of the word.[28] As already mentioned, Schultz was convicted on the grounds that the court interpreted the 1983 Egyptian Law 117 – which declares "all antiquities are considered to be public property ... [and thus] it is impermissible to own, possess or dispose of antiquities except pursuant

---

[28]   *United States of America v. Frederick Schultz*, Docket No. 02–13575 (2nd Cir 2003).

to the conditions set forth in this law and its implementing regulations"[29] –
as an ownership law, not an export-restriction law. In plain terms, the court
concluded that the NSPA applies to property that is stolen in violation of a
foreign patrimony law, clearing the way for U.S. law to be used to enforce
foreign laws in contradiction of the spirit and the letter of the 1983 enabling
legislation that allowed the United States to sign on to the 1970 UNESCO
convention.

In my mind, that is bad. But what is worse is that during the course of
Schultz's trial, we all learned of the extent of his relations with a British agent,
Jonathan Tokeley-Parry, and the extraordinary, dubious efforts undertaken
by them to remove the object in question from Egypt, fabricating provenance, making up collections that never existed, and contriving false export
and import papers. To the critics of museums – and worse, to the public
they serve – the trade in antiquities was seen to be inherently devious and
even criminal, implicating museums in the nefarious business of black market trading. The arguments that museums have been making for decades –
that we protect alienated objects and advance knowledge of them, that we
are committed to due diligence and abhor looting and the destruction of
archaeological sites, and that we work on behalf of the public to advance
their knowledge and appreciation of the ancient world and our historical
relations to it, and do so by building universal collections in their name – all
of these have been compromised by the accounts of this high-profile trial.

This, I fear, bodes ill for the U.S. museum community, which seeks to
comply with the mandate of its Enlightenment origins and the polymathic
ideal of discovering and understanding the whole of human knowledge and
into the bargain improving and advancing the condition of our human
species and the world we inhabit, for it allows the nationalist retentionist
cultural policies of foreign countries to maintain their parochial hold on
"their" antiquities and restricts the potential such artifacts hold for all of us
to understand our common past. These undermine the grounds for creating
a future of greater understanding and tolerance for the differences between
us that compose the rich diversity of our common cultural legacy.[30] All of
the arguments of Edward Said that I quoted at the top of this chapter, and

---

[29] Id.
[30] As I write this, the Association of Art Museum Directors (AAMD), an organization
      of North America's largest art museums, is drafting new principles for the acquisi-
      tion of art and antiquities that complement and elaborate on AAMD's *Professional
      Practices in Art Museums* (2001), taking into account recent U.S. legal and political
      developments in this area.

that are embraced as the founding principles of the universal museum – "I think it is incumbent upon us to complicate and/or dismantle the reductive formulae and the abstract but potent kind of thought that leads the mind away from concrete human history and experience and into the realms of ideological fiction, metaphysical confrontation and collective passion. . . . Our role is to widen the field of discussion, not set limits in accord with the prevailing authority" – will be poorly served by sustaining nationalist, retentionist cultural policies.

I began this chapter with the declaration that as public trusts, museums are like land trusts or centers for the preservation of endangered species, entrusted with the responsibility of preserving things – in the case of museums, objects of human cultural and artistic manufacture – for all of time. This responsibility is a moral one, dedicated to the protection and preservation of things made by and for humans for the advancement of their world.

I further declared that universal museums are dedicated to the proposition that the dissemination of knowledge and learning and the improvement of taste encourages refined and discriminating judgments between what is true and what is false, and that a prerequisite for this is access to objects representative of the world's diverse cultures: what I called a comparative cultural context, one that, in addition to focusing on the particular allure of a given object, opens a door onto the fact of cultural hybridity by which one culture engages with and influences another. In this respect, universal museums are a force for understanding and tolerance in the world, and the dissipation of ignorance, superstition, and prejudice.

I have also argued that museums are dedicated to the preservation of things already alienated from their first context. And I have argued against the proposed prohibition on museums' collecting unprovenienced or unprovenanced antiquities as a means of discouraging the destruction of archaeological sites and the loss of archaeological knowledge. I see this as sacrificing a known good – the preservation of the object at hand and the chance to consider it in light of any and all similar and related things – for the supposed good of future knowledge derived from unrelated, undisturbed archaeological sites. A moratorium on collecting in the service of preserving archaeological sites would work only if it were total and instantaneous, practiced both by public museums and by private collectors. So long as there is a market for antiquities anywhere, the market will be fed by any means. Far better that antiquities should be held publicly and preserved for all of time than that they should be subject to the exigencies of private collecting, forever changing unknown hands.

The value of universal museums is the promise of the Enlightenment and its embrace of humanistic values. I hold these values as real and ever promising. And I agree with the forceful statements of Edward Said in this regard:

My idea in *Orientalism* is to use the humanistic critique to open up the fields of struggle, to introduce a longer sequence of thought and analysis to replace the short bursts of polemical, thought-stopping fury that so imprison us in labels and antagonistic debate whose goal is a belligerent collective identity rather than an understanding and intellectual exchange ... humanism is sustained by a sense of community with other interpreters and other societies and periods: strictly speaking, therefore, there is no such thing as an isolated humanist.[31]

My view is that the modern tendency toward nationalist, retentionst cultural policies is a political gesture against the promise of humanism and the many contributions of the universal museum. To this end, and in light of resurgent nationalism around the world, I offer a modest proposal that would, I believe, serve to protect archaeological sites, preserve antiquities, and encourage tolerance and understanding of the world's many, diverse cultures.

I propose that museums and archaeologists should join forces to protect the world's artistic and cultural patrimony by opposing nationalist, retentionist cultural policies and by calling for a return of the *partage*. This was the practice, common early in the twentieth century, by which local governments shared archaeological finds with excavating parties, whatever their country of origin. Since the middle of the twentieth century, most "source" countries – those that host excavations, whether they be Greece, Turkey, Afghanistan, or Iraq – have passed legislation by which excavated objects are kept within their national borders as state property. Such laws restrict, indeed *forbid*, a licit trade in antiquities. And we know from decades of experience that restricting licit trade only creates and encourages an illicit one, and that an illicit trade only encourages looting and the destruction of archaeological evidence. *Partage* would itself be a licit trade and would serve to preserve archaeological evidence. It would assist the dispersal of archaeological artifacts around the world for the benefit of museums around the world and their publics. We see examples of this in our world's greatest museums, whether in Paris, Berlin, London, New York, Boston, or Philadelphia, which to this day preserve finds from excavations undertaken elsewhere, not for the benefit of local audiences here or there but for the benefit of all of us everywhere.

---

[31]   Said, *Orientalism*, xvii.

The exhibition of 2002, *Treasures from the Royal Tombs of Ur* from the University of Pennsylvania Museum of Archaeology and Anthropology, comprised objects excavated by the University of Philadelphia and the British Museum eighty years ago in what is now Iraq and acquired through *partage*.[32] What would the fate of those objects have been had they stayed in Iraq? It is hard to know. But we do know that for much of the past quarter-century they would have been inaccessible to most of the world and that most of the world would not have the chance to learn more from them or better appreciate their beauty and sophistication or the extraordinary achievement of their ancient makers. Today they likely would be lost altogether, destroyed or damaged, victims of the bomb blasts and chaotic circumstances of war.

This would likely also have been the fate of many of the great objects in the University of Chicago's Oriental Institute Museum, to which, as its director remarked in 2005, very little has been added since Iraqi laws put an end to *partage* around 1970. If only *partage* were still in effect, archaeological knowledge would be advanced, excavated objects would be shared with the world, and fewer objects would be subject to damage, destruction, and looting. As we have learned recently in Iraq and Kabul, archaeological objects and excavation sites are not protected by nationalist, retentionist policies. All too often, they are put at risk.

Antiquities are not one nation's cultural property. They are among the greatest contributions to our common, human heritage, and we should all work together to preserve them for all of time, to be studied and enjoyed by everyone everywhere. Only internationalist cultural policies serve this purpose. Nationalist, retentionist policies work against it. This, at least, is the view from the universal museum as I see it.

APPENDIX I

DECLARATION ON THE IMPORTANCE AND VALUE
OF UNIVERSAL MUSEUMS

The international museum community shares the conviction that illegal traffic in archaeological, artistic, and ethnic objects must be firmly discouraged. We should, however, recognize that objects acquired in earlier times must be viewed in the light of different sensitivities and values, reflective of that earlier era. The objects and monumental works that were installed decades and

---

[32] Lee Horne, *et al.*, *Treasures from the Royal Tombs of Ur*, (Philadelphia; University of Pennsylvania Museum of Art, 1998).

even centuries ago in museums throughout Europe and America were acquired under conditions that are not comparable with current ones.

Over time, objects so acquired – whether by purchase, gift, or partage – have become part of the museums that have cared for them, and by extension part of the heritage of the nations which house them. Today we are especially sensitive to the subject of a work's original context, but we should not lose sight of the fact that museums too provide a valid and valuable context for objects that were long ago displaced from their original source.

The universal admiration for ancient civilizations would not be so deeply established today were it not for the influence exercised by the artifacts of these cultures, widely available to an international public in major museums. Indeed, the sculpture of classical Greece, to take but one example, is an excellent illustration of this point and of the importance of public collecting. The centuries-long history of appreciation of Greek art began in antiquity, was renewed in Renaissance Italy, and subsequently spread through the rest of Europe and to the Americas. Its accession into the collections of public museums throughout the world marked the significance of Greek sculpture for mankind as a whole and its enduring value for the contemporary world. Moreover, the distinctly Greek aesthetic of these works appears all the more strongly as the result of their being seen and studied in direct proximity to products of other great civilizations.

Calls to repatriate objects that have belonged to museum collections for many years have become an important issue for museums. Although each case has to be judged individually, we should acknowledge that museums serve not just the citizens of one nation but the people of every nation. Museums are agents in the development of culture, whose mission is to foster knowledge by a continuous process of reinterpretation. Each object contributes to that process. To narrow the focus of museums whose collections are diverse and multifaceted would therefore be a disservice to all visitors.

Signed by the Directors of:

The Art Institute of Chicago

Bavarian State Museum, Munich (Alte Pinakothek, Neue Pinakothek)

State Museums, Berlin

Cleveland Museum of Art

J. Paul Getty Museum, Los Angeles

Solomon R. Guggenheim Museum, New York

Los Angeles County Museum of Art

Louvre Museum, Paris

The Metropolitan Museum of Art, New York

The Museum of Fine Arts, Boston

The Museum of Modern Art, New York
Opificio delle Pietre Dure, Florence
Philadelphia Museum of Art
Prado Museum, Madrid
Rijksmuseum, Amsterdam
State Hermitage Museum, St. Petersburg
Thyssen-Bornemisza Museum, Madrid
Whitney Museum of American Art, New York

2 FROM GLOBAL PILLAGE TO PILLARS OF COLLABORATION

Talat Halman

Distinguished ladies and gentlemen, here I stand before you – and plead guilty. I am, as Lord Elgin dubbed my ancestors, "a malevolent Turk who mutilated the Parthenon Marbles for senseless pleasure."

I declare, however, that later we Turks came to our senses about cultural heritage. We are hell-bent to cling on to everything we possess, hell-bent to recover everything that imperialists and superstates stole from us. Our "senseless pleasure" has now been replaced by pain, by pangs of conscience, by paucity of panaceas.

The task I have been assigned is to provide a response from a "source country," which denotes "a nation stolen blind," Turkey, in this instance: Turkey as a source of anguish, because it was, it still is, outrageously plundered; a source of anger, because it had, especially during the Ottoman times, squandered part of its heritage; a source of anxiety, because it vexes the imperialist establishment by making vigorous claims for properties stolen from it; a source of angst, because it is fast becoming a market country for smuggled art and antiquities.

Please don't assume, distinguished ladies and gentlemen, that I am here to vent my fury against the predators. Without absolving the crooks and the lords of the hoards, I shall attempt to explore with you and to enunciate prospects for a new regime whereby the world might share and share alike in the benefits of the lux and frux of diverse civilizations. The title of my speech is indicative: "From Global Pillage to Pillars of Collaboration." Mine is going to be a novel appeal for universal patrimony. That obviates patriotism. In the sphere of the smuggling of art and archaeology everybody is wrong and everybody is right. I feel strongly that we must do away with cultural jingoism and move in the direction of joint, collective, universal enjoyment of art and archaeology. Our current attitudes are based on selfishness and possessiveness on the part of the have-nations and greed and thievery on the part of the have-nots. As we take strides into the new millennium, we are still living through the blight of schismatic nationalism, of the purblind fanaticism of the nation-state.

Our age needs a new altruism, a dynamic idealism. We can no longer gear antiquities to guilt and recrimination. Yes, imperialism had an enormous capacity for rapacity. Cultural properties often fell victim – as they still do sometimes – to reprehensible improprieties. Nonetheless, solutions can hardly be based on the reductio ad absurdum of mere legitimacy or mechanical legislation.

Certainly heartiest congratulations go to the Washington University School of Law for organizing this symposium on "Imperialism, Art and Restitution." It is nothing short of "inspired" and "inspiring." This forum will discuss diverse aspects of cultural smuggling, museum holdings, issues of repatriation, and compensation. It will, I am confident, seek solutions. I hope that, by the end of the two-day symposium, we might be able to work out a declaration designed to propose a new international regime for art and archaeology.

We must offer our thanks to Professor John Haley and Linda McClain, the Whitney R. Harris Institute for Global Legal Studies, and its staff for organizing this important event on art and law, in other words, statutes on statues. Also, thank you, Professor John Henry Merryman, for originating the idea for this interesting event.

I hope it will be possible to avoid arguments here about who is right or wrong and why. It is senseless to mete out blame. We have all sinned. We are all guilty – imperialists, of theft; so-called source countries, of neglect and collusion; traffickers, of vandalism and venality. The time has come to create a new order of international understanding and cooperation, through a repertoire of constructive measures.

One could bemoan what happened in the past and what is still going wrong. One could ask in the form of a doggerel:

> As we small nations do nothing but blunder,
> Empires and superstates shamelessly plunder,
> Stealing what we have above ground and under,
> Tearing our resplendent collections asunder....
> Isn't it time for us victims to ponder:
> Why so much in the way of creative wonder
> Goes abroad from our lands – way yonder?

Through the centuries, willful destruction of cultural heritage took its toll of magnificent sites and monuments and objects. Both Ottoman soldiers and Napoléon's used the Sphinx for target practice; Alexander the Great, the Persians, and the Mongols burned down numerous cities in Asia Minor. Was it the Romans or the Muslims who sent the library in Alexandria up in flames? The Taliban obliterated so much of the Buddhist heritage in Afghanistan. Just three weeks ago, a leading figure of the Turkish Islamist organization known as National Vision disclosed that ten years ago they were thinking of blowing up to smithereens the breathtaking Roman pantheon of gods and kings up on Turkey's Mt. Nimrod, because, to them it was a pagan, and therefore sacrilegious, site. National Vision invoked at the time the precedent of Abraham's destroying the idols.

Compared with such actual or potential destruction, it is of course a lesser evil for imperialists to carry away objects and monuments to safety. Fearing vandalism, the German engineer Karl Humann denuded the Altar of Zeus and whisked it away (presumably with the consent of Ottoman authorities) to his homeland where Berlin's Pergamon Museum proudly and impressively displays it. Some of the carved marble from Pergamum ended up in the British Museum. Has that plunder been detrimental or beneficial? It is conceivable that vandalism might have played havoc with the treasures of Pergamum during the closing decades of the Ottoman state or in the early years of the Turkish Republic. But, assuming there was no such danger or, despite the danger, assuming no heinous destructive act was perpetrated, would it not have been a blessing to have the altar standing erect in situ? Should it not come back now to its original, authentic site, where Turkey provides security and protection?

Of all cases of international theft and illicit traffic, the least discovered and the most lightly punished are those that involve art and archaeology. Although national legislation and international conventions exist, authorities remain lax. Cars, yachts, jewelry with no historical value are often found and returned. But art objects and archaeological artifacts somehow elude official attention – many find their way into oblivion in the hands of private collectors or in basements of museums.

Cardinal sins keep getting committed in and off the field. The archaeological plunder of Iraq has been simply horrendous. Representing a "source country" – what an elegant euphemism that is, "source country" for "plundered land" – I once came up with "Ten Commandments," not that anyone is likely to heed my ironic animadversions.

First Commandment: "Thou shall not commit cultural theft."

Second Commandment: "Never sack or ransack; if you do, give it back."

Third Commandment: "Archaeological pillage is sacrilege."

Fourth Commandment: "To deny rightful owners their chance for retrieval is evil."

Fifth Commandment: "God shall tear you asunder if you plunder."

Sixth Commandment: "Thou shall not covet thy colony's patrimony."

Seventh Commandment: "Depredation is the worst depravity."

Eight Commandment: "If you leave a country destitute, you must restitute."

Ninth Commandment: "If you prey upon foreign soil, no one will pray for your soul."

Tenth Commandment: "You shall denounce grave robbers and applaud robber barons."

Ladies and gentlemen, both the problems and the prospects of world patrimony are enormously complex.

A compelling and dramatic example is undoubtedly the Elgin Marbles, which quite wisely constitute the topic of one full session at this international symposium. Almost two full centuries ago, in 1806, the Ottoman Sultan cavalierly turned them over to the British Ambassador, Lord Elgin, whose name became enshrined in them, although most scholars, quite appropriately, insist on calling them the "Parthenon" Marbles. Did Elgin steal them or receive them as a gift from the Sultan? Did the Sultan have the right to give them away? Did Lord Elgin have the right to cart them away? The British Museum claimed that it preserved and displayed the marbles authentically. Many scholars disagree. Some have advanced the argument that the museum tampered with the surfaces. It was also indicated that the sculptures were not positioned authentically: that some of the figures faced the wrong way. The vigorous Greek diplomacy to bring the marbles back to the Parthenon has met with British objections that they are safer in London, because poor air quality in Athens would do a great deal of surface damage. To obviate such objections, Greece decided to build an impressive museum on the same site. The museum itself has come under severe criticism that its architectural style is incompatible with classical aesthetics. Archaeologists also complain that the ruins of a seventh-century A.D. village will get buried under the museum.

There are no pat solutions to cultural complexities. Whose ancestors created which objects? Are the original creators the rightful owners? Or the descendants of the communities that had transported them elsewhere? Or whoever happens to be the present custodians? For instance, who legitimately owns Scythian art?

By the same token who should properly inherit the Schliemann trove? Greeks, Trojans, or their heirs, Ottomans, Russians, Germans?

Turkey is demanding the return of the objects stolen from Constantinople in 1204. It would certainly love to get back the Four Horses that the Crusaders took away from the Hippodrome in Constantinople to Venice. Would Turkey, however, be willing to relinquish to Egypt the Obelisk that was originally commissioned by Pharaoh Tutmose III about thirty-five hundred years ago and brought to and erected in Constantinople, where it still stands, twenty-four hundred years ago?

There are so many criteria and arguments for the legitimization of antiquities and other cultural properties – original creators, geographic location, length of stay, type of custodianship, authentic context, cultural milieu, enhanced value through scholarship, exhibition, publication, exposure, etc cetera. Which one or ones among these would justify claims to ownership?

Many plundered nations feel fortunate that international conventions and some national laws enable them to retrieve their stolen goods. Capable lawyers have done wonders in this respect. Those who speak for "source countries" are grateful to a number of governments and museums who have willingly sent objects in their possession back to the centuries of origin. Cultural diplomacy works best when there is goodwill on both sides. But sometimes even "source countries" that have everything to gain from rational agreements waste a golden opportunity because of myopia or mistrust.

My own country, Turkey, missed out on a remarkable opportunity in 1981/82. Allow me to tell you a heartbreaking story:

In 1962, in a village twenty miles from a major southwestern city, a peasant digging underneath a tree happened upon a Byzantine trove – silver plates, bowls, crosses, candelabra, and other exquisite objects dating back to about 570 A.D., probably from the Church of St. Nicholas near the Sion Monastery. A clever antique dealer from Istanbul got wind of this great find, showed up on the scene, and bought part of the treasure from the peasant for a pittance. The nearest archaeological museum there found out about it later, took over the remaining objects, and sent them to the archaeological museum in Istanbul.

The following year, the antique dealer contacted the Dumbarton Oaks Museum in Washington, D.C., and sold his part of the treasure in Switzerland for a million U.S. dollars. Shortly thereafter he closed his shop in Istanbul, took up residency in Athens, and then settled in Switzerland.

In 1964 the deal was disclosed, with Dumbarton Oaks acknowledging the fact that it had acquired what came to be known as the Sion Treasure. It was only then that the Turkish government demanded the return of the smuggled items. From 1964 through 1980, the Turkish initiatives yielded no positive results. A top-level Turkish diplomat in 1980 showed up at Dumbarton Oaks and told the Director that he was "there to take possession of the silver that belonged to Turkey." He was politely shown the door.

In 1981, there was a new, enlightened Director at the museum, Giles Constable, a scholar with exemplary probity. A recent appointee as Turkey's Ambassador for Cultural Affairs, I sought him out. We had a private lunch at a Washington, D.C., restaurant, where I found him quite receptive to the idea of returning the Sion Silver. However, he and I were anxious to accomplish much more than a mere return agreement. Ambitiously, we wanted to serve scholarship, restoration, exhibition, publication. The return process itself involved elaborate legal and diplomatic work. Giles Constable and I held a meeting with Derek Bok, then President of Harvard University. I also met with several members of the Harvard Corporation. They were in favor of the arrangements in principle. After their formal vote to send the Sion treasure back to Turkey, it was necessary to secure the approval of the U.S. Attorney General's Office, which came through. The endorsement from Dumberton Oaks, Harvard Corporation, and the U.S. Attorney General had been predicated to a great extent on some of the terms that Dr. Constable and I had written into the agreement. We both felt strongly that those terms were enlightened and would provide excellent advantages for all concerned, and for the world of scholarship and museums.

For one thing, many of the items had been damaged during the digging or in transit. Some had been battered or flattened for easier smuggling. Dumbarton Oaks agreed to repair the objects it had purchased as well as those in the Istanbul Archaeological Museum – completely free of charge. And Turkey would send one or two trainees to learn restoration at Dumbarton Oaks. The collection, thus restored and unified, would be exhibited in Istanbul and two years later at Dumbarton Oaks, also possibly at another U.S. museum or two, after which it would go back to Istanbul. The agreement had an article that allowed for the possibility of further exhibitions outside Turkey. It included arrangements, unilateral and joint, for publication of catalogues and scholarly works.

Giles Constable and I felt rather proud of this unique agreement and hoped that it might constitute an example for comparable arrangements internationally, that it might become a model for cultural diplomacy beyond return or restitution, that it would be beneficial in diverse ways.

What went wrong? The Turkish side, which had vigorously sought for years to get the trove back, balked. The document had all the American signatures. It was ready for one Turkish official signature, which was never affixed.

So, ladies and gentlemen, "source countries" are often not resourceful enough. Sometimes, on the verge of securing what they hanker after, they fail dismally. In this instance, Turkey had to gain everything and nothing to lose. But sometimes bureaucratic ignorance and/or legalistic apprehensions work against cultural treasures both nationally and internationally. As a result of such official sabotage, the Sion Silver did not go back, restoration work lagged, no Turkish restorers were trained, there were no exhibitions or publications. Turkey lost; everyone involved lost.

I keep bemoaning the regrettable failure of the Turkish government. But, while commending the goodwill of Dumbarton Oaks, Harvard, and the Attorney General in this instance, I must condemn many museums in the United States and in Europe for concealing or flaunting some of their stolen pieces. Many of them offer hypocritical defenses:

"We acquired these items a long time ago. . . . Statutes of limitation apply."

"If these had stayed in their country of origin, they would have disappeared or been destroyed."

"There is no proof that any of these were stolen – maybe they were given as gifts."

"No, you may not inspect our basements, but you should take our word for it that these objects are not in our museum."

"Our national legislation prohibits the return of the items even if we would rather return them."

"These may have come from your soil, but they were not created by your ancestors. They are yours by conquest, by default, by your illegitimate acts."

"They appear to be yours, but we excavated them, we did the scholarly work on them, we did all the scientific publications."

These paltry or pathetic excuses contain some half-truths, to be sure.

It is true that some poor countries are extremely rich in their archaeological assets. Turkey is a prime example. Its mainland – the Anatolian peninsula – is host to more than forty identifiably different ancient civilizations. It possesses an estimated twenty thousand mounds and tumuli, three thousand ancient cities, and no four than twenty-five thousand monuments. Each year, more objects are dug up than the total number of objects in all of the British museums. How can an underdeveloped country where the per capita national income is barely $3,000 U.S. per annum afford to excavate, restore, preserve, and exhibit this vast treasure? Impressive improvements have taken place, but so much more needs to be done. It has been estimated that if the total cultural budget of all European nations were used for archaeology in Turkey, it would fall short of Turkey's annual needs.

The shame of abandoning certain sites to make way for dams, for instance, the unforgivable episode that involved submergence of Zeugma, makes me shudder. I keep hoping that the Turkish Ministry of Culture and Tourism will respond to pressure from international organizations, nongovernmental organizations (NGOs), and public opinion to spare other sites like Hasankeyf from a similar fate.

The shortsightedness of certain governments has in the past resulted in great opportunities lost. One infuriating example is what transpired in Turkey in connection with an offer that had been made by Mr. Gulbenkian in the early 1960s at a time when a military government was in power. Mr. Gulbenkian, a citizen of Turkey although he had virtually never lived there, wanted to make a gift of his fantastically rich art collection, including many priceless Ottoman art objects. He also offered to set up a fund to create a museum in Istanbul to house his collection and to defray the cost of maintaining the museum. Furthermore he proposed that he might fund the creation of an orchestra whose expenses his foundation would pay for. In every conceivable way, this was a munificent offer. Turkey had nothing to lose, but a great deal to gain. Yet, taking a mind-boggling decision, the Turkish government declined to accept the offer. Thereupon, Mr. Gulbenkian established the museum and created the orchestra in Lisbon, Portugal.

True, neglect and incompetence facilitate pilferage and smuggling. But does that disqualify Turkey from its status as a custodian any more than thefts of paintings disqualify many advanced nations? The country is blessed with archaeological riches that defy the imagination. Its surplus could fill hundreds of museums in other countries. Turkey could sell, donate, exchange countless items. Yet, most of its scholars, archaeologists, and cultural administrators are passionately reluctant to part with any item – even though they know that Turkey will get, in return, a wealth of items from other countries. But the bickering goes on. The insistence on possession is relentless. It leads the world nowhere. We must now unite for "one world of art and archaeology." That requires a new system of ethics, a universal deontology, a worldwide collaboration.

Because the prevailing patterns of proprietorship are predicated upon narrowminded nationalism as well as crass possessiveness, the world is denied the opportunity – which I identify as a universal right – to view and study and enjoy creative arts everywhere. Everything in global patrimony belongs to all of us – to all nations, to all human beings. We are all compatriots in world civilizations. Perhaps we should coin the terms "com-patrimony" and "com-patrimonists."

Because of the need to cover up stolen objects, some museums in industrialized countries are, in part, thieves' dens. Because of the concern to lose what they possess or the reluctance to share scholarly knowledge, many museums in underdeveloped countries have become citadels.

There is a crying need for openness, honesty, altruism, constructive cooperation.

Permit me to propose a set of new principles for the future world order of art and archaeology:

1. World inventory: Entire holdings of all museums to be registered in a world inventory supervised by the United Nations Educational, Scientific, and Cultural Organization (UNESCO).
2. Amnesty: An international amnesty to be issued for all cultural objects acquired by museums prior to 1975.
3. Repatriation: All objects illegally acquired by museums after 1975 to be returned to their countries of origin.
4. Stronger antismuggling laws: New national legislation and international measures to reduce smuggling of art and antiquities.
5. Sale and exchange: New legislation for museum-to-museum sales and exchanges of art and antiquities.
6. Integrity of sites: An international ban on tampering with the authenticity and integrity of archaeological sites.
7. International fund: Creation of an art and archaeology fund (AA Fund) with income to be derived from a percentage of gross receipts at all museums, of all museum-to museum sales of cultural properties, of fees and penalties for illegally acquired objects, a portion of royalties, and so on.
8. Use of AA Fund: Income to be used for the creation and renovation of museums, restoration of sites and objects, international traveling and cyberexhibitions, production of books, Compact disks (CDs), documentaries, and so forth.

Would the world create and comply with such a regime?

Is all this feasible? Is it a panacea? Or is it pure fantasy? A utopia that will never come about? Utopia is always worth a try. It is better to be guided by utopia than myopia. "Nothing happens," said the American poet Carl Sandburg, "unless first a dream." I agree with Anatole France, the prominent French author, who once observed: "If it weren't for utopias, there would be no cities and man would still be eking out a miserable life in caves."

Ladies and gentlemen, we must have faith in the prospect for better conditions for art preserved and antiquities conserved. Setting up a new and rational system is not an idle dream. If we strive hard enough, we can achieve it. In many ways – in war and terrorism, in guilt and destruction – we continue to be savages. But the world has, nonetheless, taken giant strides – thanks to dreams fulfilled through determined efforts and enlightened work.

Who would have predicted in 1900 that life expectancy would rise from thirty-five to seventy by the year 2000?

Who would have foreseen in the latter part of the nineteenth century that man would fly and even travel faster than the speed of sound?

Who would have thought that slavery would be abolished and colonies emancipated?

Who would have imagined, even twenti-five years ago, that he could reach into his pocket, pull out a cell phone in Zimbabwe, and chat with a friend in Japan?

Who in the early twentiech century would have expected a world organization like the United Nations composed of independent sovereign states each with an equal vote, from Burma to Britannia, from Algeria to America?

Who would have foreseen, say, sixty years ago, the eradication of measles, malaria, polio?

Ladies and gentlemen, minor and major miracles are never out of the realm of possibility. They do occur and will continue to in science, medicine, scholarship, technology.

Imperialism is dead. Restitution is feasible, almost routine. Art is forever. Despite instances of savagery, humankind will preserve its civilizations and creativity. International law is capable of making a compellingly constructive contribution to a better world. The eponymous creator of the Whitney R. Harris Institute for Global Legal Studies was right in affirming that "the struggle for peace, law, and justice in the world is eternal." We can, however, confidently assert for our part that without having to wait for an eternity, we shall be able to create a new just order for the world's art and archaeology, museums, and cultural institutions.

3 MUSEUMS AS CENTERS OF CULTURAL UNDERSTANDING

Willard L. Boyd

The concept of a museum is primarily Western in origin. It is a human construct designed to learn through the acquisition, preservation, and interpretation of collections of objects. However, a museum is more than a warehouse of objects. It is a place of ideas about objects. Whose objects? Whose ideas?

Traditionally, museums defer to the curators' judgment as the acquirers of the objects and the authenticators of the ideas emanating from the objects. However, exhibition labels seldom acknowledge specific curatorial authorship, thus leaving visitors with the impression that it is an Olympian institution rather than a mere individual speaking. People, not gods, make museums.

Even as the people who are the museum have become more professional during the past fifty years, their judgments and actions have been and are increasingly challenged. Curatorial "expertness" does not trump public concerns about what is collected and how it is exhibited.

Because museums conserve the past, they are not oriented toward new ideas and new ways. Museums tend to stick with the familiar rather than reach out to the unfamiliar. Too often they justify the status quo as the upholding of standards and decry change as politically correct pandering. Instead of blinders, professionals of all types need peripheral vision. They have little perception of how others perceive them. In the case of museums we live in a time when the intellectuals and publics in our own and different cultures no longer unquestioningly genuflect before the majesty of traditionally Western-oriented museums.[1]

Times change. Even museum perspectives change with the times. We are in an era of rapid policy evolution with respect to the acquisition, retention,

[1] Boyd, Museums as Centers of Controversy, 128 *Daedalus* 185 (1999).

and exhibition of museum collections. Since World War II there has been a
sea change in the attitude of large American museums. Art museums have
widened their scope beyond Western art and "classical" antiquities. Art historians who have moved into non-Western fields begin to sound like cultural
anthropologists. Meanwhile, archaeologists and cultural anthropologists are
emerging from a period of guilt over their predecessors' ideas and methods.
It is a sign of growing respect for "otherness" that museums have moved away
from the term *primitive* when referring to the cultural objects of Oceania,
Africa, and the Americas. Even totem poles are rising in artistic estimation.
In 1981 the Field Museum reopened its Northwest Coast Indian and Inuit
exhibit with the counsel of an advisory committee of clan representatives.
One of the committee members was commissioned to create a totem pole
that was installed during a large public ceremony in front of the museum.
When the pole was not included in a book on public sculpture in Chicago,
the museum asked why not. The reply was that the pole was only a native
carving. The next edition of the book included the totem.

   With the ending of political colonialism and the rise of multinational cultural forums, the collection policies of museums have come under increasing
scrutiny. We are in an age of cross-cultural divides about the acquisition,
retention, and exhibition of museum collections. Museums cannot be
impervious to these differing perspectives if they are to be intellectu-
ally and ethically credible in a world where the views of others also
count.

   According to a *Christian Science Monitor* feature on General John Abizaid,
U.S. commander in charge of Mideast Forces:[2] "Abizaid often stresses the
cross-cultural imperatives of the war on terrorism, and the importance
of nonmilitary remedies." He told a congressional committee: "What will
win the global war on terrorism will be people that can cross the cultural
divide."

   Museums need to cross cultural divides with respect to collections and
exhibitions, and nonlegal means are important in doing so. When a museum
moves beyond cultural objects made for the marketplace, more than connoisseurship and money are involved. In crossing cultural divides, we need
to be respectful of other perspectives and places. The term *retentionist* as
applied to source countries sounds like a pejorative and is inappropriate,
especially because museums are also retentionists.

   It is the nature of all people to be protective and proud of their heritage.
Even in a global society, we live our life locally. Tom Friedman used the

---

[2]   *See* text at www.csmonitor.com/2004/0305/p01 s02-usmi.html

metaphor of "The Lexus and the Olive Tree" to make the point that while all people want some of the material benefits of globalism, they still treasure the heritage of place.

Understanding and mutual respect go a long way in joining people together where there are differences. Universalism is more likely to be achieved through cross-cultural collaboration than through either unilateral or multilateral declarations.

Law changes to reflect the times even as it is rooted in the need for societal stability. Cultural property and cultural heritage have different legal and societal meanings. The first suggests property law and the second human rights law. They are not, however, mutually exclusive, but integrating them across cultural divides calls for understanding and respect, open-mindedness and goodwill, and above all patient listening to each other.[3]

Both illegal and legal trading of cultural objects for financial purposes go back to time immemorial. As George Stocking points out:

Material culture was, in a literal economic sense, "cultural property". The very materiality of the objects entangled them in Western economic processes of acquisition and exchange of wealth.[4]

However, we offend many when we view their cultural treasures only in economic terms. Such objects are beyond monetary appraisal. Indeed they are profaned when regarded in other than respectful spiritual terms.[5]

So much for the preaching. How well do I practice it? Not all that well, but better than if I had not tried. I am clearer in my mind as to the acquisition and exhibition of museum collections. I am less clear about retention and repatriation of collections.

---

[3] Merryman, Cultural Property, International Trade and Human Rights, 19 *Cardozo Arts & Ent. L.J.* 51 (2001); Wilkie, Public Opinion Regarding Cultural Property Policy, 19 *Cardozo Arts & Ent. L.J.* 97 (2001); Hughes, The Trend toward Liberal Enforcement of Repatriation Claims in Cultural Property Disputes, 33 *Geo. Wash. Intl L. Rev.* 131, 134–135 (2000); Shapiro, Repatriation: A Modest Proposal, 31 *N.Y.U. J. Intl L. and Pol.* 95, 96–100 (1998); Gerstenblith, Identity and Cultural Property: The Protection of Cultural Property in the Unites States, 75 *B.U. L. Rev.* 559, 567–586 (1995); Merryman, Two Ways of Thinking about Cultural Property, 80 *Am. J. Intl L.* 831 (1986); Merryman, Thinking about the Elgin Marbles, 83 *Mich. L. Rev.* 1881 (1985).

[4] *History of Anthropology*, Vol. 3, *Objects and Others Essays on Museums and Material Culture*, p. 5, University of Wisconsin Press (1985).

[5] O'Keefe & Prott, *Law and Cultural Heritage*, Vol. 3, 839–840 (1989); Shapiro, supra n. 3, at 97. *See by analogy* Rakotoarisoa, Intangible Heritage: Do We Have the Right?, *ICOM News* #2 p. 11 (2004).

ACQUISITIONS

Starting in the early 1970s, the Field Museum's accession policy became very restrictive.[6] This was triggered by both the UNESCO Convention on the Means of Prohibiting and Preventing the Illicit Import, Export, and Transfer of Ownership of Cultural Property[7] and the Convention on International Trade in Endangered Species of Wild Fauna and Flora.[8] Since the Field Museum focuses on environmental biodiversity as well as archaeology and ethnography, its accession policy provides that the museum and staff "shall be in full compliance with laws and regulations, both domestic and foreign, governing transfer of ownership and movement of materials across political boundaries."

Similar institutions have similar provisions because they regularly do field work in other countries and need both work and transit permits. If the institution does not comply with the laws of the host country, its staff does not get permits. Moreover, these institutions are deeply concerned with the destruction of archaeological sites, cultural groups, and environmental habitats. In addition to basic research, they are increasingly drawn into issues of protection and preservation. For these reasons, American cultural and biological institutions nowadays adhere to the laws of the source nation, and movement into the United States primarily takes the form of loans, exchanges, and traveling exhibits. These institutions have changed as knowledge, needs, and values have changed.

Indeed, the law also changes. The recent decision in *U.S. v. Schultz*[9] has made clear that the United States will enforce foreign cultural patrimony laws.[10] Three federal appeals courts – the Second, Fifth, and Ninth Circuits – have now taken this position.[11] It is noteworthy that the Egyptian law applied in *Schultz* provides "for licensure of certain archaeological missions, and for

[6] *U.S. v. McClain*, 545 F.2d 988, 997 n. 14 (1977).
[7] *See* http://www.unesco.org/culture/laws/1970/html_eng/page2.shtml
[8] *See* http://www.cites.org
[9] *U.S. v. Schultz*, 333 F.3d 393 (2nd Cir. 2003), *cert. denied, Schultz v. United States*, 157 L. Ed. 2d. 891 (2004).
[10] For a proposed U.S. uniform state cultural patrimony statute, see Gerstenblith, supra n. 3, at 641–688.
[11] *U.S. v. McClain*, 545 F.2d 988 (5th Cir. 1977), *rehearing denied*, 551 F.2d 52 (5th Cir. 1977), *and appeal after remand*, 593 F.2d 658 (5th Cir. 1979); *U.S. v. Hollinshead*, 495 F.2d 1154 (9th Cir. 1974). For discussion of these cases, see Hughes, supra n. 3, at 138–44.

circumstances under which antiquities may be donated by the government to foreign museums in appreciation of those missions' work."[12]

National organizations of the American museum community opposed judicial recognition of cultural patrimony laws primarily on the legal grounds that U.S. courts do not enforce cultural property export restrictions of other countries.[13] They argued that an export license is only relevant where imports are embargoed under the 1983 Cultural Property Implementation Act. That act is Congress's limited implementation of the 1970 UNESCO treaty. Pursuant to that legislation, the President, after consultation with the Cultural Property Advisory Committee, can restrict the import of specified archaeological and ethnographic objects where the President determines that such cultural property is in jeopardy from pillage.[14] However, on June 28, 2004, the Association of Art Museum Directors (AAMD) published a "Report on Acquisition of Archaeological Materials and Ancient Art."[15] "The report is the work of a Task Force comprised of AAMD members, and is part of a continuing process by which AAMD examines professional practices for the acquisition and display of works of art in all fields." The report affords acquisition guidelines for members, which include the following:

II. A. 2. Member museums should make a concerted effort to obtain accurate written documentation with respect to the history of the work of art, including import and export documents. Member museums should always obtain the import documentation when the work of art is being imported into the U.S. in connection with its acquisition by the museum.

    II. D. 1970 UNESCO Convention: In recognition of the November 1970 UNESCO Convention on the Means of Prohibiting and Preventing the Illicit Import and Export and Transfer of Ownership of Cultural Property, member museums should not acquire any archaeological material or work of ancient art known to have been

[12] *U.S. v. Schultz*, supra, n. 9. This type of sharing is often referred to as *partage*.
[13] *U.S. v. An Antique Platter of Gold*, 991 F. Supp. 222 (1997), *aff'd*, 184 F. 3d 131 (2nd Cir. 1999) (Brief of Amici Curiae in support of the appeal of Michael H. Steinhardt – American Association of Museums, Association of Art Museum Directors, Association of Science Museum Directors, and American Association for State and Local History). *See also U.S. v. McClain*, 545 F. 2d 991–992 n.1 (5th Cir. 1997); Merryman, Cultural Property, International Trade and Human Rights, 19 *Cardozo Arts & Ent. L.J.* 51, 52–61 (2001); Merryman, The Free International Movement of Cultural Property, 31 *N.Y.U. J. Intl L. & Pol.* 1, 3–9, 13–14 (1988).
[14] 19 U.S.C. §2602 a(1)(A).
[15] *See* http://www.aamd.org

"stolen from a museum, or a religious, or secular public monument or similar institution" (Article 7b of the Convention). In addition, member museums should not acquire any archaeological material or work of ancient art known to have been part of an official archaeological excavation and removed in contravention of the laws of the country of origin.

Member museums should not acquire any such works of art that were removed after November 1970 regardless of any applicable statutes of limitation and notwithstanding the fact that the U.S. did not accede to the Convention until 1983.

Although not inclusive of ethnographic and other cultural property covered by UNESCO treaty, these AAMD guidelines constitute a significant ethical step forward in reducing illegal trade in cultural objects.

Instead of fighting a losing legal and public relations battle against source countries, the movement of cultural property will be greatly advanced by the cooperation and respect exemplified in the AAMD guidelines.

For example, source country patrimony laws might be modified to authorize export of some objects to foreign museums and collectors. Such legal exportation would result in greater dissemination of knowledge, accurate provenance, and elimination of damage to the objects as well as the sites. Moreover, the sale proceeds from legal exports could fund local museums and site protection and preservation.[16] But the question is, Will American museums and collectors respect such liberal laws or claim they are merely an exercise of police power that US courts should not enforce? It is American refusal to recognize any legal limitation on collecting that has driven source countries to enact wall-to-wall patrimony laws.

As the AAMD guidelines demonstrate, the time has come to respect the perspective of site countries and to recognize the legitimacy of their concerns. Museum associations are churning out ethics codes that espouse such respect even though actions belie that rhetoric. Consequently, aggrieved groups must resort to confrontation as in the case of Native Americans and

---

[16] For an extensive discussion on this approach, see the Japan Society Web site at http://www.Japansociety.org for a transcript of April 9, 2003, Cultural Property Forum: The Export Policies of China, Korea, and Japan; Merryman, Two Ways of Thinking about Cultural Property, 80 *Am. J. Intl L.* 831, 846–849, 852–853 (1986). *See also* Merryman, Cultural Property, International Trade and Human Rights, 19 *Cardozo Arts & Ent. L.J.* 51, 52–58 (2001) (limit source country retention to national "treasures"); Rudenstein, Cultural Property: The Hard Question of Repatriation, 19 *Cardozo Arts and Ent. L.J.* 69, 80–82 (2001); Hughes, supra n. 3, at 145–146; Pearlstein, Claims for the Repatriation of Cultural Property: Prospects for a Managed Antiquities Market, 28 *Law & Pol'y. Intl Bus.* 123, 140–150 (1996) (proposal for a managed, self-policing antiquities market).

Holocaust survivors.[17] Ethical credibility requires that dealers, collectors, academics, and museum professionals of all perspectives must now talk and work together actively to implement the ethics they separately espouse.[18] Ethically we have a long way to go, however. In a *New York Times*, August 20, 2004, story on the return of a stolen Egyptian relief, Martin D. Ficke, a special agent for Immigration and Customs Enforcement, is reported as commenting that "New York continues to be a hub of art smuggling through its airports and seaport," and specifically, "There's a market in museums, auction houses, curators. . . . And that keeps us pretty busy."[19]

Ethics require more of us than the law requires.[20] Ethically all American collectors have the joint responsibility to act affirmatively and voluntarily to stop illicit trade.[21] Associations of museums, dealers, and private collectors need a joint statement on good practices that is forthright and clear. If all American collectors conduct themselves ethically, we need not fear the redeployment of the U.S. Customs Art Fraud squad to fight terrorism and financial fraud.[22] Indeed, American collectors will be in the vanguard of General Abizaid's legion of people who can cross the world's cultural divides.

Site countries and museums are publishing inventories of cultural objects and sites, and Web lists of stolen objects are proliferating,[23] so that it is difficult to make the case for a good faith purchaser. The media thrive on art theft. To cry foul, a foreign consul need only go to the media in the U.S.

---

[17] Boyd, Museums as Centers of Controversy, 128 *Daedalus* 185, 190–192 (1999).

[18] Wilkie, supra n. 3, at 102–104; Merryman, supra n. 13, at 9–14.

[19] Pogrebin, Stolen Artwork from Temple Will Be Returned to Egypt, *New York Times*, Aug. 20, 2004, at A23.

[20] Boyd, Museum Accountability: Laws, Rules, Ethics and Accreditation, 34 *Curator* 165, 173–174 (1991).

[21] *See generally* Messenger, The Ethics of Collecting Cultural Property (2nd ed.) (1999); Ethical Considerations and Cultural Property, 7 *Intl Journal on Cultural Property* #1 (Special Issue 1998).

[22] D'Arcy, U.S. Customs Art Squad Reassigned to War on Terror, *The Art Newspaper* (London) Jan. 2004.

[23] *See* ICOM Red Lists of African Archaeological Cultural Objects at Risk, Latin American Cultural Objects at Risk, and Emergency List of Iraqi Antiquities at Risk at http://icom.museum/redlist; Culture without Context, *Newsletter of the Illicit Antiquities Research Centre* at http://www.mcdonald.cam.ac.uk/IRAC/cwoc; Pickard, Policy and Law in Heritage Conservation, 320–323 (2001) (European Conventions on Protection of Architectural [Granada] and Archaeological [Malta] Heritage); Hamma, Finding Cultural Property Online, 19 *Cardozo Arts & Ent. L.J.* 125 (2001); Bibas, The Case against Statutes of Limitation for Stolen Art, 103 *Yale L.J.* 2437, 2460–2469 (1994). For additional links dealing with illicit trade in cultural property, *see* ICOM Useful Links at http://www.icom.museum/traffic_links.html

locality where a museum, a dealer, or a collector holds the object. Public shaming can often bring about repatriation.[24]

Attitudes are also shifting in other cultural property importing countries. The *Wall Street Journal* of February 18, 2004, reported:

> Earlier this month saw "Not for Sale," a two-day Swiss-British conference, held in Geneva, on the traffic in artifacts from Iraq, Afghanistan and elsewhere. Bringing together an unusual group of antiquities dealers, collectors, academics, museum professionals, politicians, diplomats and law-enforcement officials from around the world, it was organized to discuss the implementation of new laws passed by Britain and Switzerland, and to consider strategies to better policing and tracking down of illegally excavated as well as stolen antiquities.
>
> Both countries were known for being clearinghouses for stolen antiquities. To rectify that, they are now acceding to the (UNESCO) Convention (bringing to 102 the number of countries acceding to the Convention). In addition, last December Britain passed the Dealing in Cultural Objects (Offences) Act, which makes it illegal to knowingly deal in stolen artifacts. . . .
>
> In addition, the two countries have agreed on the need for more cooperation among art professionals, academics and law-enforcement agencies; to set up expert task forces to work with law enforcement; and to create databases to track stolen artifacts.[25]

REPATRIATION

The UNESCO treaty applies to acquisitions made after a country implements the treaty. What about museum collections acquired prior to that time? I am less sure about what you do when a museum is requested to repatriate a cultural object(s) it has held for a long time. I do know that stonewalling will not work in the global information age. It is better to be open and to seek to build a relationship with the claimant.[26]

As the UNESCO treaty does, the AAMD guidelines apply to prospective acquisitions. Nevertheless, the guidelines set forth good practice with respect to prior acquisitions:

l. D. AAMD recognizes that some works of art for which provenance information is incomplete or unobtainable may deserve to be publicly displayed, preserved, studied, and published because of their rarity, importance, and aesthetic merit.

---

[24] Wilkie, supra n. 3, at 101–103; Shapiro, What the New Millennium Might Bring, 19 *Cardozo Arts & Ent. L.J.* 105, 106 (2001).

[25] Zainab Bahrani, British and Swiss Get Tough about Smuggling in the Fray, *Wall ST. J.*, Feb. 18, 2004.

[26] Boyd, Museums as Centers of Controversy, 128 *Daedalus* 185, 197–199 (1999).

AAMD affirms that art museums have an obligation to such works of art, which in the absence of any breach of law or of these principles may in some cases be acquired and made accessible not only to the public and to scholars but to potential claimants as well.

II. F. If a member museum gains information that establishes another party's claim to a work of art acquired after the date of this Report, even though this claim may not be enforceable under U.S. law, the museum should seek an equitable resolution with the other party. Possible options that should be considered include: transfer or sale of the work of art to the claimant; payment to the claimant; loan or exchange of the work of art; or retention of the work of art.

Similarly, the Code of Ethics of the International Council of Museums (ICOM)[27] calls for dialogue:

4.4 Return and Restitution of Cultural Property . . .
In response to requests for the return of cultural property to the country or people of origin, museums should be prepared to initiate dialogues with an open-minded attitude based on scientific and professional principles (in preference to action at a governmental or political level). In addition the possibility of developing bilateral or multilateral partnerships with museums in countries that have lost a significant part of their cultural or natural heritage should be explored.

This section intimates that it is preferable for museums to take an initiative "based on scientific and professional principles" rather than to leave it to governments to take actions based on political considerations, which are more likely to take precedence over cultural policy concerns.

What happens if you cannot reach an AAMD "equitable resolution" with a claimant or develop an ICOM "partnership" with other museums? There is always recourse to impartial conflict resolution through conciliation, mediation, arbitration, and litigation. This is easier said than done. How do you get parties to the table and what principles and laws might apply? What principles and laws govern repatriation? Do they apply ex post facto?

There are various relevant declarations, but usually they are neither explicit nor universally recognized. Two examples of such declarations are the Declaration on the Importance and Values of Universal Museums and the Draft Declaration on the Rights of Indigenous People. The Declaration on the Importance and Value of Universal Museums,[28] issued in

---

27   *See* http://icom.museum/ethics.html#4
28   57 *ICOM News* #1 at 4 (2004). The signers of the declaration are The Art Institute of Chicago; Bavarian State Museum, Munich (Alte, Pinakothek, Neue Pinakothek); State Museums, Berlin; Cleveland Museum of Art; J. Paul Getty Museum, Los Angeles;

December 2002 and signed by the directors of eighteen U.S. and Western
European museums, reads in part:

The international museum community shares the conviction that illegal traffic in
archaeological, artistic, and ethnic objects must be firmly discouraged. We should,
however, recognize that objects acquired in earlier times must be viewed in the light
of different sensitivities and values, reflective of that earlier era. The objects and
monumental works that were installed decades and even centuries ago in museums throughout Europe and America were acquired under conditions that are not
comparable with current ones.

   Over time, objects so acquired – whether by purchase, gift, or partage – have
become part of the museums that have cared for them, and by extension part of
the heritage of the nations which house them. Today we are especially sensitive to
the subject of a work's original context, but we should not lose sight of the fact that
museums too provide a valid and valuable context for objects that were long ago
displaced from their original source. . . .

   Calls to repatriate objects that have belonged to museum collections for many
years have become an important issue for museums. Although each case has to be
judged individually, we should acknowledge that museums serve not just the citizens
of one nation but the people of every nation.

   Although it is true that the foregoing is a unilateral declaration by the
directors of nineteen significant Western art museums and that it is particular rather than universal in approach, it, nevertheless, is a noteworthy
statement of the museum "retentionist" view of repatriation. The declaration would carry greater bona fides if it were explicit as to the action the
signers are now taking to stop current illegal traffic in cultural objects, such
as requiring export licenses as a condition precedent of new acquisitions.[29]
By referring to prior purchases and gifts of collections, the declaration raises
appropriate legal issues to be considered from differing cultural perspectives
when the acquisition took place.

   Solomon R. Guggenheim Museum, New York; Los Angeles County Museum of Art;
   Louvre Museum, Paris; the Metropolitan Museum of Art, New York; the Museum of
   Fine Arts; Boston; the Museum of Modern Art, New York; Opificio delle Pietre Dure,
   Florence; Philadelphia Museum of Art; Prado Museum, Madrid; Rijksmuseum, Ams-
   terdam; State Hermitage Museum, St. Petersburg; Thyssen-Bornemisza Museum,
   Madrid; Whitney Museum of American Art, New York; the British Museum,
   London.
[29] As to these bona fides see Petridis, *Exhibition Review: Arts of Africa, Asia, Oceania,*
   and the Americas, Musée du Louvre, Pavillon des Sessions, Paris, France, African Arts
   34, 3 (2001): 74–77, 95–96.

To be truly universal, museums need to look beyond their own cultural traditions and laws to those of the source nation as well. In this way all the laws applicable at the time of prior transactions can be considered. This more universal approach is reflected in Article 12 of the Draft Declaration on the Rights of Indigenous People (1994):[30]

Indigenous peoples have the right to practice and revitalize their cultural traditions and customs. This includes the right to maintain, protect, and develop the past, present and future manifestations of their culture, such as archaeological and historical sites, artifacts, designs, ceremonies, technologies and visual and performing arts and literature, as well as the right to the restitution of cultural, intellectual, religious and spiritual property taken without their free and informed consent or in violation of their laws, traditions and customs.

Applying Article 12 to repatriation cases would not be inconsistent with U.S. and European law. It is settled law in the Western civil and common law that transactions can be vitiated in the case of fraud, undue influence, mistake, and theft.

It is true that many contested objects have been in museum collections for long periods. There is no legal consensus as to when a claim for restitution of cultural property is barred by time. Courts consider what is equitable under the circumstances.[31] Given the reluctance of courts to enforce stale claims, it is important to make a persuasive case for repatriation on the merits. Justifiable bases for repatriation are comprehensively set forth in volume 3 of O'Keefe and Protts's 1989 seminal treatise, *Law and the Cultural Heritage*.[32]

Museums cannot hide behind fiduciary duties where a good case for repatriation is made. U.S. museums have deaccession policies which are subject to the oversight function of the attorney general in the state where the museum is incorporated. When a museum governing board takes action to deaccession for purposes of repatriation, the attorney general should be apprised of the action and the rationale for it.

Since the western museum raison d'etre is to preserve and protect objects, the claimant should demonstrate that the objects when transferred will be inalienable and, consistent with the claimant's traditions, will be under the perpetual care of a recognized cultural custodian and will be appropriately accessible.

---

[30] *See* http://www.unhchr.ch/huridocda/huridoca.nsf/(Symbol)/E.CN.4.SUB.2.RES. 1994.45.En?OpenDocument
[31] Bibas, supra n. 23.
[32] *See also* Shapiro, supra n. 3, at 103–105.

Given the dangers of terrorism, war, civil disturbance, natural disasters, and inadequate funding for facilities and storage, the museum and claimant should work out an agreement by which some of the objects remain deposited with the repatriating museum so that if a disaster occurs in either place a portion of the collection will be saved.

If the museum and the claimant cannot mutually agree as to the disposition of the objects, an impartial third party could conciliate, mediate, or arbitrate. Coming, often as strangers as well as protagonists, from different perspectives makes it hard for the parties to agree on a method of dispute resolution which both parties would consider impartial. Judicial litigation is a last resort.

Although claiming to be internationalists, American museums may not be willing to utilize an international forum. For example, Article 4 of the 1976 Convention on the Protection of the Archaeological, Historical, and Artistic Heritage of the American Nations provides for an Inter-American Council to settle disputes among the parties to the convention.[33] The United States, however, is not a party to the convention.

My own repatriation experience relates to Native Americans. In the late 1980s I was asked by the American Association of Museums to participate with a few museum colleagues in discussions with the Montana congressman Melchert's administrative assistant, Clara Spotted Elk. She was interested in how Congress might reconnect Native Americans with their tribal heritage residing in museum collections. Many of these collections are located far from where tribes live; also, sadly, tribal members were often barred access to collection storage.

After those discussions, Michael Fox, then Director of the Heard Museum, proposed the Phoenix Dialogue, consisting of twelve people – six Native Americans, three archaeologists and anthropologists, and three museum people. The dialogue was the prelude to the Native American Graves Protection and Repatriation Act (NAGPRA). Although there was a push by the

---

[33]   15 *Intl Legal Materials* 1350, 1351 (1976). *See also* Merryman, International Trade and Human Rights, 19 *Cardozo Arts and Ent. L.J.* 51, 52–58 (European Court of Justice), 61–64 (European Court of Human Rights) (2001); Reppas, The Deflowering of the Parthenon: A Legal and Moral Analysis on Why the "Elgin Marbles" must be returned to Greece, 9 *Fordham Intell. Prop. Media & Ent. L.J.* 911, 954–975 (1999) (related regional and international laws); Gegas, International Arbitration and the Resolution of Cultural Property Disputes: Navigating the Stormy Waters Surrounding Cultural Property, 13 *Ohio St. J. on Disp. Resol.* 129, 151–166 (1997) (arbitration as the proper forum); Prunty, Toward Establishing an International Tribunal for the Settlement of Cultural Property Disputes: How to Keep Greece from Losing Its Marbles, 72 *Geo. L.J.* 1155, 1167–1182 (1984) (proposed international court for cultural property dispute settlement).

Native Americans and the other two museum representatives to file a unanimous report, the archaeologists dissented in part. As one of the museum members, I filed a separate opinion to the dialogue report that dissented on the issue of applicable substantive law. I also set forth my individual concern in May 14, 1990, testimony before the U.S. Senate Committee on Indian Affairs.

In part I said:

I fully subscribe to the portions of the majority report relating to the role and responsibilities of museums and the exchange of information between museums and Native American groups. I also fully agree to the need for an impartial process to resolve disagreements. I depart from the Panel's proposal for *ex post facto* change of the substantive law applicable at the time Native American remains and cultural objects came into the possession of museums and the law applicable to Museum fiduciary duties respecting the stewardship of collections. I believe that all pre-existing legal standards and rights, including those existing under Native American customary law, must be respected and considered in the resolution process. To make major shifts now in the applicable substantive laws would in my judgment bring results far beyond the ability of all of us to foresee.

During the dialogue, I was impressed by the understandable concerns of Native Americans about the insensitive treatment by some museums of their cultural heritage. I also was strengthened in my conviction that generally museums have played, and continue to play, a major role in multicultural learning in a pluralistic society.

Even with continuing cooperative working relationships, I know there will be times when differences arise which must be resolved impartially and fairly. In a democratic society, there must be an accessible process through which to weigh and resolve such differences in an open and constructive manner. In the Dialogue the view was clearly expressed that Native Americans have not fared well in federal tribunals and that a local process would be preferable. At the Field Museum we have developed a policy which provides a local process. It provides for conciliation, impartial dispute resolution, and application of Native American as well as other pertinent law. The Field Museum "repatriation" policy tries to balance Native American concerns with the Museum's threefold concerns about collection preservation and scholarship, the fiduciary duty for collections, and the scholarly and public need to understand the sum as well as the parts of the human condition in an increasingly interdependent world.[34]

I then went on to propose in some detail a possible legislative mandated alternative dispute resolution process that would be subject to judicial review.

[34] Hearing before Senate Select Committee on Indian Affairs, May 14, 1990, pp. 119–121.

Any legislation ought to contain a three-step process to encourage conciliation, decision, and finality. Legislation should first encourage and then facilitate good faith efforts by the parties to reach mutually agreeable solutions. Failing voluntary resolution, an impartial administrative tribunal should be available to resolve the differences. Finally, explicit provision must be made for judicial review of the tribunal's decision in order to provide finality and to satisfy constitutional requirements.

Any tribunal should be a truly impartial decision mechanism. Such a tribunal should be made up of equal numbers of Native Americans and museum professionals. Neither group should be given greater representation in order to preserve the tribunal's impartiality and meet the test of procedural due process.

The impartial panel should be given latitude as to how it crafts its decision with respect to possession and stewardship of the materials in question. Legally and philosophically, both museums and Native Americans hold cultural material of prior generations in trust for future generations. Neither should be free to dispose of the material without restrictions. Accordingly, the panel should have the latitude to order reconsecration, repatriation with conditions, continued study of the objects, joint custody, or any combination of these possibilities.

Ultimate judicial review of the resolution process is essential to assure constitutionality of an administrative tribunal. Such judicial review should generally defer to the factual findings made by the administrative tribunal. All adjudication of the parties' relevant legal rights, on the other hand, must be subject to *de novo* review.

I believe that "standing" to initiate any dispute resolution process should be broadly defined to include any descendant group which is biologically and/or culturally affiliated with the original group. I also believe that any individuals who have any reasonable or good faith interest whatsoever, be it scientific, social, or otherwise, should be permitted to submit written and oral statements regarding any claim. Nevertheless, there needs to be a process to aid the Museum and tribunal to determine which claimant among several may have the strongest claim.

With respect to the standards for repatriation, I caution against legislation regarding the appropriate "burden of proof." Such legislation may very well result in *ex post facto* alteration of pre-existing substantive rights. Repatriation based on such legislated standards could constitute a taking under the Fifth Amendment. At most, the legislation should simply outline the order in which the parties are to submit arguments and proofs.

I believe that all the existing appropriate legal standards should be a part of the adjudicating process. The panel must consider Native American and state and federal law. Within each of these types of law, the panel must consider varied concepts of property law, constitutional law, and contract law. The panel must also consider the different rights uniquely held and the obligations owed by each of the interested individuals, groups, museums, sovereign and quasi-sovereign entities. In particular, the panel must be cognizant of the legal fiduciary responsibility for conserving and protecting collections.[35]

---

[35]   Id. at 124–127.

I concluded my testimony by stressing the role of museums in advancing cross-cultural understanding:

As you approach this complex situation, I hope you will consider the enormous contributions museums have made over centuries to knowledge and education. As human institutions, they have their failings as all humans do. Yet it is because of their central mission of collecting that we have preserved the cultural history of so many people. Museums have made extraordinary contributions to our under-standing of each other, as well stated by Walter Echo-Hawk when he wrote in 1986:

> Since their inception, museums in the United States have had a relationship with Native Americans that has been both beneficial and antagonistic. Museums played a vital role in the preservation of Native American culture during crisis periods in which the federal government actively sought to assimilate the Indian into the mainstream of American society.
>
> Today, these collections provide a means for all Americans to better understand, appreciate, and respect past and present-day American Indians. . . . Museums have played, and can continue to play a role as a bridge between cultures.

And Mr. Echo-Hawk correctly concludes that, "The relationship between museums and Indians has not always lived up to its fullest potential."[36]

At best my dispute resolution proposal and ex post facto substantive law argument were perceived as arcane. And so NAGPRA came into being with only a few of the larger anthropological/archaeological museums expressing reservations as to some of its provisions.

Suffice it to report that NAGPRA has brought museums and tribes closer together. Although there is potential constitutional "takings" vulnerability in the law, no museum has successfully challenged the act on that ground. The Field Museum trustees are greatly troubled by the fact that the law does not prohibit tribes from reselling repatriated cultural objects. As a consequence, the Field staff has been instructed by the board to negotiate an inalienable restriction with the tribe.

Since Congress appropriated inadequate funds to carry out the legislation, the Field Museum provides the equivalent of one coach airfare to enable a tribal representative or representatives to visit the museum. When tribal representatives visit, they are put in touch with Chicago's American Indian Center and the museum's Native American trustee.

Whenever the museum repatriates, the Illinois Attorney General is notified first, and the board itself officially repatriates by resolution. In some instances the Museum is asked by tribes to hold repatriated objects

---

[36] Id. at 128–129

indefinitely because they either do not have or cannot agree on an appropriate depository.

Because NAGPRA applies only to U.S. museums, private collectors who desire their collections to go intact to an institution must export them to a foreign museum. Ironically, the United States may need export controls on Native American collections. On the other hand, some foreign museums are voluntarily repatriating Native American objects as well as remains.

EXHIBITIONS

Museums need to be open to the representatives of the cultures represented in their collections. In particular, joint ventures build respect and mutually beneficial relationships. The classic case in point is the longtime relationship of the Oriental Institute of the University of Chicago with Egyptian scholars and governmental authorities. Joint research and exhibit ventures with source countries should be the norm and are especially crucial with respect to encyclopedic museum collections.

When it creates exhibits, the Field Museum includes representatives of the cultures and environments encompassed in the exhibits. For example, in the early 1900s the Field Museum purchased a Maori meeting house from an Englishman who had purchased it from a German who had acquired it in New Zealand. The current curator was concerned about how the present day Maori from the town of origin would feel about the museum's possession of the house. The museum connected with the Maori whose forebears were from that house. Young Maori were engaged to rehabilitate the house. The museum received long-term loans of portions of the house that remained in New Zealand. With the help of a corporate sponsor and the New Zealand government, a good-sized delegation of Maori traveled to Chicago for the rededication. Forty-eight hours before the event the Maori entered into an extensive palaver in their hotel. Some argued for repatriation of the house. The final vote was in favor of the house's staying at the Field Museum. The young Maori felt it was their joint project with the museum and the elders argued that this is an opportunity to educate people who do not know who the Maori are.

The Maori exhibit team was greatly interested in the Museum's Pawnee earth lodge, which was built jointly with a Pawnee advisory group. The Maori were impressed that the earth lodge is used for public programs, so they insisted that the museum make the meeting house available for meetings just as an active house would function.

In another instance, the Field Museum was approached by a large American foundation that felt that the museum has a major African collection and might be willing and able to remount an exhibit from the point of view of Africans and African Americans. The exhibition team was coheaded by an art historian whose father was a cultural leader (sultan) in the Cameroons and an African-American community activist. Several local African Americans on the Advisory Committee wanted the museum to dismantle the Egyptian exhibit that had just opened because it did not conform to their view. The museum did not do so. In one section of the Africa exhibit a label explains that a particular group of objects were taken from their original location by a British punitive expedition.

When exhibiting human remains and sacred objects from foreign countries, the Field Museum looks to the exhibition policies of those countries and the cultural practices of the people represented.

Recognizing the importance of place in understanding cultural context, both the Egyptian and African exhibits at the Field Museum explore ways the environment influences culture and culture impacts the environment.

Since the future of the Field Museum depends on cross-cultural relationships globally as well as locally, the museum's mission statement reflects this interdependency. The section, "Collections: World-Wide Knowledge Database," concludes by stipulating that

in discharging its collection trusteeship, the Museum recognizes the special relationship it has with the people whose cultures and habitats are represented in the collections. We will nurture these special relationships so together we can enhance greater understanding of cultural traditions and environmental surroundings for the benefit of all humankind.

Another section, designated "Linkages – Working with Others," asserts, "The Museum has an obligation to seek out and collaborate with researchers and teachers who reside in areas from which our collections come."

The last section, "Cultural Understanding and Mutual Respect: Listening to Each Other," concludes that

the Museum subject matter directly relates to the great issues of the present and the future: environmental and cultural diversity and their interrelationships. There are differing scholarly and public viewpoints on these concerns. While the Museum does not take institutional positions on these issues, it must serve as a center of free inquiry, a marketplace for multiple points of view on these matters. In doing so it serves as a forum where relevant controversy can be aired. In this way the Museum can be a "door in the wall" of our differences and inspire greater knowledge, understanding and respect for our varied natural environments and cultural heritages.

CONCLUSION

If it seeks to be international, a museum needs to be inclusive rather than exclusive. It is a custodian of collections for diverse publics and environments. Where the museum purports to have a multicultural mission, it must by definition embrace culturally diverse perspectives. Scholarly research and exhibits will be enriched by this universal approach.

At root, museum collections are about human relationships. When human relationships are open and engaging, museums prosper. Common sense and ethical precepts should take precedence over arcane and divisive legal duels when dealing with museum collections. In sum, I have drawn the same conclusion about tangible cultural property that Michael Brown has about intangible cultural property, namely, that we need to negotiate our way to more balanced and working relationships.[37]

A stellar example of this approach is the 2002 agreement entered into between the American Museum of Natural History and the Confederated Tribes of the Grand Ronde Community of Oregon maintaining the Willamette Meteorite at the museum and recognizing the Tribe's spiritual relationship to the meteorite. "The agreement reflects mutual recognition of and respect for the traditions of both the Tribe and the Museum."[38] In the twenty-first century a museum must be a center for cultural understanding and mutual respect.

[37] Brown, Who Owns Native Culture?, pp. 242–246, 247, 252 (2003).
[38] *See* at http://www.amnh.org., *see also* Shapiro, supra n. 3, at 105–108; Gerstenblith, The Public Interest in the Restitution of Cultural Objects, 6 *Conn. J. Int'l. L.* 197, 241–246 (2001); Maranda, *Heritage, Objects, Collecting: The Need for an Ethical Approach*, ICOM Intl Committee for Museology, 11–12 (2000).

4 IMPERIAL APPROPRIATIONS OF THE PARTHENON

William St Clair

One reason why the case of the Elgin Marbles offers an excellent paradigm for issues of imperialism, art and restitution is that we have two and a half thousand years of experience. Indeed, in the appropriations of the Parthenon, we have what is probably the most fully documented example in history of the interlocking links, the changing perceptions, and the current issues. I begin with two general points.

First, the appropriation of the Parthenon was part of the appropriation of Hellenism as a whole, a process that began in the ancient Hellenistic and Greco-Roman worlds, was resumed in the Western European tradition during the Renaissance, made significant scholarly, historical, archaeological, and scientific advances from the seventeenth century onwards, and is still continuing. Indeed, from the perspective of the present century, we can see that the export of parts of the building by Lord Elgin, the most drastic of all the past appropriations, occurred towards the peak of that long historical process, and that the central role of Hellenism in Western culture and education began to go into relative decline not long after. Second, in the long history of the Parthenon, it has been the viewers who had the visual experiences, who selected what was important to them in the act of viewing, who made the meanings, who internalised them, and who may also have acted upon them, both individually and collectively. Without viewers the Parthenon is a meaningless heap of marble, and viewers have never been the inert recipients of meanings recommended to them by others.

To recover the meanings that different constituencies of historical viewers have made is, of course, inherently extremely difficult and the evidence for some periods is sparse.[1] My approach is to attempt to situate changing

---

[1] The same issues arise when we try to assess the impact and influence of the reading of printed writings where the role of readers has often been ignored or downplayed.

viewerly responses within wider contexts, often unarticulated, that we can only know about from elsewhere. For this purpose, a prime resource are the narratives that have been advanced to legitimate the appropriations, and the physical and other means that the appropriators have used to try to persuade viewers to regulate their responses in accordance with these narratives. It is with these that we should engage when we consider restitution.

From the moment it was conceived in the fifth century BC, the Periclean Parthenon was a monument to imperialism. As had its predecessors, it asserted the identity of the people of Athens not only against non-Hellenes but against other Hellenic city states such as Sparta, Corinth, or Argos. But, since the cost of building was, to a large extent, financed by monetary contributions forcibly levied from the numerous other Hellenic cities under Athenian domination, the grandeur of the building emphasised that imperial meaning more obviously than either the temples of other Hellenic cities or the predecessor buildings in Athens. To Plato, who was deeply interested in the effects on minds of the viewing of works of art, the Periclean building programme was not only an extravagant waste of money on public display but an example of how art can be used to corrupt the citizenry.[2] One fourth-century Athenian, the orator Isocrates, thought that the Parthenon had succeeded in its aim of celebrating and legitimating the Athenian empire. As he wrote: 'Pericles . . . so adorned the city with temples, monuments, and other objects of beauty that even today visitors who come to Athens think her worthy of ruling not only the Hellenes but all the world.'[3] But for many fifth-century non-Athenians, we may confidently conjecture, the Parthenon was not a monument to the glories of contemporary Hellenic civilization, but a humiliating reminder of the recent assumption by Athens of a hegemony over their own cities.[4] Certainly, once the Athenian empire was broken up, as it had been by the time of Isocrates, there was no rush among the formerly subject cities to re-establish it.

For my investigation into how our view of the past is changed by shifting the main site of cultural formation from authors to readers, see *The Reading Nation in the Romantic Period* (Cambridge 2004).

[2] *Gorgias* 518–519.

[3] *Antidosis* 234.

[4] The few references and allusions to the monument in surviving ancient writings are noted and commented upon by Savas Kondaratos, The Parthenon as Cultural Ideal, in *The Parthenon and Its Impact in Modern Times*, general editor, Panayotis Tournikiotis (Athens: Melissa, 1994) 23–28.

For many years it has been common to describe the Parthenon as a monument to democracy. The European Union, which is helping to finance the current conservation programme on the Athenian Acropolis, is following the United Nations Educational, Scientific, and Cultural Organization (UNESCO) and some United States government agencies in promoting the iconic image of the monument on official documents as a symbol of all that is best in the shared Western democratic heritage. It is, of course, possible for democracy at home to coexist with empire abroad. It is true too that when the Periclean Parthenon was built, Athens had, briefly, a democratic form of government – although one confined to the free male citizens. In a famous passage Thucydides set out in the funeral oration of Pericles a statement of the ideals of the Athens of that time and contrasted them with those of other cities.[5] But there is nothing symbolic of democracy about the iconography of the Parthenon itself, and the heavy work of quarrying, transporting, and construction was done by slaves.[6] The modern meaning, while not exactly untrue or unhistorical, exists in the mind of viewers, including viewers of representations, and of those who have tried to influence them, including Pericles, not in the original fifth-century text of the monument. Indeed, uncomfortable though it may be to admit it, the iconography of the Parthenon lends itself more easily to appropriation by fascist ideologies than by democratic. In ancient mythology, the Hellenes were often presented as engaged in an ongoing struggle against uncivilized barbarians symbolically represented as giants, amazons, and half-human monsters. The metopes of the Parthenon portray gruesome scenes of personal life and death combat between Hellenes and centaurs, an aestheticisation of inter-racial violence.

In discussing the state of the Hellenic world in the fifth century, Thucydides offered a fascinating aside. If, he says, the city of Sparta, which had no grand temples, should ever be abandoned, posterity would be reluctant to believe that it had once been so strong. If, however, Athens were to become a ruin, posterity would wrongly guess its power to have been twice what it actually was. Thucydides has been proved right.[7] In recent centuries those who admired the Spartans, of whom there have been many, had no monuments round which to cluster their narratives – indeed the

---

[5] Book 2, 35–46.
[6] For a thoughtful series of essays that discuss the possible effects of democracy on Athenian art, see Deborah Boedeker and Kurt A. Raaflaub, editors, *Democracy, Empire, and the Arts in Fifth-Century Athens* (Harvard 1998).
[7] Book 1, 10.

rejection of art by the Spartans was part of their appeal.[8] Of the many types of political system that existed in the Hellenic world, empires, democracies, oligarchies, tyrants, enlightened despots, monarchies with hereditary military elites, and others, the Parthenon by the sheer fact of its imposing continuing presence has tended to overwhelm the memory of cities other than Athens, centuries other than the fifth, and Hellenic political systems other than democracy. Furthermore, later generations have actively cooperated in shaping the viewerly experience towards that selected memory. During the nineteenth century, for example, almost all the non-fifth-century buildings that formerly stood on the Acropolis were removed. In order to promote the special claims of fifth-century Athens on the modern viewer, the visible remains of over two thousand years of other Athenian pasts were destroyed.

The Parthenon was in use as an ancient temple for nearly a thousand years. During that time a succession of non-Athenians, beginning with Alexander of Macedon, adopted the building to try to legitimate their claims to be the inheritors of classical Athens. A fine fourth-century head of Alexander in Pentelic marble, with many surviving traces of red colouring, apparently the base paint for representing his golden-coloured hair, was found near the Erechtheion on the Acropolis in 1886. It was exhibited in New York in 2004 and 2005, a fine example, incidentally, of how, when museums cooperate in lending items from their collections, large constituencies of viewers, historians, archaeologists, scholars, and art historians, as well as the general public, derive benefits that are otherwise entirely beyond reach.[9]

To help with these post-Periclean appropriations, the ancient Parthenon was architecturally altered to drive home the message that the city of Athens was now under external domination. New features were added to the building, but the main change was to construct monuments on the Acropolis, in some cases so close up against the Parthenon as to interpose themselves between the temple and its viewers.[10] Although these architectural additions usually presented themselves as homage to the building, we can be confident

[8]   See Elizabeth Rawson, *The Spartan Tradition in European Thought* (Oxford 1969).
[9]   Acropolis Museum 1331. See the full description, discussion, and illustration in Dimitrios Pandermalis, editor, *Alexander the Great, Treasures from an Epic Era of Hellenism* (New York: Alexander S. Onassis Public Benefit Foundation, 2004).
[10] The additions are described and in some cases illustrated by Manolis Korres, 'The Parthenon from Antiquity to the 19th Century', in *The Parthenon and Its Impact in Modern Times*, general editor, Panayotis Tournikiotis (Athens: Melissa, 1994) 138–140.

that the experience of viewers, and the impact of the monument on their minds, was different from what it had been before the additions. But how did the viewers of the post-Periclean centuries of antiquity regard it? Was it a saddening reminder to the local Athenians of a great age lost and irretrievable, or a source of pride and inspiration to try to emulate it? Did the tourists who came from all over the multi-ethnic Greco-Roman world accept the justificatory narrative of the Roman empire; gratefully agree that the Hellenic heritage, of which they now had a share, was in safe hands; and feel strengthened in their loyalty to the imperial rulers under whose protection they lived?

Admiration for fifth-century Athens has been so widespread in both the ancient and the modern worlds that it is useful to recall that many have disagreed. The Christians who took over control of the eastern Roman empire in the fourth century AD closed the academies that had been founded by Plato and Aristotle, an action that represented the completeness of the triumph of the incoming monologistic theocracy over the pluralistic, enquiring, intellectual scepticism on which the achievement of classical Athens had been founded. The temple was converted into a church and the Virgin Athena became the Virgin Mary. In ancient times, when only priests normally entered the temple, the main view of the Parthenon for citizens was from the outside as they progressed on foot across the open spaces of the Acropolis. The external sculptural decoration, especially the frieze that wends round all four sides of the buildings, was designed to keep the eyes of viewers on the move. As far as the Christian Parthenon was concerned, by contrast, the main viewerly experience occurred when Athenians visited the building as worshippers. Those who entered the Parthenon, whose classical lines were now increasingly obscured by other buildings, encountered three vaults of rising height drawing their eyes upwards to the Christian religious images. In order to appropriate and subvert the Parthenon, the Christians changed the main view from mobile to static, from outside to inside.[11]

When the Ottoman Turks conquered the Byzantine empire in the fifteenth century, they converted the church into a mosque and built a minaret that, by a deception of the eye, appeared to rise from the centre of the roof. But, although they made few architectural changes, the main view was again changed. During the Ottoman centuries few Greeks or visitors were permitted to enter the fortress. From the town of Athens, almost all that could be

[11]   See William St Clair and Robert Picken, The Parthenon in 1687: New Sources, in Michael Cosmopoulos, editor, *The Parthenon and Its Sculptures* (Cambridge 2004) 166–195.

seen of the Parthenon was its minaret, the visual assertion of the supremacy of the successor empire. So powerful was the minaret as a symbol of Oriental domination that in contemporary Western engravings the Acropolis is sometimes wrongly shown with two minarets.

For the second thousand years of its existence, the Parthenon was presented to viewers not as a monument to classical Athens, let alone to democracy, but as a symbol of the completeness of the defeat of the values that classical Athens had embodied. That was part of the general legitimating narrative of all the main successor empires that took over the building, the Byzantine Christians from the east, the Roman Catholic crusaders from the west, and the Moslems from the east.

It was the Christian/Moslem Parthenon that the first wave of educated travellers from Western Europe discovered when they began to arrive in Athens in the late seventeenth century. Unlike their predecessors who were dependent on unreliable local traditions, they had a full knowledge of the ancient Greek and Latin authors. Within a short time, they had retrieved a full and largely accurate understanding of the main architectural and artistic characteristics of the Periclean predecessor and of its religious and civic purposes. During the eighteenth century, as a result of the excellent, careful, and accurately measured work by the second wave of archaeologists, architects, and artists, engravings of the recovered details of the fifth-century Parthenon were diffused throughout the Europeanised world. Buildings modelled on the Parthenon, as mediated to architects by engravings, are to be found in many countries. Berlin by the early nineteenth century had become the Athens on the Spree. Edinburgh was the Athens of the North.[12]

I think it is fair to say that Greek revival architecture both represented and presented the ideals of the European Enlightenment, scholarly, exact, scientific, humanist, questioning, international. Although there was admiration for ancient Athenian art and architecture, the Enlightenment appropriation was not seen within the limiting contexts of art or architectural history or of connoisseurship. The Enlightenment was engaged in an attempt to extend the boundaries of the recovery of Hellenism as a whole, of which ancient art was only part. Figure 4.1, for example, shows a typical visual attempt to offer an understanding of how the ancient Parthenon may have appeared

---

[12] Architectural copies are discussed by Panayotis Tournikiotis, 'The Place of the Parthenon in the History and Theory of Modern Architecture' in Tournikiotis 201–257.

Figure 4.1. The ancient Parthenon as imagined in the eighteenth century

Figure 4.2. The ancient Academy of Athens, a companion piece

as a building.[13] Its companion Figure 4.2 shows that it was the ideals of the ancient academy of Athens that the Enlightenment appropriators wished to promote, an attitude of mind not just an architectural style.[14] These

13 H. W. Williams, *Select Views in Greece* (London 1829).
14 Ibid.

and similar images were carried by engravings and re-engravings across the Europeanised world.[15]

In European countries, by the end of the eighteenth century, such an aura already attached to the building in a faraway country that only a handful of citizens had seen that the Parthenon was only copied when the most dignified of public monuments were commissioned, such as the Valhalla in Bavaria and the Scottish National Monument. These copies were mainly built, in imitation of the Acropolis of Athens, in positions of prominence on outcrops of high ground. In Scotland, where a full-scale replica was intended, the sponsors ran out of money before it could be completed, so Edinburgh has its own ruined, or rather partially built, Parthenon, which provides a visual contrast to the mediaeval castle, the closely packed old town, and the older values that the Enlightenment hoped to supersede. Figure 4.3 shows the Edinburgh Parthenon under construction beside the astronomical observatory and above the Royal High School recently rebuilt in the style of the Propylaia on the Athenian Acropolis.[16] Figure 4.4 shows a vision of Enlightenment Edinburgh that closely resembles the visions of ancient Athens offered by artists of the time.[17]

In the United States, by contrast, the Parthenon was routinely copied to give dignity not only to public buildings but to commercial and financial institutions and large private plantation residences. With these later representations and adaptations, as with the Parthenon itself, we may be sure, a mismatch soon developed between the aspirations, intentions, and experiences of those who first constructed them and those of successor generations. It seems unlikely, for example, that many present-day viewers

[15] For example, in the German and French bilingual book by C. Frommel, *Ansichten aus Griechenland* (c. 1830) and in the engravings used to illustrate the innumerable editions in several languages of Barthelemy's *Voyage d'un Jeune Anacharsis en Grèce*, which also draw on Williams.

[16] *Modern Athens, Displayed in a Series of Views of Edinburgh in the Nineteenth Century... from original drawings by Mr Thomas H. Shepherd* (London 1829) 48.

[17] Done in 1866 by J. Dick Peddie, reproduced in colour in *The National Monument to Be Completed for the Scottish National Gallery on the Model of the Parthenon at Athens* (London: Adam and Charles Black, 1907). For another colour reproduction of a fine picturesque view of Edinburgh as the emerging new Athens showing the Calton Hill as an acropolis with its Parthenon in the distance and St Anthony's Chapel playing the role of the Monument of Philopappos, see J.C.B Cooksey, *Alexander Nasmyth 1758–1840* (Paul Harris 1990) C26.

Figure 4.3. The Edinburgh Parthenon under construction

of the plain replica of the Parthenon in Wall Street, New York, built on the site where George Washington took his oath as the first president of the United States, and long since dwarfed by banks that flaunt an imperialising ethos of global private capitalism, are strengthened in their adherence to the

Figure 4.4. A vision of Enlightenment Edinburgh as the new Athens

ideals of a well-informed, public-spirited, and participative citizenry that
the early republic wished to promote.[18]

Let me now turn to the physical removal and export abroad of portions of
the Parthenon and to the justifications for these appropriations that have
been offered to viewers. In 1687, in a war between an alliance of Western
countries and the Ottoman Turks, a shell fired by the invading army struck
the building, which was being used as a gunpowder store. The Parthenon was
blown apart by the blast and has been a ruin ever since, although with some
restoration. When, after the surrender of the Acropolis, the commander of
the Western armies, Morosini, attempted to remove the large pedimental
sculptures from the building to take home to Venice as a trophy, his ropes
and tackles broke, and the largest and most visible surviving sculptures were
shattered. Only a few – mainly small – pieces of the Parthenon left Athens
at that time.

Morosini's bungled attempts to export sculptures from the Parthenon
had little or nothing to do with admiration for the Hellenic heritage. He
and his armies were simply asserting their military power by taking war
booty from a conquered land, just as the ancient Romans had taken ancient
Greek art to Rome and Byzantium, and earlier Western armies had plundered Byzantium. If Morosini had taken, and not just destroyed, parts of the
Parthenon, his justificatory narrative would have been right of conquest.
This episode is a useful reminder to those who wish to judge present day
public policy on restitution issues in accordance with backward-looking
criteria on what was legal at the time. International law recognised a right
of conquest at least until 1918, and that is the only legitimating narrative
for the presence of some pieces held in museums in Britain and other
countries.

To give just one example, among the objects in Western museums for
which the allegedly legal justification rests on right of conquest are the bronze
heads and figures that were taken from the African kingdom of Benin, in
present day Nigeria, by an invading British army in 1897. These objects,
artistically and technologically of extremely high quality, were central to
the beliefs and rituals of the court of Benin for hundreds of years. They
remind modern viewers of all races that Africa had local artistic traditions

---

[18]   The present building was constructed between 1834 and 1842, the previous building
having been demolished in 1812. See Charles J. Ziga, *New York Landmarks* (New York
1993) 9.

comparable to those of Europe. Indeed the first Europeans to see the Benin bronzes could only explain them by postulating and exaggerating European influence. The circumstances in which they were acquired were described by A. P. R. Pitt Rivers, a British military officer who was part of the expedition and who was among the first in the West to appreciate their historical and artistic value.

In 1896 an expedition, consisting of some 250 men, with presents and merchandise, left the British settlements on the coast, and endeavoured to advance towards Benin city. The expedition was conducted with courage and perseverance, but with the utmost rashness. Almost unarmed, neglecting all ordinary precautions, contrary to the advice of the neighbouring chiefs, and with the express prohibition of the King of Benin to advance, they marched straight into an ambuscade which had been prepared for them in the forest on each side of the road, and as their revolvers were locked up in their boxes at the time, they were massacred to a man with the exception of two, Captain Boisragon and Mr Locke, who, after suffering the utmost hardships, escaped to the British settlements on the coast to tell the tale.

Within five weeks after the occurrence, a punitive expedition entered Benin, on 18th January, 1897, and took the town. The king fled, but was afterwards brought back and made to humiliate himself before his conquerors, and his territory annexed to the British crown.

The city was found in a terrible state of bloodshed and disorder, saturated with the blood of human sacrifices offered up to their Juju, or religious rites and customs, for which the place had long been recognised as the "city of blood."

What may hereafter be the advantages to trade resulting from this expedition it is difficult to say, but the point of chief interest in connection with the subject of this paper was the discovery, mostly in the king's compound and the Juju houses, of numerous works of art in brass, bronze, and ivory, which, as before stated, were mentioned by the Dutchman, Van Nyendaeel, as having been constructed by the people of Benin in 1700.

These antiquities were brought away by members of the punitive expedition, and sold in London and elsewhere. Little or no account of them could be given by the natives, and as the expedition was as usual, unaccompanied by any scientific explorer charged with the duty of making inquiries upon matters of historic and antiquarian interest, no reliable information about them could be obtained. They were found buried and covered with blood, some of them having been used amongst the apparatus of their Juju sacrifices.

A good collection of these antiquities, through the agency of Mr. Charles Read, F.S.A., has found its way into the British Museum; others no doubt have fallen into the hands of persons whose chief interest in them has been as relics of a sensational and bloody episode, but their real value consists in their representing a phase of art – and rather an advanced stage – of which there is no actual record, although we cannot be far wrong in attributing it to European influence, probably that of the Portuguese some time in the sixteenth century.[19]

A photograph taken on the spot in 1897 shows a heap – or rather a wall – of the bronze heads and other figures stacked, higglety pigglety six or ten feet high, awaiting removal to the coast and export to London.[20] In London many were then sold at public auction, in order to defray the costs of the military intervention, and they have since made their way to many collections, public and private, with a selection being presented to the British Museum. The Benin case exemplifies the most direct form of imperialism, the use of armed force by one country to take – in this case loot – the resources of a weaker country.

The Benin bronzes also exemplify another imperial narrative, the attempt to justify the destruction of the context that gave the objects their original meaning by reconceptualising them as 'works of art' in accordance with post-romantic Western aesthetics, a point I discuss later in relation to the Parthenon. Unfortunately, they also illustrate another consideration relevant to issues of restitution. In present [2005] circumstances, there are is no guarantee that if the objects were returned, the authorities in the localities concerned would be able to ensure that they would be suitably preserved, conserved, and displayed.

Let me now turn to Lord Elgin. From the beginning, before he even left Scotland, Elgin had developed a well-informed admiration for the Hellenic heritage and for Hellenic architecture in particular. His original purpose had been to continue the Enlightenment agenda of appropriation by imitation by employing artists and moulders to make accurate drawings and plaster casts so that Western artists and architects would have reliable models on which to base Western neo-Hellenic art and architecture. It was only when, by a stroke of political fortune, Elgin found himself able to remove pieces of the building that he seized his moment. Over the next twenty years or so, his agents were able to remove most of the best surviving sculptures that had previously formed part of the building. Incidentally, the claim made by supporters of the status quo, that about half the surviving sculptures are in Athens – apparently an attempt to introduce some kind of legitimating

---

[19] Lieutenant-General A. P. R. Pitt Rivers, *Antique Works of Art from Benin, Collected by Lieutenant-General Pitt Rivers, DCL, FRS, FSA* (printed privately 1900) Preface.

[20] Reproduced in *Royal Art of Benin, The Perls Collection* (New York: Metropolitan Museum of Art, 1992) 16.

justification by '*partage*' into the discussion – is only true in an unimportant and misleading sense. With few exceptions, for example, the metopes in Athens are so badly effaced as to be unrecognisable.

The 'firman', the document upon which the claim that the Marbles were legally acquired by Lord Elgin ultimately rests, consists of a letter of four pages that was sent in May 1801 by the Caimacam, the second highest official in the Ottoman Empire, (temporarily in charge while the Grand Vizier was on campaign), to the Governor and Chief Justice of Athens. Since much of the recent published writing about this firman appears to me to be based on misunderstandings – driven, in some cases, by a wish to hack away at any suggestion that Elgin's appropriation might had official authorisation – it may be worth offering a full comment.

The word *firman* appears to have been used by Western visitors in the whole region from India to the Balkans to mean official permission.[21] Travellers in the Ottoman Empire seem usually to have obtained a firman, equivalent to a personal passport, that carried the official insignia, 'tougra', of the Ottoman Porte, and carrying this document could help open doors. Richard Pococke, for example, who was in Athens in 1740, noted that the English consul 'introduced me to the Waiwode, to whom I made a very handsome present; and on shewing my firman, he said, he was there to obey the Grand Signor's commands; so that I saw every thing in and about Athens with the utmost freedom.'[22] In 1755 the French artist Le Roy obtained permission to draw and set up ladders and scaffolds in the Acropolis with the help of the French consul.[23] But by 1800, perhaps because it was wartime, Elgin's secretary, Hunt, was advised that 'your imperial Firman will not open to you the gates of one Turkish fortress; it will be necessary therefore, to procure admission to the Acropolis by a present of ten piastres or its equivalent in Coffee and Sugar.[24] Elgin's 'firman' of 1801 was not a routine document like a passport that usually carried the tougra but a specially prepared official letter of far higher authority.

Two official versions were prepared by the Ottoman government, one in Turkish, and the other in Italian, the lingua franca of the eastern Mediterranean. Both letters, the Turkish and the Italian, were taken by Philip

---

[21] Used this way, for example, in a semi-official collection of documents, Jean Henri Abdolonyme Ubicini, *La Question d'Orient devant l'Europe. Documents officiels, manifestes, notes, firmans, circulaires, etc.* (Paris 1854).

[22] Richard Pococke, *A Description of the East* (London 1755) 169.

[23] Roger Middleton editor, Introduction to *Julien-David Le Roy, The Ruins of the Most Beautiful Monuments of Greece* (Los Angeles 2004) 9.

[24] Hunt papers, in possession of the author, hitherto unpublished.

Hunt, Elgin's secretary, to Athens in 1801 and used to enforce the removals. When Hunt appeared before the 1816 Select Committee of the House of Commons, he described how he asked Elgin to apply for a firman, and 'as I had been before deceived with respect to the pretended contents of a fermaun, I begged that this might be accompanied by a literal translation; the fermaun was sent with a translation, and that translation I now possess. It is left at Bedford, and I have no means of directing any person to obtain it; I would have brought it if I had been aware I should be summoned by this Committee before I left Bedford'[25] The document then disappeared until I discovered it among the Hunt papers in 1962. The Turkish version, which was delivered to the Ottoman addressees, is likely to have perished with the other Ottoman records in the Greek War of Independence, and no copy was found when I arranged for an official search in the archives in Istanbul.

David Rudenstine of the Cardozo Law School in New York has suggested that the Italian version of the firman is some kind of forgery, rigged up by Elgin and Hunt to provide legitimation. He puts great weight on the fact that the document is not signed and therefore, he claims, would not be accepted as legal proof in a modern court.[26] However, the Italian version of the firman is documented in detail in the historical record and its authenticity as an official Ottoman document, its provenance, and its pedigree are all secure. That it is genuine is further confirmed by the fact that it is written on paper from a mill in the Veneto known to have been used by the Ottoman Porte, in the handwriting of Pisani, the dragoman. As for the notion that the only documents that we should be willing to accept as evidence are originals personally signed, if we were to take that seriously, we would have no knowledge of any kind about ancient Hellas or indeed about most periods of the past.

It was by presenting the official letter from the Acting Head of the Ottoman Government to the Governor and the Military Governor in Athens that Hunt was able to persuade them to permit the removal of the sculptures from the Parthenon, although removals from the building do not appear to be allowed for by the wording. The key phrase at the end of the document appears to mean that Elgin could take away any pieces of stone he found in digging, not that he could take pieces of the building. Hunt, a representative of the

[25] *Select Committee Report* page 141.
[26] David Rudenstine, Lord Elgin and the Ottomans: The Question of Permission in *Cardozo Law Review*, 23, January 2002, page 452, and A Tale of Three Documents: Lord Elgin and the Missing Historic 1801 Ottoman Document in *Cardozo Law Review*, 22, page 1865.

British state with a representative of the central Ottoman government at his side, threatened to have the officials removed from their posts, or sent to the galleys, if they did not comply. The officials were at the same time given large monetary inducements. Since the third edition of my book *Lord Elgin and the Marbles* was published in 1998, I have been able to examine the financial accounts that are in the possession of the present Lord Elgin. Since they are written in a mixture of languages and currencies they are not at first easy to understand and have not been given any attention by previous researchers among the Elgin papers. But to me, as a former official of the British Treasury, there are few types of evidence better than itemised financial accounts for revealing what really went on.[27]

The Military Governor received payments in the first year alone equivalent to thirty-five times his annual salary. The Governor was given more, and even larger amounts that do not appear in the accounts were paid to officials in Constantinople. The firman, in form a favour granted by the Sultan to the official representative of an ally, who happened to be interested in antiquities, was in practice a private mining concession to extract antiquities from the Acropolis of Athens. The paradigm point is this. No administrative or judicial system can be expected to withstand such a weight of political influence and money. This is imperialism in action, destroying not only monuments but the local administrative and legal infrastructure. And there are plenty of lesser Elgins at work today bribing officials, breaking pieces from ancient buildings, encouraging destructive digging of archaeological sites, making collections of 'unprovenanced' antiquities, and destroying knowledge about the past.

Later, because of doubts about the legality of what had been done under the authority of the 1801 firman, Elgin and later ambassadors obtained other firmans whose effect was to give an amnesty to those who might have broken the law and that, by permitting the export of Elgin's collection from Ottoman jurisdiction, implied that he was the legitimate owner. It is because of these later firmans, whose texts do not surviv, but are well attested in the record as having been obtained with huge inducements and political pressures, that some lawyers, notably John Merryman, have concluded that Elgin had good title to the collection and the right to sell it to the British state. Although, in my opinion, we should not make policy today by guessing at what may or may not have been legal long ago and far away, I doubt whether the argument is decisive. Decisions by public officials to exceed their authority that are

---

[27] Extracts published in William St Clair, The Elgin Marbles: Questions of Stewardship and Accountability in *International Journal of Cultural Property*, (2) 1999.

obtained by inducements are questionable under most systems of law, and I know of no lawyer who says that Ottoman law was exceptional.

I now turn from the firman to the legitimating narrative. From the moment that the first sculptured metope was cut out from the building, put on a cart, and loaded on a British warship, Elgin's Hellenism contained an inescapable contradiction. How could the violence that he had done to the monument be explained as the actions of a lover of Greek art? How could his removal of the best surviving sculptural pieces be an act of homage? Elgin was publicly attacked as a plunderer as early as 1803 before any of the Marbles had even reached England.[28] The answer was to present the export as a 'rescue'. During the quarter-century before Elgin, the building had suffered greatly from an unprecedented inflow of Western tourists and naval and military servicemen of many Western countries. Eager to acquire even the smallest carved fragment as a souvenir, they had created a lively market for broken-off pieces that the Ottoman soldiers of the fortress were able to supply. Elgin's removals put a stop to the casual pillage and pilfering, which had done more damage in a few years than had occurred in the century since Morosini. To that extent, he was able to claim, with some justice, that he was performing an act of rescue. Or, put another way, to illustrate the paradigm point, he had rescued the Marbles from the consequences of a free market in antiquities encouraged by a booming Western demand in a state that had weak administrative and judicial institutions.

But how could the Elgin appropriation continue to be justified when, with the establishment not long afterwards of an effective modern Greek state, the dangers from which the exported pieces had been 'rescued' no longer existed in Athens? And when those pieces that had been exported faced other risks, such as air pollution in the nineteenth and early twentieth centuries, aerial bombing in the twentieth, and terrorism in the twenty-first, that were higher in London than in Athens? The answer was to add a narrative of stewardship to that of rescue. Elgin had 'placed them in security for ever'. That was the defence of his supporters as early as 1810 in reply to criticisms in the British press.[29]

---

[28]   *The Gentleman's Magazine . . .* for the year MDCCCIII. Volume LXXIII. Part the Second, page 103, not previously known to me or noticed by others as far as I can see.

[29]   *The Gentleman's Magazine and Historical Chronicle. From July to December 1810. Volume LXXX. Part the Second.* page 335, not previously known to me or noticed by others as far as I can see.

In developing and promoting the rescue and stewardship narrative in the nineteenth and twentieth centuries, the British appropriators of the Parthenon were following the justificatory narrative of the British empire, an institution that for most of its history struggled with similar contradictions. Like the lands of the overseas colonial empire, the legitimating narrative of the Marbles proclaimed, they had not been taken by force. They had been legitimately – and legally – acquired with the consent of the then rulers of the country. They had been saved from chaos and barbarism and were being carefully looked after by an imperial protecting power that had their best interests at heart. I say that this was the legitimating narrative of the British empire, but it has been deployed by many other empires. The Athenians had a rescue narrative for their empire and were forever accusing the rescued cities of ingratitude when they did not accept it. They also had the beginnings of a stewardship narrative in the appointment of *hellenotamiai*, 'stewards for Hellas' of the centralised imperial treasury, although these stewards did not prevent the revenues of the subject cities from being misappropriated into public works in Athens. And of course present day American-led imperialism also deploys a rescue and stewardship narrative, for example, to justify the invasion and occupation of Iraq.

The Elgin Marbles played a role in the legitimating narrative of empire. The presence in central London of the greatest works of art hitherto attained by the mind of man – as they were connoted by nineteenth-century Western artists, art historians, critics, and many others – helped to reinforce the claim that the British empire was essentially different from other empires, past and present. It was exceptional, benign, caring, intellectual, and artistic, founded on consent, scarcely an empire at all but a temporary trusteeship during which non-independent territories were being prepared for the equality of democracy and independence.

In the nineteenth century, the Parthenon in Athens and the Elgin Marbles in London offered different, and to some extent reciprocal, meanings to different viewerships. In independent Greece, the monument was central to a long pursued national Westernising agenda, although that was not its meaning abroad.[30] Figure 4.5 shows a typical representation of the Parthenon in the early nineteenth century as it was received by viewers in the West through engravings and accounts by travellers. The scene is vaguely

---

[30] In addition to the usual sources that discuss this aspect, such as William St Clair, *Lord Elgin and the Marbles* (Oxford revised edition 1998), see the important study by Anastasia-Helen Yalouri, *Global Fame, Local Claim: The Athenian Acropolis as an Objectification of Greek Identity* (Oxford: Berg, 2000).

Figure 4.5. The denuded Acropolis of Athens, being viewed in the nineteenth century as a symbol of ruin of empire

Oriental, peaceful, largely deserted except for sheep, but with weapons that are needed for local control.[31] This is a colonial Parthenon, one that mainly serves the psychological and political needs of Western admirers of Hellenism. Colonel Napier, of a family famous as conquerors in India, contemplates how far Athens had fallen. As Byron wrote, 'Fair Greece Sad Relic.' The Parthenon is a lesson in what happens to great nations when, as Cecil Rhodes later declared, they become effeminate and lose their will to rule.

Meanwhile in London, as Figure 4.6 illustrates, the Elgin Marbles were shown not only divorced from their Athenian geographical, climatic, historical, religious, and architectural context, and displayed as 'works of art' in accordance with European post-romantic aesthetics, but incorporated into a metropolitan, 'universal', museum that, by the sheer extent and miscellaneity of its collections, celebrated British national and imperial success.[32] And they were shown outside in.

Let me now turn to another aspect of the Parthenon that is central to the tradition of appropriation by the West. Since the Renaissance, the main Western

---

[31]   Major General Edward Hungerford Delaval Elers Napier, *Excursions along the Shores of the Mediterranean* (London 1842) frontispiece to second volume.
[32]   *British Museum Elgin Room* an engraving by L. Jewitt, 1840s.

British Museum, – Elgin Room.

Figure 4.6. The Elgin Room in the British Museum in London, the experience offered to metropolitan viewers at around the same time

tradition of monumental sculpture has been marble, uniformly white. This tradition not only was practiced but was supported by a body of art historical and aesthetic theory. The essence of sculpture, wrote Winckelmann in the eighteenth century, is pure form, as distinct from painting which uses colour. Form is essentially different from colour. White is the essence of purity, the essence of classicism. In fact, by the late eighteenth century the Enlightenment archaeologists had discovered that the Periclean Parthenon and its sculptures had not been white marble but had been brightly painted, gilded, and heavily adorned and criss-crossed with metal attachments, including reins, bridles, weapons, and wreaths, also painted. These discoveries, which meant that the whole Western understanding and practice of classicism had been wrong, and which was reconfirmed again and again by innumerable ancient sculptures recovered from the earth by excavation, caused consternation among artists and their patrons all over Europe and North America, for if the Periclean artists had painted their statues, should not the moderns follow their example? That would make modern marble art look 'Oriental' and in the case of female nude statues, pornographic? All through the nineteenth and much of the twentieth century, many artists and archaeologists ignored or contested the truth of the archaeological discovery. Others were prepared to say that the ancients had simply shown bad taste in painting their statues and the sculptures from the Parthenon were more authentic with the colour gone.

The metal parts of the artistic composition, which contradicted the Winckelmann theory even more directly, were also ignored or explained away as of no consequence to modern viewers. So powerful is the persisting ideology of classicism-as-form that its influence is evident in even the most unlikely places. In the British Museum, for example, the explanatory gallery that was opened in 1998 – financed, incidentally, by a collector of mostly 'unprovenanced' antiquities – offers viewers reconstructions of how the Parthenon sculptures might have looked in ancient times. With the help of computers, these reconstructions restore the limbs and heads that either are in Athens or have been lost, and they add back the lost colour. But they omit the metal altogether. What, in the case of the Parthenon frieze, is a straightforward composition with a strong narrative line, is made incomprehensible to viewers.

But there was a more sinister side to the cult of whiteness. In the nineteenth century Robert Knox, an Edinburgh anatomist, who also wrote about the Elgin Marbles, offered an apparently scientific anthropology of the different qualities of different races, the brave northener, the cowardly Jew, the untrustworthy Oriental, and so on.[33] Drawing on Knox, a false history was constructed that the ancient Hellenes were a white blue-eyed people closely related racially to the northern Anglo-Saxon and Germanic peoples who were their true successors. In the promulgation of this racist theory, the Elgin Marbles, and the white casts that were more often seen than the original marbles, played an explicit role. In an important recent study, *Chromophobia*, David Batchelor, an art historian and critic, notes that the fear of colour in the Western art tradition is not a small or light matter. The fear, he shows historically, long predates Winckelmann and lies deep and unacknowledged in many attitudes, including of course those of European and American imperialism. As Batchelor writes:

Chromophobia manifests itself in the many and varied attempts to purge colour from culture, to devalue colour, to diminish its significance, to deny its complexity. More specifically: this purging of colour is usually accomplished in one or two ways. In the first, colour is made to be the property of some "foreign body," usually the feminine, the oriental, the primitive, the infantile, the vulgar, the queer or the pathological. In the second, colour is relegated to the realm of the superficial, the supplementary, the inessential or the cosmetic. In one, colour is regarded as alien and therefore dangerous; in the other, it is perceived merely as a secondary quality of experience, and thus unworthy of serious consideration. Colour is dangerous, or it is trivial, or it is both.[34]

In the light of subsequent events, the opening sequences of Leni Riefenstahl's film *Olympiade*, which celebrates the 1936 Olympic Games, should send a chill through every present-day viewer. The film opens with a vision of ancient Athens, with the deserted Parthenon emerging from the mists of time. White statues of ancient athletes and enticing women give way to the beautiful bodies of their modern white successors. We see the torch carried to Berlin, the nations marching in military formations past Hitler, some giving the Nazi salute, and we hear the approving roar of the crowd.

During the Nazi period, German classical scholars came forward to lend their professional support to the fascist ideologies of the day. Ernst Buschor, for example, in a book published in Germany during the war, picking up the Knox/Nazi racial narrative, described the ancient Greeks as a Nordic

---

[33] See Robert Knox, *The Races of Mankind* (London 1850) 400, 596; *Great Artists and Great Anatomists, A Biographical and Philosophical Study* (London 1852) 137; *A Manual of Artistic Anatomy for the Use of Sculptors, Painters, and Amateurs* (London 1852) 34, 134, 172.

[34] David Batchelor, *Chromophobia* (London 2000) 22–23.

people who had entered from the North.[35] He followed this with a little book, *War in the Age of the Parthenon*, which was distributed to soldiers and students. With its photographs of serene classical funerary monuments as well as scenes of fighting and death shown on vases and sculptures, the book offers encouragement and comfort to German soldiers by linking them to a great, and avowedly honourable, tradition of heroic war. The struggles between Hellenes and centaurs in the metopes of the Parthenon, although not said outright to be symbolic representations of the current war, are among the many scenes of violence recommended for aesthetic appreciation. In a preface, Buschor makes explicit the Nazi element of the appropriation by dedicating his book to the soldiers 'who have died for the Great Hellenic heritage on the borders of the west'.[36]

During the Second World War, in proportion to its population, Greece suffered more than any occupied country, with the possible exception of Poland, with plundering of its stores of food, starvation, deportation, atrocities, collective reprisals against whole towns, and the extirpation of the Jews of Thessalonika.[37] In the Nazi appropriation of Hellenism, the ancient Greeks were of the noble West; the modern Greeks were of the despised East. In Greece itself, as far as the occupying armies were concerned, the heritage lay only in the stones.[38] In 1946, an archaeological survey of the war damage found that the Parthenon and the other ancient Hellenic buildings had scarcely been scratched.

Meanwhile the Elgin Marbles in London had undergone a transformation that was also a result of the cult and ideology of whiteness. In 1928, the British government accepted an offer from an art dealer, Sir Joseph, later Lord, Duveen, to finance the building of a new Elgin Gallery at the British Museum. Among the motives of the British government in accepting Duveen's money, which was known to be tainted, was a wish to consolidate the claim to be

[35] Ernst Buschor, *Hellas, Bilder zur Kultur des Griechentums herausgegeben von Hans von Schoenbeck und Wilhelm Kraiker* (August Hopfer Verlag Burg B. M. 1943).

[36] Ernst Buschor, *Das Kriegertum der Parthenonzeit* (Munich 1943). 'Die auf griechischem Boden und an anderen Rändern des Abendlandes für das Grosse Griechische Erbe fielen.'

[37] See Mark Mazower, *Inside Hitler's Greece: The Experience of Occupation, 1941–44* (New Haven, London: Yale University Press, 1993).

[38] For example, *Fürungen durch Griechenland* (Eine Vortragsreihe des Deutschen Wehrmachtsenders Athens c. 1942) an illustrated booklet produced in Athens by the German army of occupation for the use of trooops made scarcely any mention of Greek history after antiquity.

the legitimate stewards of the Marbles and of the heritage of which they were an embodiment. As Neville Chamberlain, the Prime Minister, wrote privately to his sister on September 26, 1937, as Europe moved inexorably towards war, 'I think he [Duveen] has made sure that they [the Marbles] will never leave London but of course some day they may be bombed out of existence.'[39] The motives had parallels in the building of the imperial capital city of New Delhi that we can now see as an attempt to assert a confidence in the legitimacy and permanence of British rule in India, which was already crumbling.[40]

It was in 1937 and 1938, when Riefenstahl was editing her film for release, that another type of appropriation of the Parthenon was occurring in London. During these years, in response to the wishes of the Duveen, and encouraged by small bribes paid by his agents, the labourers of the British Museum scraped the surfaces of many of the sculptures with metal chisels and harsh abrasives in an effort to make them appear more white. The damage was done over a prolonged period without the knowledge of any of the curatorial staff. An inquiry under a judge, Lord Macmillan, concluded that 'the damage is obvious and cannot be exaggerated.'

As all archaeologists, historians, and art historians have long known, progress in understanding the ancient Hellenic past can proceed only as a result of careful attention to minute detail, and much progress has recently been made by new methods. The careful historical, archaeological, and scientific work done in recent decades on the site in Athens has added immeasurably to our understanding of the Parthenon and is continuing to do so. We can now read the initial results of the researches of Sarantis Symeonoglou, in which he believes he has identified a number of the artists of the Parthenon frieze, whom he calls Master A, Master B, and Master C. Symeonoglou reconstructs how the artist in charge, that is, Pheidias, is likely to have designed and allocated the carving, making use of the relative strengths of the artists, one in drapery, another in horses, another in faces, and so on. Symeonoglou's conclusions derive from months of minute study of the surfaces of the slabs of the Parthenon frieze that are in Athens.[41] Two points are relevant to our paradigm here. First, genuine research can only be fully effective if all the surviving slabs can be seen together so that close comparisons

---

[39]   Quoted by St Clair 1999 from Chamberlain papers, NC 18/1/1022, University of Birmingham Library.

[40]   See, for example, Robert Grant Irving, *Indian Summer. Lutyens, Baker, and Imperial Delhi* (New Haven, London: Yale University Press, 1981). The buildings include many features that emphasise the promise that India will soon become self-governing.

[41]   Published in Michael Cosmopoulos, editor, *The Parthenon and Its Sculptures* (Cambridge 2004).

can be made. Second, all research on the surfaces of many of the pieces from the Parthenon at present in London has been compromised.

The potential scale of the losses to knowledge inflicted by Duveen, and therefore to our and future generations' ability to understand and appreciate the Parthenon, has been graphically revealed by the recent work of Vincenz Brinckman and other German archaeologists and researchers in a work entitled *Bunte Götter Die Farbigkeit Antiker Skulptur.* They have shown how, by a study of the fine incisions left by the original artists on the architectural sculptures from the temple of Aphaia at Aegina, and above all by the pattern of surface erosion and patina affecting the differently coloured parts of the sculptures in different ways, which are still discoverable on the surfaces, they have been able to recover the original colour scheme of the whole pedimental composition.[42] They have recovered not just broad patches of blues, reds, yellows, and other colours used on the figures, but details of the elaborate coloured meander patterns of ornamentation on the hems of garments. It has long been known that the colour applied to ancient sculpture made it easier to see and understand, especially in the case of architectural sculptures such as those on the Parthenon, which had to be viewed from a distance. What the German archaeologists have also demonstrated is that colour brings out details of the plasticity of ancient sculpture that the eye cannot otherwise appreciate. Far from form and colour being opposed, as the Winckelmann aesthetic chromophobic tradition wrongly assumes, they reinforce one another.

From 1938 for sixty years, the authorities of the British Museum, in their desperation to maintain public confidence in the rescue and stewardship narrative, plunged into contradictions that deepened with every year. While claiming to be advancing scholarship, they impeded research and caused false information about ancient art to pass into circulation among archaeologists, art historians, and the public. While claiming to be the legitimate guardians of a monument to ancient Athenian democracy, the British Museum authorities repeatedly broke the laws, regulations, conventions, and standards of openness, accountability, and official conduct that are central to modern British democracy.[43]

[42] *Bunte Götter, Die Farbigkeit Antiker Skulptur* (Munich 2003). Catalogue of an exhibition held at the Glyptothek München, 16 December 2003–29 February 2004.
[43] Examples are noted in William St Clair, The Elgin Marbles: Questions of Stewardship and Accountability in *International Journal of Cultural Property*, (2) 1999, and in The Damage to the Marbles: Trusteeship and Accountability at the British Museum, *The Stakeholder*, journal of the Public Management Foundation, in a special supplement October 2001.

On 1 June 1998, Chris Smith, then the British Secretary of State for Culture, Media, and Sport, deployed the official rescue and stewardship narrative for what was to be the last time, in the House of Commons.[44] The narrative was repeated by outside supporters. The piece by Brian Sewell, the art critic of a London newspaper, did not disguise its racist assumptions:

Athens has managed very well without the Marbles since Lord Elgin rescued them in the first quinquennium of the 19th century. The Turks, whose Ottoman Empire then embraced all Greece and most of the Balkans, paid them scant regard, occasionally knocking off their vulnerable part for sport or to oblige passing travellers with souvenirs, but the Greeks themselves did far worse damage by grinding them down for mortar. Witnessing this, Elgin felt it his duty to save them from further depredation.... But who were these Greeks, early in the 19th century, and who are they now? They are not the Greeks of the ancient pre-Christian city societies that still capture the imaginations of all educated, romantic, oppressed and hopeful people who dream of democracy. They are not the Greeks whose language, literature and philosophies have formed the course of culture in the western world these past 2,000 years ... Ancient Greece, the mother of us all, subsided into a feeble, superstition-ridden, near-pagan agrarian society with not an idea in its head, its stock corrupted by Saracens, Sicilians, Normans, Bulgars, Venetians, Turks and any old Levantine, and I dare say that even the Scandinavian Varangians on their way to guard Byzantium planted a flaxen seed or two.[45]

The late Auberon Waugh, one hopes under a guise of irony, joined in the racist sneers, thinking it amusing to call the Greeks

some short-legged, hairy-bottomed foreigners, who have nothing whatever to do with the Ancient Athenians but who happen to occupy the space, being descended from Turkish invaders over the centuries.[46]

When the British Museum authorities were forced to admit both to the scale of the Duveen damage and to the attempted institutional cover-up, the rescue and stewardship narrative was revealed to have long been a sham. As in British India after the Amritsar massacre of 1919, it was not only the events themselves but the disingenuousness of the official responses, and the underlying attitudes that came to the surface, that convinced many people in Britain and elsewhere that the whole Elgin appropriation, whatever might

---

[44] 'The Parthenon sculptures were legally and properly acquired. They have been kept in very good condition – very great care has been taken of them ever since.' *Parliamentary Report*, Commons, 1 June 1998.

[45] Brian Sewell, We must never lose OUR marbles, Istoria List Archive, 18 May 1998, published in the *London Evening Standard* shortly before.

[46] *Daily Telegraph* 30 November 1999.

have been the case in the past, was now invalid and that the Marbles must go back.

The rescue and stewardship argument received yet another blow in July 2004 when eight of the sculptured marble blocks of the west side of the Parthenon frieze went on public view in the Acropolis Museum in Athens. For nearly two and a half thousand years the west frieze remained in its place. Apart from occasional washing and some nineteenth-century pinning to hold it more securely in place, there were few interventions. When in the 1970s it was realised that air pollution caused by recent industrialisation in the Athens area was damaging the monuments, a makeshift canopy was placed over the frieze so as to prevent acid rain from running over the surfaces. Then, in 1993, as part of the ambitious internationally funded programme of conservation, the topmost part of the Parthenon west porch was temporarily raised to permit the west frieze blocks to be lifted out intact and full-scale marble replicas installed in their place. They can now be examined close up by viewers for the first time ever.

As anyone can now see at once, the surfaces are quite different from those on the pieces taken to London, and from the other pieces of the frieze that were found in excavations in the nineteenth century after Elgin's departure and have been on show in Athens for many years. They look mostly brown, variegated with patches of white and orange. As has long been known, the local Pentelic marble from which the Parthenon, including its sculptural elements, was constructed is unusually rich in iron. Over the centuries, as the marble interacted with the atmosphere, the building became the distinctive rich golden colour that has been much admired. As anyone can also now see from the numerous marks of the artists' chisels and other tools that are visible on the brown but not the white parts of the surface, the brown is the original surface. Any parts of the frieze that are at present white or cream have lost a layer of marble and are, in varying degrees, damaged. The bright white gulleys caused by the rundown of pre-1978 acid rain are a pitiful sight. Scientific work showed that the surface consists of two monochromatic layers, called by the researchers the epistoma (30 to 100 micrometers) and the epidermis (80 to 120 micrometers). After international consultations, the Greek authorities decided on a laser process that vaporizes the dirt that had settled from particles in the air but that leaves the marble, and its colour, unchanged. The technique is similar to that used in eye surgery. In accordance with modern archaeological ethics, parts of the surfaces have been left uncleaned in order to enable future generations to make use of future techniques – the conservation equivalent of leaving part of an archaeological site undug.

What do the west frieze blocks reveal about their recent history? It can be seen that since Elgin's day, the block of a rider trying to control his unruly horse had lost the head of the male figure. When this serious damage occurred has not yet been determined – one possible time is during the Greek War of Independence of 1821–33 during which the Acropolis was besieged more than once – but it is tourist not war damage. To a large extent, the counterfactual claim that the Parthenon sculptures would not have survived if Elgin had not 'saved' them depends upon this lost head. The wonderful news for all those who value the Parthenon is that about 50 per cent of the monochromatic layers still survives – on some pieces far more. This is, by several orders of magnitude, the largest area of original marble surface of the Parthenon frieze that now exists, all but a few patches of the rest of the surfaces having been lost either through centuries of weathering or, in the case of many pieces in the British Museum, by deliberate scraping off. The west frieze in Athens is now, by far, the most precious resource that has survived anywhere for improving our understanding of the sculptured frieze of the Parthenon, how it was made, and how it appeared in ancient times. Since the monochromatic layers are the nearest we can ever get to the frieze as it existed in Pericles' day, it is also a resource that can be expected to yield more knowledge as new generations bring new techniques to bear. Visitors can see the traces of cobalt blue paint that is undoubtedly ancient, and some red about which there is uncertainty. By benign neglect and minimal intervention until action was unavoidable, the Greek authorities have saved for posterity not just the west frieze but knowledge itself.

However, even before its final collapse, the rescue and stewardship narrative was giving way to another justification that may have sounded more convincing because it appeared to be rooted in a more modern ideology. And here too we have a paradigm. Among the most pervasive and powerful forces of the present day is a belief that the main purpose of an organisation is to please the consumer of the goods and services that the organisation provides. If the customer does not like the product, change the product. Duveen, in his picture-dealing business, secretly altered old master paintings to make them fit the preconceptions of potential buyers. If the public expected Greek sculpture to be white, Duveen's response was to make them white.

One of the features of the recent attempts to construct a new legitimating narrative for the Elgin Marbles has been the eagerness of museum curators to adopt the ideology of consumerism and to press it upon the public. For example, the British Museum's appointed spokesman is on record as commending as 'a suitable last word on the affair' the following conclusion of a newspaper report: 'I doubt if the average visitor or even the average art-lover would notice any change but that of colour. But then how many average visitors ever gave them more than a passing glance'. In 1999 the editor of *The Times*, who had been given a privileged official briefing, commented that 'the brutal truth is that the marbles almost certainly look better than they would have looked without the chisel and carborundum'. If the rescue and stewardship story has been quietly dropped, the 'all-the-better-for-a-good scraping' argument is still alive and well. It can to be found, for example, in the official history of the British Musem written by a former director that was prepared as part of the celebration of the museum's anniversary in 2003.[47]

For the consumerist attempt at legitimation, too, scholars have stepped forward to offer their support. I quote from an argument offered by Mary Beard, an academic classicist, my colleague at Cambridge:

Perhaps we should not be thinking of the museum in terms of a stark contrast between academic and consumerist goals. The very idea of the museum is in a sense a trade-off, a difficult negotiation, between those two. Try replacing the word "consumerist" with "access" or "outreach".[48]

If I have understood her correctly, Beard assumes that because public museums in Britain are now encouraged to widen their appeal to groups who previously felt excluded and unwelcome – indeed 'outreach' is part of the conditions under which they receive their grant from public funds – the curators are faced with what she assumes is a dilemma. The curators, she implies, instead of – or maybe in addition to – using their skills to present and explain the strangeness of the past to viewers of all backgrounds, should be willing to change the appearance of the antiquities to make them more attractive to the hitherto excluded. They should, she implies, make Greek antiquities look more familiar by moving them more into line with the expectations of the viewers, even if these expectations are based on misunderstandings and prejudices. The fact that it is the socially disadvantaged

---

[47]   D. M. Wilson, *The British Museum: A History* (London: British Museum Press, 2002) page 243.
[48]   Mary Beard, What Are We All Really Talking About? *The Art Newspaper* 99, January 2000, 18–19. While not repeating this argument, Beard does not withdraw from it in her book, *The Parthenon* (2002).

who are to be condescended to and misinformed in this way offers an apparently liberal veneer to a consumerism that more educated viewers would not tolerate.

The consumerist ideology was also recommended by another British academic, Sir John Boardman, who now out-duveens Duveen. 'Cleaning for display in museums,' Boardman declares in discussing the pre-war whitening of the Parthenon sculptures in London, 'has attempted to restore them to something like their pristine white.' 'From an aesthetic point of view, monochrome sculpture is far easier to appreciate.' He says that he himself finds it 'easier to appreciate sculpture in a mainly monochrome state.' 'Weathered surface detracts from appreciation.' The duty invariably placed on the trustees of museums to preserve the collections entrusted to their care for the benefit of future generations and for future research, Boardman impatiently dismisses as 'the demands of rather self-indulgent archaeologists who are prone to put their own academic needs before all other.'[49]

Again we see the persistence of long-exploded archaeological errors in the unlikeliest places. At what stage, one has to ask again, were the Parthenon sculptures ever the 'pristine white' that Boardman admires and wishes to see offered to viewers? He can only be referring to the moment during the building of the temple in the fifth century when the marble sculptors, on a change of shift, left the scaffolds with their drills and their chisels, and the painters and the metal workers arrived to take their place with their brushes, their paint pots, and their boxes of metal. Apart from the absurdity of wishing to fake up for modern viewers the appearance of sculptures before they were even completed, and forcing ancient art to conform with errors and prejudices about whiteness, there probably never was such a 'pristine' time. It is more likely that the marble carving, the marble painting, and the putting in place and painting of the metal features, all proceeded together.

What is significant – or a paradigm – about the articles by Beard and Boardman is not only their attitude to the whitening and to the question of where the pieces of the Parthenon at present in London can best be displayed. Their contention that museums can legitimately alter originals in order to make them easier to look at, that it is part of 'education' to protect the public from the intrinsic difficulty of understanding ancient art, and that a modern 'aesthetic' that is never free of ideology – sometimes unattractive and dangerous ideology – and that is forever changing should override the

---

[49] John Boardman, The Elgin Marbles: Matters of Fact and Opinion in *International Journal of Cultural Property* 9, 2000.

duty to preserve, to explain, and to question by research shows how far the consumerist ethos has taken hold even among those whom we might have expected to resist it.

At the beginning of 2002, a different justification for keeping the Marbles in London was offered to the British people. Since then the authorities of the museum have sought to revive the notion of a 'universal museum', in which all the arts of all the civilizations of the world can be seen together. In the British Museum, they say, you can see Greek art in context, alongside Egyptian, Assyrian, and Chinese art. To send back the Marbles to Greece, they say, would destroy the ability to compare differing styles of art. The labels in the British Museum have been altered to reflect this new claim.

The ideal of a universal museum was part of the aspiration of the European Enlightenment, carried into effect in many Western countries during the nineteenth century. The world's art, so the argument ran, should no longer be the private preserve of aristocracies. The general public too should be given some experience of the greatest artistic achievements of the ancient and modern worlds, the originals of which were mostly in private palaces or in galleries in faraway countries. This genuine attempt to widen access was done, in the case of sculptures, by plaster casts; in the case of paintings, by having professional artists make excellent copies, engravings, and later photographs.[50]

The recent attempt by eighteen museums to claim to be 'universal museums' has, however, little to do with the humanist ideals of the past, or to a desire to widen access. For a start, most of these museums are only interested in showing original pieces. Only a handful have even some antiquities from even some of the many civilisations that once existed. Even if you were to put all the collections of the eighteen together, they would still only offer a small and unrepresentative sample. And, as for the suggestion that the eighteen museums are the best context, it is hardly likely to appeal either to the mobile viewers who live in the developed West or to the citizens of those and other countries that cannot afford to travel to them. But, in any case, the idea that a museum in a northern country is the best context in which to appreciate an ancient monument such as the Parthenon is absurd. As a friend of mine from Eastern Europe said when she heard this line being

50   Examples noted by Susan Pearce and Ken Arnold, editors, *The Collector's Voice; Critical Readings in the Practice of Collecting, Vol 2. Early Voices* (Aldershot: Ashgate, 2000).

offered on television by the previous British Museum director, 'Is he saying I cannot appreciate the Alhambra by going to Spain to look at it because there are no Greek temples nearby? Is he suggesting that parts of the Alhambra should be broken off and sent to museums which have strong collections of Chinese art?'

The published Declaration on the Importance and Value of Universal Museums deserves to be looked at closely. The declaration talks about 'the universal admiration for ancient civilizations [which is] so deeply rooted today'. Note the ritual repetition of the word 'universal'. But can the authors of the declaration really believe that those who visit museums all 'admire' all the civilizations whose artefacts they see there? Not every ancient culture deserves to be 'admired' – very few in fact – nor is every broken pot worthy of the connoisseurship approach. The aim of the eighteen museums appears to be to create an autonomous 'aesthetic' realm where Greek antiquities, drastically decontextualised from their local, historical, and cultural contexts, are contrasted with museum objects from elsewhere. When the director of the British Museum, speaking of the proximity of the display rooms, declares that 'the connections between cultures are now more explorable. For instance between Egypt and Mexico', he must know that there were no connections of any kind between these two ancient civilisations and that any similarities in artistic style that visitors may detect are fortuitous.[51] Museum curators, it seems, instead of fulfilling what has long been regarded as their primary educational role of encouraging viewers to achieve a critical understanding of the complexity and variety of human experience, to appreciate the historic differences, and to question their assumptions, are now trying to legitimate the status quo that results from past imperialism by promoting the late Victorian, post-romantic aesthetics advocated by Ruskin and Pater. And here we have another paradigm point. It is this ideology, which seeks to separate the aesthetic from the historical, that encourages the trade in 'unprovenanced' antiquities that is doing such damage to knowledge.

The arguments from the Greek authorities and their many supporters for the return of those parts of the Parthenon that are at present abroad have also changed in recent years. The claim used to be couched in overtly national terms. 'We are the Greeks; the Marbles are ours; give them back'. I was never able to support it. But the present proposal is not like that. It makes no

[51]   Interview with Neil MacGregor in *Art Newspaper* no 136 May 2003, page 18.

claim for ownership. It avoids all questions about legality and past rights and wrongs and is not concerned with such counterfactuals as to what might have happened to the Marbles if Elgin had not taken them. Instead, it considers what is best from the perspective of our generation. And, seen that way, the proposal rightly puts the needs of the monument and of its viewers first, enabling the scattered fragments to be placed together and viewed and studied from the outside, in the changing natural light for which they were designed.

Personally, I should like to build other features on to the Greek government proposal. There is no need, for example, for the return to be simply a transfer from one museum management to another. The two governments and parliaments have the opportunity to devise new forms of trusteeship that are tailor-made to the needs of the monument in the twenty-first century. A new trusteeship could, for example, lay specific duties on the trustees with regard to conservation, display, access, record-keeping, needs of scholars, consultation, and accountability. Such a new form of trusteeship could draw on expertise and resources from other countries besides Greece who share in the Hellenic heritage, including international organisations. That would be real universalism.

Let me now offer some provisional conclusions. Over its long history the meanings attributed to the Parthenon by viewers and by those who have sought to influence viewers have changed frequently. The Parthenon has been a monument both to various historic empires and to the colonial state, a celebration of classical Hellas and of its defeat, a symbol of Enlightenment and democracy but also of nationalism and fascism. The pieces from the monument taken abroad have been given different meanings from those left at the site. Nor did these changes only occur in the mind of different generations of viewers. The stones themselves have been altered to fit the political and ideological agendas of the appropriators.

We can also note that during the centuries since the Parthenon was first studied by Western antiquarians, we have seen a struggle between what we may call the scholarly, scientific archaeology of the Enlightenment that makes a genuine effort to understand the material remains of the past, and how they have come down to us in material form, in all their complexity, on the one hand, and the imputed meanings invented and advocated by various appropriators to meet the perceived political and ideological needs of a changing present on the other. In that ongoing struggle, the record shows how frequently those who have the most knowledge, and therefore the greatest responsibility, have allowed themselves to be co-opted. Of one point we may be certain. Those who think that by possessing the stones of the Parthenon they possess the Hellenic, the Enlightenment, or the democratic heritage reveal how little they understand these ideals. The outcome is not certain. Meanwhile, as evidence about the wishes of citizens continues to mount, we can recall Pericles' words in which he contrasted his city with others where power was in the hands of the unelected few. 'We Athenians decide public questions for ourselves.'[52]

[52]   Book 2, xl, 1–4.

5   WHITHER THE ELGIN MARBLES?

John Henry Merryman[1]

In 1985 I published an article entitled "Thinking about the Elgin Marbles"[2] in which, at perhaps unnecessary length, I examined the legality and morality of Lord Elgin's acquisition of a substantial number of the Parthenon Marbles.[3] The dramatic actress Melina Mercouri was then Greece's Minister of Culture and was conducting an emotionally compelling international campaign for return of the Elgin Marbles to Athens. Her argument was

[1]   My thanks to William Clair and Kate Fitz Gibbon for their helpful suggestions.
[2]   Merryman, Thinking about the Elgin Marbles, 83 *Mich. L. Rev.* 1880 (1985). The article is republished in John Henry Merryman, *Thinking about the Elgin Marbles: Critical Essays on Cultural Property, Art and Law* 24 (2000), cited herein as *Critical Essays.*
[3]   Elgin removed, or took from the ground where they had fallen or from the fortifications or other structures in which they had been used as building materials, pedimental sculptures, metopes and portions of the frieze. The frieze, a 3-foot-high horizontal band carved in low relief, originally extended 524 feet around the Parthenon's inner chamber. Elgin acquired 247 feet of the frieze. The metopes, a series of ninety-two 4-foot-square panels sculpted in high relief, surrounded the top of the Parthenon's outer colonnade and recounted assorted historical and mythical battles. Elgin acquired fifteen metopes, predominantly from the south side Lapith and Centaur group. The pediments, the low triangles at the ends of the building formed by the pitch of the roof, were filled with sculptures in the round. Elgin acquired seventeen pedimental sculptures. In addition, he collected assorted architectural fragments from the Parthenon.

The objects that Elgin acquired in Athens and are now held by the British Museum are customarily called the *Elgin Marbles.* Greeks and others sympathetic to the Greek campaign for their return to Athens often prefer to refer to them as the "Parthenon Marbles." That terminology does not work well here because more than half of the known existing Parthenon Marbles were not taken by Elgin and remain today in Athens. To preclude the resulting ambiguity I continue to refer to the Marbles in the British Museum as the Elgin Marbles.

based in part on the claim that they had been stolen. Leaning heavily on William St Clair's *Lord Elgin and the Marbles* [4] for the pertinent history, I examined that claim and concluded that the acquisition was legal and, by the standards applicable in that time and place, ethical. That conclusion still seems right to me, but it should come as no surprise that others appear to disagree.[5]

The award of the 2004 Summer Olympic Games to Greece stimulated renewed arguments for the return of the Elgin Marbles to Athens, where a new Acropolis Museum was to be built near, but not on, the Acropolis to receive them in time to display them during the Games.[6] This time, however, the Greek position, as presented by the Greek Minister of Culture Evangolos

---

[4] William St Clair, *Lord Elgin and the Marbles* (2d ed. 1983). The third edition was published in 1998.

[5] Dean David Rudenstine has published a series of articles in which he disagrees with crucial parts of William St Clair's history and with my conclusions about the legality and morality of Elgin's actions. See Rudenstine, "The Legality of Elgin's Taking: A Review Essay of Four Books on the Parthenon Marbles," 8 *Int'l J. Cultural Prop.* 256 (1999); id. "Cultural Property: The Hard Question of Repatriation," 19 *Cardozo Arts & Ent. L.J.* 82 (2001); id. "A Tale of Three Documents: Lord Elgin and the Missing, Historic 1801 Ottoman Document," 22 *Cardozo L. Rev.* 1853 (2001); id. "Lord Elgin and the Ottomans: The Question of Permission," *23 Cardozo L. Rev. 449* (2002). John Moustakis, in an interesting student note, "Group Rights in Cultural Property: Justifying Strict Inalienability," 74 *Cornell L. Rev.* 1179 (1989), argued that Greeks as a group have a property interest in the Marbles and that such group rights are, or should be, inalienable. Thus, as do most other writers on the Elgin's removals (who are legion), Mr. Moustakis adopts the cultural nationalist position, which I discuss below.

[6] A superstitious person might conclude that the Acropolis Museum project was accursed. A first architectural competition in 1976 that failed to produce an acceptable proposal was followed by further troubled competitions in 1979 and 1989. Finally, in 2001, a fourth, successful competition was won by the New York – based Swiss architect Bernard Tschumi. When work began on the Tschumi project it was complicated and interrupted by opponents. Residents of the Makroyanni neighborhood and archaeologists concerned to protect the seven layers of archaeological remains said to lie beneath the site engaged in tenacious political and judicial action. Litigation that eventually reached the highest Greek courts intermittently ordered work at the site to stop or permitted it to proceed, and the prospect that the museum would be completed in time for the Olympic Games continued to recede. In the *Art Newspaper* of April 2004, at p. 9, Martin Bailey reported that the Greek government had halted construction in order to preserve important archaeological evidence at the site, but work on the new museum was soon resumed. In the event, the museum was not built in time for the Olympic Games, and the Elgin Marbles remained in London.

Venizelos, was significantly different. Greece announced that it did not claim ownership of the Elgin Marbles. The argument was that whatever one might think about whether the Elgin Marbles belong *to* Greece, they belong *in* Greece. The new Greek position has made it unnecessary to reargue the ownership issue here. We can focus our attention on the question whether the Elgin Marbles should return to Athens or remain in London, in the British Museum.

Who should decide that question? It appears that the British and the Greeks have been speaking to each other about the Elgin Marbles.[7] Perhaps they will reach an agreement. If they do, does that end the discussion? Is the problem solved? Or is it possible that such a settlement, while agreeable to the Greek and British national interests of the moment, might conflict with the broader international interest that all of us share in the welfare and disposition of the London Marbles? If there is such a conflict, how should it be resolved?

The international interest is expressed in the premise, stated in the preamble of the 1954 Hague Convention,[8] that cultural property is "the cultural heritage of all mankind." This statement, which is echoed in other international instruments,[9] is the culmination of an innovation in international law that began in the midnineteenth century.[10] Should a settlement of the

---

[7] In its 2003 Report at <http://unes.doc.unesco.org/001307/130725e.pdf6> UNESCO's Intergovernmental Committee for Promoting the Return of Cultural Property to Its Countries of Origin or Its Restitution in Case of Illicit Appropriation reported: "Outside the Secretariat's efforts and the Committee's framework, on 12 November 2002 the Greek Minister of Culture, while in London, had separate meetings with the British Secretary of State for Culture Media and Sport, and with the new Director and Chairperson of the Board of Trustees of the British Museum. On 18 March 2003 an additional meeting took place in London with representatives from the Department for Culture, Media and Sport, and from the Greek Ministry of Culture. A UNESCO representative also attended." There have also been references in the public media to British-Greek talks about the Elgin Marbles.

[8] 1954 Hague Convention for the Protection of Cultural Property in the Event of Armed Conflict, in UNESCO, *Conventions and Recommendations of UNESCO Concerning the Protection of the Cultural Heritage* (1985), p. 13.

[9] Thus the Preamble to the 1970 UNESCO Convention on the Means of Prohibiting and Preventing the Illicit Import, Export, and Transfer of Ownership of Cultural Property states that "the protection of the cultural heritage can be effective only if organized both nationally and internationally among states working in close cooperation." The convention is set out at p. 57 of the UNESCO publication cited in fn. 9.

[10] This development, whose origin is the so-called Lieber Code, is described in Merryman, "Two Ways of Thinking about Cultural Property", 80 *Am. J. Int. L.* 831 (1986), reprinted in *Critical Essays* 66. The content of articles 34–36 of the *Lieber Code* may

London Marbles question be expected to recognize and protect this international interest? Suppose, for example, that Greece and the United Kingdom agreed that the London Marbles would be sent to Greece on long-term loan in return for business concessions and trade preferences granted to Britain. Is this the way decisions should be made about the fate of great works of art?

The obvious alternative to a bilateral settlement is a multilateral one in which the various national and international interests are properly represented, argued and considered. To whom should such arguments be addressed? A case decided by the United States Supreme Court, *Austria v. Altmann*,[11] suggests that Greece might have standing to sue the United Kingdom in an American court under a provision of the Foreign Sovereign Immunities Act of 1976.[12] If so, we could face the surreal prospect of what is essentially a replevin action, brought by the claimed owner, Greece, against the purchaser in good faith, the United Kingdom, from the alleged trespasser *de bonis asportatis*, Lord Elgin, in a U.S. District Court. The mind reels. And, in an only slightly less exotic case, whose alleged jurisdictional basis also rests on the Foreign Sovereign Immunities Act, the heirs of the Russian Suprematist artist Kazimir Malevich have sued Amsterdam's Stedelijk Museum in the Federal District Court for the District of Columbia to recover works by the artist held by the museum.[13]

Rather than second-guess a U.S. trial court, we can imagine that Greece brings an action against the United Kingdom before a hypothetical International Cultural Property Tribunal that is charged with making informed, principled decisions concerning the proper allocation of disputed cultural property. What should the tribunal decide? Should the Elgin Marbles continue to repose in London or can Greece establish good reason to move them to Athens?

---

have been influenced by an 1813 decision of the Vice-Admiralty Court of Halifax, Nova Scotia: *The Marquis de Someruels*, Stewart's Vice-Admiralty Reports 482 (1813). The judge in that case, Dr. Croke, clearly was influenced by a French work published in 1796: *Lettres à Miranda*, by Quatremère de Quincy, a Frenchman who opposed Napoléon's seizure of works of art during his Italian Campaign. See Merryman, "Note on *the Marquis de Someruels*," 5 *Intl. J. Cult. Prop.* 321 (1996).

[11] *Republic of Austria v. Altmann*, 541 U.S. 677 (2004). The case was remanded to the federal district court in Los Angeles but was settled before trial when the parties agreed to submit the case arbitration in Vienna.

[12] 28 U.S.C. s. 1605(a)(3).

[13] The case is discussed by Sylvia Hochfield in "Who Owns the Stedelijk's Maleviches?" *ARTnews*, April 2004, p. 64.

I shall try to convince the reader that there are weighty reasons why the Elgin Marbles should remain in London, in the British Museum. In doing so, I consider three[14] distinct varieties of what lawyers call "arguments" and others might variously refer to as "patterns of discourse" or "narratives," which we can call *nation-*, *world-*, and *object*-centered. Such arguments would be addressed to the tribunal and would have to be considered by it in reaching its decision. We begin with the nation.

I. THE NATION

When she was the Greek Minister of Culture, Melina Mercouri, as had Lord Byron before her,[15] eloquently and passionately argued that the Elgin Marbles should be returned to Greece, where they belong because they are Greek. They were created in Greece by Greek artists for civic and religious purposes of the Athens of that time. The appealing implication is that, being in this sense Greek, they belong among Greeks. This is the argument from cultural nationalism, which to some readers may seem to be more an assertion than a reasoned argument. They may wonder whether it is self-evident that an object made in a place belongs there, or that something produced by artists of an earlier time ought to be returned to the territory now occupied by their cultural descendants, or that the present government of a nation should have power over artifacts historically associated with its people or territory.

In its best sense, cultural nationalism recognizes the relation between cultural property and cultural definition. For a full life and a secure identity, people need exposure to their history, much of which is represented or illustrated by objects. Such artifacts are important to cultural definition and expression, to shared identity and community. In helping to preserve

---

[14] The alert reader will observe that all of my argument's components seem to come in threes. Is this an expression of some fundamental truth about the structure of argument? An indication of the author's limitations? An expression of the German folk wisdom that *alle gut kommt en drei?* Whatever.

[15] Byron's version of historical events and motivations has strongly influenced modern attitudes toward the Marbles. Byron's attack on Elgin was carried on in conversations and correspondence but took its most influential form in his poetry, particularly in *The Curse of Minerva* (1811) and in *Childe Harold's Pilgrimage* (1812), canto II, stanza XII. *Childe Harold*, in particular, was an immediate best-seller in several languages, quickly entered the culture and engendered the French epithet *Elginisme* to refer to one who removed cultural property from its site.

the identity of specific cultures they help the world preserve texture and diversity. They nourish artists and generate art (it is a truism among art historians that art derives from art). Cultural property stimulates learning and scholarship. A people deprived of its past is culturally impoverished. As one of John Steinbeck's characters asked in *The Grapes of Wrath*: "How will we know it's us without our past?"[16]

There is, however, little danger that the Greeks will ever be deprived of the opportunity for ample direct contact with their past. Greece is full of monuments of antiquity, and its museums contain extensive collections of Greek art of all periods. As to the Parthenon sculptures themselves, something over half of those presently known to exist remain in Athens.[17] Lord Elgin took some of the best pieces, and it is undeniable that some of those left in Athens are in worse condition today than those that were taken to London, for reasons we will discuss below. But what remains in Greece still is substantial and representative.

Even if all of the Parthenon Marbles were in London, it would not be obvious that the Greeks were culturally deprived. If the British had attempted to appropriate the identity of the Marbles, disguising or misrepresenting their origin, then the Greeks, and all the rest of us, would rightly object. But in the British Museum the Marbles have always been presented openly and candidly as the work of Greek artists of extraordinary genius and refinement. Presented as they are, spectacularly mounted in their own fine rooms in one of the world's great museums, the Elgin Marbles honor Greece and generate admiration and respect for the Greek achievement. No visitor to the British Museum could come away with any other impression.

Cultural nationalism is a sword with two edges. The Elgin Marbles have been in England since 1821 and in that time have become a part of the British cultural heritage. They have entered British culture. They help define the

---

[16] For a fuller discussion of the relationship between objects and national cultures see Merryman, "The Public Interest in Cultural Property," 77 *Calif. L. Rev.* 339 (1989), republished in *Critical Essays*, p. 93.

[17] In commenting on this statement Mr. St Clair wrote in February 2004, in a letter to the author: "I also think that the summary about 'half the marbles' being in Athens is misleading –partly because the monument is far more than its sculptural decoration but also because the pieces in Athens are, with few exceptions, in far worse condition. With the exception of one metope and a section of frieze that could not be removed without huge damage to the building, Elgin took all the best surviving pieces. So the estimate of 'half ' that I know is widely quoted is, if not technically untrue, rather misleading to those who do know the fuller picture."

British to themselves, inspire British arts, give Britons identity and community, civilize and enrich British life, stimulate British scholarship. One can argue that in these terms the Greek claim is more powerful than that of the British, but it is not unreasonable to perceive the two positions as roughly equivalent.

Later chapters in this volume discuss Native American Graves Protection and Repatriation Act (NAGPRA) of 1991.[18] Under this remarkable law, American museums have been required to publish inventories of the American Indian and Native Hawaiian human remains, funerary objects, sacred objects and objects of cultural patrimony that they hold and, on request, return them to their culture of origin. The analogy to the cultural nationalist argument in the Elgin Marbles case is tempting. If it was right to return their artifacts to the Indian tribes and Hawaiians, as I think it was, by the same logic should not the Marbles return to Athens?

There are, however, significant differences between the two cases. Most important, under NAGPRA cultural objects are returned to the living cultures that originally made and used them. The objects involved were essential to the religious and ceremonial lives of those cultures, whose members today share the values and beliefs and seek to perform the same ceremonies and participate in the same rituals as the ancestors who made the objects. Repressed and fragmented by American imperialism, they want to regain the means that will enable them to heal and restore their cultures. On their return, the objects will be put to their traditional uses.[19]

Modern Greeks relate differently to the Parthenon Marbles and to the Classical culture in which they were created and employed. That culture is "dead." To the extent that its values, beliefs and accomplishments are shared by modern Greeks they also are shared by every other participant in Western culture, including the British. There is no serious interest in or possibility of putting the Elgin Marbles to their ancient Greek ceremonial uses. They are now in a museum in London. If they return, they will go into a museum in Athens. NAGPRA, a fascinating cultural enterprise about which we all have much to learn, is not an applicable precedent for the Marbles case.

[18]   25 USC sections 3001–3006 (1990).
[19]   Compare the Afo-A-Kom incident: The Afo-A-Kom is a five-foot-tall sculpture that appeared on the New York art market in 1973, was said to embody "the spiritual, political and religious essence" of the Kom people of Cameroon, became the object of impassioned public and private discussion and was voluntarily returned to the Kom in May 1974. The case is described in John Henry Merryman and Albert E. Elsen, *Law, Ethics and the Visual Arts* (4th ed. 2002) p. 267.

The cultural nationalist argument tends to merge and become confused with two others, which might be called economic nationalism and political nationalism. Economically, whoever has any of the Parthenon Marbles has something of great value. It is inconceivable that they would ever be put on the market, although if a pedimental figure, a metope or an element of the frieze were offered for sale it would bring an enormous price. The more relevant economic consideration is that the presence of the Marbles in a public collection nourishes the tourist industry. Possession is obviously necessary in order to exploit that kind of economic value. For Greece to claim it, however, merely re-argues in another form the question of ownership, an argument that I believe it would lose. And in any event, we have seen that Minister of Culture Venizelos did not propose to press that argument.

Political nationalism treats the presence of the Marbles in England, or in any other place than Greece, as an offense to Greeks and the Greek nation. Here the demand for the return of the Marbles is based on national pride. No candid observer can deny the power of political nationalism in world affairs. A Greek government that secured the return of the Marbles would be wildly popular. A Greek politician who could claim credit for the return would be a national hero. But political nationalism comes loaded with heavy baggage: a troubling history of exploitable superstition and prejudice, an unsavory record as the religion of the state and a tool of demagogues, a source of international economic, social, political and armed conflict. To most observers, its assertion does not argue persuasively for the return of the Elgin Marbles to Greece.

Returning to cultural nationalism, does it make the case for the return of the Elgin Marbles? I have argued elsewhere[20] that its attraction is a relic of nineteenth-century romantic nationalism, dramatized and popularized by Byron's life, death, and poetry and kept alive by Greeks and Hellenophiles. Still, the plea that the Marbles are Greek and belong in Greece has an undeniable appeal. There is a romantic strain in most of us, and at some deep psychological level we are all helpless Hellenophiles.

Despite its emotional pull, however, the power of Greek cultural nationalism weakens if we recall that many of the known surviving Parthenon Marbles are already in Greece and that those in the British Museum openly honor Classical Greek artists and the Greek achievement. And, as we have

---

[20] See the discussion of cultural nationalism in Merryman, "The Retention of Cultural Property," 21 *U.C. Davis L. Rev.* 477 (1988), reprinted in *Critical Essays* at pp. 122, 133–137.

seen, cultural nationalism is a two-edged argument that is also available to the British. One can admire the Greekness of the Elgin Marbles and respect their specific cultural importance to Greeks without concluding that they belong in Greece.

II. THE WORLD

We have seen that a number of international instruments state that "cultural property belonging to any people whatsoever" is "the cultural heritage of all mankind." These words in the Hague Convention of 1954 announce the principle of cultural internationalism: that everyone has an interest in the preservation and enjoyment of cultural property, wherever it is situated, from whatever cultural or geographic source it derives. The United Nations Educational, Scientific, and Cultural Organization's (UNESCO's) legitimacy as an international agency concerned with cultural property stands on that premise, and UNESCO pronouncements build on it. Thus in 1976 UNESCO promulgated a Recommendation[21] whose Preamble states that the international circulation of cultural property

is a powerful means of promoting mutual understanding and appreciation among nations.... [and] would also lead to a better use of the international community's cultural heritage which is the sum of all the national heritages.

And the Preamble to the 1970 UNESCO Convention[22] states that

the interchange of cultural property among nations ... increases the knowledge of the civilization of man, enriches the cultural life of all peoples and inspires mutual respect and appreciation among nations.

What do these various statements of cultural internationalism say or imply about the proper disposition of the Marbles? I identify three [sic] main factors: *education, cultural enrichment,* and *better use.*

Education

Museums are educational institutions whose exhibitions of art from other times and places help us understand, appreciate and respect our own and

[21] 1976 UNESCO Recommendation Concerning the International Exchange of Cultural Property, in UNESCO, *Conventions and Recommendations of UNESCO Concerning the Protection of the Cultural Heritage* (1985) p. 101.
[22] 1970 UNESCO Convention on the Means of Prohibiting and Preventing the Illicit Import, Export, and Transfer of Ownership of Cultural Property *id.* p. 57.

other peoples' cultures. The exhibited collections of the British Museum, the Metropolitan Museum, the Louvre and other great museums temper, if they cannot totally eliminate, cultural parochialism. In the case of the Marbles, their installation in the British Museum has had and continues to have, as Elgin hoped, a strong educative impact, quickly commanding respect not only for Greek art but for the civilization that produced it. Today Greek achievements in art, drama, literature, philosophy and science permeate Western culture. If all of Classical Greek art had remained in Greece, our world today would be a significantly different one.

Cultural Enrichment

At a fundamental level, most learning is comparative. It has truly been said that "thinking without comparison in unthinkable." At a different level, what we know is enriched, acquires breadth and depth, by comparison. In London, the educative impact of the Elgin Marbles on visitors to the British Museum is significantly enhanced by their proximity to great works of Mesopotamian, Egyptian, Asian and other great cultures, with which they can conveniently be contrasted and compared. Every visitor to the British Museum, even one who enters totally focused on viewing the Marbles, must pass great monuments of other cultures on the way to the room in which the Marbles are exposed. Most visitors will find it impossible to pass by without pausing for a few moments before some of them. This kind of opportunity makes every visit to the British Museum an experience in comparative education. In Greece, where the museums understandably are filled with Greek art, this kind of comparative viewing and learning experience is not available to the viewer; nor would moving the Elgin Marbles to Athens provide it.

Better Use

Recall that the 1976 UNESCO Recommendation, quoted above, says that the interchange of cultural property "would also lead to a better use of the international community's cultural heritage." What does "better use" mean? The quoted text does not tell us what the drafters had in mind, so we are free to speculate. Does exposure to a larger and more widely distributed number of the world's people constitute a better use? Consider the great quantities of redundant works that are hoarded in Greece, where they will never be accessioned, studied, published or exhibited. They merely languish, deteriorating, in storage. Would distribution abroad of such works constitute a "better use" of them? Would selling or exchanging them for objects from other cultures in order to enrich Greek private and museum collections constitute a "better use?"[23]

It would seem so. In the Recommendation's context, it is "the interchange of cultural property" that can lead to a "better use." Such interchange can serve a variety of desirable objectives, one of the most obvious of which is the wider distribution of the works of a given culture. That version of "better use" would not be achieved by the return of the Elgin Marbles to Athens, which would narrow rather than broaden the distribution of Classical Greek sculpture. Interchange can, however, also serve the important purpose of reintegration of dismembered works, which is better discussed in the next section of this chapter.

I conclude that all three [sic] of the world-centered arguments – education, cultural enrichment and better use – favor (pace the very important integrity interest discussed below) retention of the Elgin Marbles in the British Museum.

III. THE OBJECT

Finally, we consider object-centered considerations applicable to decisions about the possible relocation of the Elgin Marbles. I can think of three [sic] such considerations, which, in declining order of relative importance, we can call *preservation, truth,* and *distribution/access.*[24]

Preservation

Preservation takes priority for obvious reasons. If the Elgin Marbles are destroyed, people of all cultures will be deprived of access to them, and considerations of integrity and distribution become irrelevant. Damage short of destruction, whether through inadequate care, the action of the elements or the hazards of war, terrorism or vandalism, threatens the same values. If the Marbles now in London would be better preserved in Athens, that would be a powerful argument for return.

In the British Museum, the Marbles are well mounted, maintained and guarded. The Museum's record is of course not perfect, marred by the

[23] For a discussion of retentionism and its consequences see "The Retention of Cultural Property," 21 *U. C. Davis L. Rev.* 477, republished in *Critical Essays* at p. 122.
[24] For a fuller discussion see "The Nation and the Object," 3 *Intl. J. Cult. Prop.* 61 (1994), republished in *Critical Essays* at p. 158.

"cleansing" episode in 1937–38 which Mr. St Clair has so vividly described.[25] The extent of damage to the Marbles from that unseemly chapter in their history is differently estimated by Mr. St Clair, Ian Jenkins and John Boardman.[26] To an interested foreign observer it might appear that Mr. St Clair has taken care not to underestimate the damage, while Mr. Jenkins and Professor Boardman, with comparable scrupulosity, are at pains not to overestimate it.

There seems to be little doubt, however, that the sculptures that remained on the Acropolis after Elgin departed have been more seriously eroded by exposure to a variety of hazards, including vandalism, souvenir hunting and *nefos*, the marble-devouring smog of Athens. Eventually, most of the remaining sculptures were taken down and removed to a safer environment, while the smog continues to consume the temple itself, which is made of the same marble as the sculptures. If one had to make a decision based solely on concern for the physical preservation of the Elgin Marbles, moving them to Athens would be difficult to justify. Even if they would be placed in a museum there, as the Greeks plan, rather than reinstalled on the Parthenon, what reason would there be to expect that they would be safer in Athens over the next two centuries than they have been in London over the past two centuries? Under present conditions, the preservation interest does not seem to argue for moving the London Marbles from London to Athens.

Integrity

The second international concern is related to the integrity of the work of art. If we think of the intact Parthenon as an integrated work, with more power, beauty and cultural significance than the sum of the dismembered parts, then it makes sense to argue that the sculptures should be reinstalled on the temple. That result could of course be achieved by moving the Parthenon to London and there reuniting it with the sculptures, but not even the British have advanced such a proposal. The only reasonable way to reintegrate the

[25] St Clair, "The Elgin Marbles: Questions of Stewardship and Accountability," 8 *Intl. J. Cult. Prop.* 291 (1999).

[26] The differing opinions on damage to the Marbles from the cleansing episode are stated and contested in William St Clair, "The Elgin Marbles: Questions of Stewardship and Accountability," 8 *Intl. J. Cult. Prop.* 391 (1999); John Boardman, "The Elgin Marbles: Matters of Fact and Opinion," 9 *id.* 233 (2000); and Ian Jenkins, "The Elgin Marbles: Questions of Accuracy and Reliability," 10 id. 55 (2001).

Elgin Marbles with the Parthenon is to send them to Athens. Accordingly, the integrity argument clearly favors the Greek position.

There is, however, the serious difficulty that the Marbles cannot be reinstalled on the Parthenon without exposing them to certain destruction from the combined effects of the elements and the smog of Athens. The preservation and integrity interests are in direct conflict, and in that case preservation must prevail. At a time when the sculptures remaining on the Parthenon and the remaining Caryatids on the Erechtheion have had to be taken indoors by the Greek authorities to preserve them from further erosion, it cannot seriously be proposed that the Marbles should be restored to their places on the temple.

In fact, the Greek proposal is to transfer them from a museum in London to a museum in Athens. There they would be nearer the Parthenon and, if the new Acropolis Museum were completed, in sight of it. That remaining distance, however, appears to be critical. Being near the Parthenon is not enough. "Close only counts in horseshoes."[27] Under present conditions, true reintegration of the integrity of the temple is impossible without exposing the Marbles to unacceptable hazards.

Distribution

The other object-centered interest is in an appropriate international distribution of the common cultural heritage, so that all peoples have a reasonable opportunity for access to their own cultural achievements and those of others. How should this distribution/access consideration affect the allocation of the Elgin Marbles? It is true that Greek antiquities can be found in major museums and private collections throughout the world and that some of the greatest Greek antiquities are abroad. But it is difficult to argue that Greece itself is in this sense impoverished. Greek museum and private collections are enormously rich in Greek antiquities of all periods. One of the reasons people go to Greece is to enjoy its wealth of cultural treasures, including the number of surviving Parthenon Marbles that remain in Athens.

The distribution argument actually seems to work in favor of the dispersion, rather than concentration in one place, of the works of a culture. Thus the late art critic John Canaday argued that American art should be "spread

[27] The text quotation, another bit of folk wisdom, is commonly heard on golf greens when a putt rolls close but fails to drop into the cup. It is also heard in other sports contexts and has crept into more general usage. A popular variant is "Close, but no cigar."

around," not kept at home. The idea of "missionary art" that makes a culture vivid and comprehensible abroad is, as we have already seen, an appealing one that promotes international understanding and mutual cultural respect. If all the works of the great artists of Classical Athens were returned and kept there, the rest of the world would be culturally impoverished.

Dispersion of related objects may also offer an important preservation value. As this is written, religious fundamentalism and international terrorism are serious preoccupations throughout much of the world. Serbs deliberately destroyed the Mostar bridge and other Islamic buildings and artifacts. The Taliban deliberately destroyed the Bamiyan Buddhas and thousands of other works of art in Afghanistan, fully informed of their world importance and despite international appeals that they be preserved. An entire major collection of Rodin's sculpture, including lifetime casts and unique works, was destroyed in the attack on the World Trade Center on September 11, 2001. Paranoia might be a poor guide to cultural property policy, but we have seen enough to know that the Marbles might seem to some terrorists or religious fundamentalists to be an attractive target.[28] Would it be safer to keep the Parthenon Marbles divided between London and Athens, as they now are, rather than put all those irreplaceable eggs in one Athenian basket?

Criteria for an appropriate international distribution of the artifacts of a culture do not yet exist; the dialogue until now has been dominated by demands for repatriation and by deference to cultural nationalism. But on the facts it seems difficult to argue convincingly on distributional grounds for the return of the Elgin Marbles to Athens. If we focus instead on the question of access, there is no apparent reason to suppose that the Elgin Marbles would be more accessible to the world's people in Athens than they now are in London.

Reviewing the object-centered arguments, it appears that they lead in different directions. The most powerful of them, preservation, seems not

---

[28] Religious fundamentalism can strike art anywhere. The following Associated Press report appeared in the January 11, 1983, *San Francisco Chronicle*, datelined at Fort Worth, Texas: "Wealthy businessman Cullen Davis, a born-again Christian, destroyed more than $1 million worth of gold, silver and ivory art objects because they were associated with Eastern religions, evangelist James Robison said yesterday. Robison told the *Fort Worth Star Telegram* that he and Davis used hammers to smash the carvings, which Davis had donated last September to help Robison pay off debts. The evangelist decided not to accept the gift after recalling a verse in Deuteronomy: 'The graven images of their gods shall we burn with fire for it is an abomination to the Lord thy God.' Robison said he considered Davis's actions 'a good testimony for his Christian faith.'

to advance the Greek cause, since there is no apparent basis for arguing that the Elgin Marbles would be safer in Athens than they are in London. The integrity argument favors reuniting the Marbles with the Parthenon, but that is not at present possible without exposing them to unacceptable hazards. There are no developed criteria for surely applying the distribution criterion, but it does not appear that the present distribution of Classical Greek antiquities would be improved by returning the Elgin Marbles to Athens.

CONCLUSION

The precise question before the hypothetical International Cultural Property Tribunal is whether, excluding any ownership considerations, the case has been made to move the Elgin Marbles from the British Museum in London to a museum in Athens. In concluding that the case has not been made I have considered nation-centered, world-centered and object-centered arguments on behalf of the Greek position and found them unpersuasive. On the facts of the Elgin Marbles case, all of these arguments (with one caveat), as I have understood them, favor the British position.

Some readers may think that I concede too little weight to cultural nationalism, much less than it generally receives in popular literature and the media. Even in serious international cultural property fora, interested parties sometimes play the cultural nationalism card with significant effect. There are, of course, many circumstances in which the relation between an object and a nation or a people justifies legal recognition and protection. The Native American Graves Protection and Repatriation Act (NAGPRA) and the Afo-A-Kom case provide obvious examples. Too often, however, nationalist sentiment and the befogging rhetoric that supports it have been allowed to displace reasoned argument. I believe that public debate about the Elgin Marbles has been seriously afflicted by this malady.

Conversely, my argument gives substantially greater weight to cultural internationalism than it typically receives in popular literature and the media. Although the international interest is confidently stated in several important international instruments,[29] excerpted above, in practice it often loses its power when confronted by a national claim, even when that claim is, by objective standards, excessive. How the law and politics of cultural

---

[29]   See nn. 22 and 23 and accompanying text, supra.

property reached such an unbalanced state cannot be explored here. In this chapter I have compensated for both effects by giving less effect to nationalism and more to internationalism, in an effort to take a more balanced position.

The caveat concerns possible restoration of the integrity of the dismembered Parthenon by restoring it as well as possible to its original harmony and grandeur. Such a project would face a number of difficulties. Most importantly, it would require marshaling and reinstalling in their original places on the temple all of the surviving sculptures now found in Athens, London, Paris, and Munich, plus bits and pieces of the fabric of the Parthenon now held abroad.

Even if those nations would agree to submit their Parthenon holdings to such a project, we have seen that it is presently not feasible because of the chemical vulnerability of the marble of which the sculptures and the temple were made. Athens, as do other modern cities, has a corrosive atmosphere that would damage and eventually destroy the sculptures, just as it is currently eroding the few sculptural fragments remaining on the Parthenon and the fabric of the building itself.

It seems reasonable to suppose that the modern technology that produces Super Domes could be employed to isolate and protect the Parthenon from the Athenian atmosphere. Would such a project be worth the expense? Would the resulting change in the dramatic Athenian skyline, where the romantic ruin of the Parthenon now hangs in the sky, visible for miles around, be acceptable? Finally, would reintegration of the sculptures with the temple really be feasible? Or has the building been so reduced over the last two centuries by the combined actions of the elements, the smog, souvenir hunters and vandalism that the result would risk being more a travesty than a restoration?

We do not know the answers to such questions. In the present state of our knowledge and under present conditions, for the reasons set out above, the Elgin Marbles should remain in London.

6 THE BEAUTIFUL ONE HAS COME – TO RETURN

The Return of the Bust of Nefertiti from Berlin to Cairo

Kurt G. Siehr[1]

I. HISTORY

1. Ancient History

"The queen's [Nefertiti's] bust is the best-known work of art from ancient Egypt – arguably from all antiquity."[2] The limestone bust of Nefertiti – her name means "The Beautiful One Has Come" – is at present exhibited in the Egyptian Museum in Berlin. Nefertiti was the wife of Pharaoh Akhenaton (also known under the name Amenhotep or Amenophis IV of the eighteenth Dynasty) ruling from 1353 to 1336 B.C. in the new capital el-Amarna, about two hundred kilometers north of the old capital Thebes, and the founder of the new monotheistic cult of the Sun god Aton.[3] We do not know very much about Nefertiti. She might have been a princess of the Indo-Iranian empire Mitanni in central and northern Mesopotamia, and it is still unknown whether she became a co-regent under a different name, fell into disgrace, retired prematurely or passed away rather early.[4]

2. Modern History

For a long time Akhenaton and his innovation were unknown to historians and to archaeologists as well. This is mainly due to two factors: Akhenaton

---

[1] The symposium organizers requested that the author and Stephen Urice take opposing positions on the question whether the bust of Nefertiti should remain in Berlin or be returned to Egypt. As lawyers both of us might have argued either position.

[2] Dorothea Arnold, "The Workshop of the Sculptor Thutmose," in: Dorothea Arnold, *The Royal Woman of Amarna. Images of Beauty from Ancient Egypt* (New York 1997) 41 *et seq.*, at p. 65.

[3] Cf. Nicolas Reeves, *Akhenaten. Egypt's False Prophet* (London 2001) 43 *et seq.*

[4] Reeves (N.3) p. 157 *et seq.*; Joyce Tyldesley, *Nefertiti. Egypt's Sun Queen* (New York 1998) 139 *et seq.*

had a different residence and his successors abolished most traces of the Aton cult he favoured. It was he who abandoned former traditions, irritated the powerful class of priests and introduced a kind of solar monotheism.[5]

The site of what was later known as Tell el-Amarna was already surveyed by the engineers and savants attached to Napoléon's Egyptian expedition of 1798–99.[6] During the nineteenth century it was visited by John Gardner Wilkinson (1797–1875) in 1824 and 1826, by Karl Richard Lepsius (1810–84) in 1843 and 1845, by William Matthew Flinders Petrie (1853–1942) and by Howard Carter (1874–1939) in 1892.[7] At the beginning of the twentieth century the Deutsche Orient-Gesellschaft (German Oriental Society) headed by the Egytologist Ludwig Borchardt (1863–1938) received permission for excavations in Egypt. This took place in Tell el-Amarna, the presumed residence of Akhenaton. On 6 December 1912 the bust of Nefertiti was excavated in the workshop of the sculptor Thutmose together with some unfinished portrait busts of her. As was usual at that time, the finds were divided between Egypt and the foreign holder of the excavation licence. In this partition the painted bust of Nefertiti was part of the German share. The bust was shipped to Germany, given to the wealthy wholesale merchant James Simon (1851–1932) as one of the sponsors of the excavations in Tell el-Amarna, lent and in 1920 finally donated to the Berlin museums and in 1923 unveiled and exhibited to an astonished public in the Egyptian Museum in Berlin.

In 1939 the Berlin museums were evacuated and the cultural treasures removed to secure shelters for safekeeping. The bust of Nefertiti was ultimately sheltered in a salt mine at Merkers/Kaiseroda in Thüringia. In 1945 it was evacuated by the American Army and its Monuments, Fine Arts and Archives branch, shipped to the U.S. Central Collecting Point in Wiesbaden and finally made accessible to the public.[8] In 1956 Nefertiti returned to West Berlin. The East German Democratic Republic tried in vain to recover the bust, which was formerly exhibited in a museum on "Museum Island,"

---

[5]   Cf. Jan Assmann, *Ägypten. Eine Sinngeschichte* (2d ed. Frankfurt/Main 2000) 243 et seq.

[6]   Cf. *Desciption de l'Ègypte ou recueil des observations et des recherches qui ont été faites en Egypte pendant l'expédition de l'Armée française publié sous les ordres de Napoléon Bonaparte* (reprint 1995) vol. IV, plate 63 no. 6 ("une ancienne ville").

[7]   Cf. Reeves (n. 3) p. 13–22.

[8]   Cf. Walter I. Farmer, *The Safekeepers. A Memoir of the Arts at the End of World War II* (Berlin/NewYork 2000) p. 46 *et seq.*; Thomas Carr Howe, *Salt Mines and Castles. The Discovery and Restitution of Looted European Art* (Indianapolis/New York 1946) 286–287.

after 1945 part of East Berlin.[9] The intra-German debate on "Who owns Nefertiti?" became moot when East and West Berlin were reunited in 1990.

3. Recent Developments

When the bust of Nefertiti was exhibited in Berlin in 1923 and rapidly became one of the favourite attractions of the Egyptian Museum the Egyptian government officially asked Germany to return it. This they did in at least four different ways:[10]

- In 1925, Egypt refused to grant any excavation permission to Germans unless Germany returned the bust of Nefertiti or, at least, agreed to arbitration on the question of return. Germany declined.
- In 1929 Egypt offered valuable antiquities in exchange for the return of Nefertiti. Germany declined in 1930.
- In 1933 German diplomats and politicians wanted to return the bust but Hitler refused to do it.
- In the 1950s Egypt inquired whether Germany might be inclined to talk about the return of the bust of Nefertiti. These efforts had no success.

Apart from this there are many declarations by Egyptian politicians and cultural officials that the bust of Nefertiti should be in Egypt and exhibited in the Cairo Archaeological Museum. I think there are five very good reasons that could be pleaded in favour of a return of this prominent piece of Egyptian archaeological cultural property to the country of origin. Whether these reasons would convince a court today or in the future cannot be predicted.

II. RETURN OF NEFERTITI

1. Division of Spoils of 1913

There are three different attitudes towards the finds of archaeologists excavating in foreign countries: take all, take nothing, and take half of it. In the early days of archaeology, before local rules on the protection of national

---

[9]   Reinhard Mußgnug, *Wem gehört Nofretete?* (Berlin/New York 1977) p. 10 *et seq.*
[10] Cf. Rolf Krauss, "1913–1988: 75 Jahre Büste der NofretEte/Nefert-iti in Berlin", in: 24 *Jahrbuch Preußischer Kulturbesitz.* 87–124, at p. 102–116 (1988) and 28 *Jahrbuch Preußischer Kulturbesitz* 123–157, at p. 123–125 (1992); Gert v. Paczensky, "Der Fall Nofretete", in: Gert v. Paszensky/ Herbert Ganslmayr (eds.), *Nofretete will nach Hause. Europa – Schatzhaus der "Dritten Welt"* (München 1984) 260 *et seq.*, at 286 *et seq.*

treasures were introduced, permission to excavate and to keep the finds was a simple application of the regular rules of treasure trove known almost everywhere since ancient times.[11] Where the excavation site was uninhabited and, in effect, a no-man's-land, as often was the case in nineteenth-century Egypt, excavation became a sort of competition governed by the principle "First come, first served". In these early incidents of what came later to be called the "rape of Egypt," excavation teams took all the finds and transported them to Europe or America.[12] When the Rosetta Stone was discovered in 1799 by French invaders, nobody asked Egyptians whether this precious document should stay in Egypt or might be taken by the discoverers and exported to Europe. In 1801 it was only a matter between the French and the British whether the Rosetta Stone would go to Paris or to London.[13]

During the nineteenth century Mediterranean source countries introduced legislation protecting national cultural treasures. This was also done in Egypt, at this time again part of the Ottoman Empire governed by a viceroy.[14] Excavation licences had to be applied for, and, they were if granted, the finds of the excavation campaign had to be equally divided between Egypt and the foreign licence holder. This regime of "take half of it" was still valid when in 1911 the Germans started excavating some parts of Tell el-Amarna.[15]

When in December 1912 the German excavation campaign was successful and on January 20, 1913, the division had to be made, it seems to be very likely that Borchardt, eager to preserve the bust of Nefertiti for Germany, either did not reveal the find to the Egyptian antiquities authority (headed by the French Egyptologist Gaston Maspero, 1846–1916, but

---

[11] Since ancient times it has been a common rule that the finder who actually took the treasure into his possession became the owner of half and the other half became the property of the owner of the land. Cf. *Institutiones Iustiniani* 2, 1, 39; M. Radin, *Handbook of Roman Law* (St. Paul, Minn. 1927) 343; M. Kaser, *Das römische Privatrecht,* vol. 1 (2d. ed. München 1971) § 102 I 3 (p. 426–427); G. Hill, *Treasure Trove in Law and Practice from the Earliest Time to the Present Day* (Oxford 1936) 1 *et seq.*

[12] Brian M. Fagan, *The Rape of the Nile* (Wakefield, R.I./London 1992); Hill (n. 11) 280: Egypt – "The Eldorado of treasure hunters."

[13] James Cross Giblin, *The Riddle of the Rosetta Stone. Key to Ancient Egypt* (New York 1992) 25 *et seq.*

[14] Ordonnance du 15 août 1835 portant mesures de protection des antiquités, in: A. Khater, *Le régime juridique des fouilles et des antiquités en Égypte* (Cairo 1960) 271 *et seq.*

[15] Cf. Article 4 Décret du 17 novembre 1891 arrêtant les conditions auxquelles des autorisations de fouilles peuvent être délivrées, in: Khater (*supra* n. 14) at 282; Article 11 Loi n° 14 du 12 juin 1912 sur les antiquités (in force since 1 July 1912), in: Khater (supra n. 14) at 286.

represented at the division by the junior official Gustave Lefebvre, 1879–1957, with less professional competence) at all or diligently hid the bust underneath some unimportant antiquities or Gustave Lefebvre as an epigraphist and papyrologist did not recognize the importance of the bust of Nefertiti. Whatever might have happened in Egypt in 1913, it seems to be undisputed that the Egyptian antiquities authority did not know of the bust of Nefertiti until it was exhibited in Berlin in 1923 and that they never knowingly agreed that this piece should belong to the legitimate share of the German half of the finds of Tell el-Amarna.[16] It is, however, a well-settled principle since the early days of cultural property legislation that every export of national cultural treasures has to be expressly permitted by the country of origin. Such permission was not given by the Egyptian antiquities authority with respect to the export of the bust of Nefertiti.

If this were true, what would be the effect of such a lack of a valid division agreement and export licence? This is a legal question. But which law must provide the answer? Is it Egyptian law, German law, or international law, or must all these laws agree? Another problem is whether the law in force in 1913 has to be consulted or whether current law has to give the answer. Of course, matters of title with respect to the bust of Nefertiti have to be decided according to conflict-of-law rules of the forum state. If Egypt decided to sue the Berlin Egyptian Museum for restitution of the bust, German courts would apply German conflicts rules. Without going into the details of a complicated matter it may suffice to say that the museum as the donee of an object governed by German *lex rei sitae* and *lex contractus* would have to return the donated object under the German rules of unjust enrichment (§ 816 I 2 BGB) because the bust under the Egyptian *lex rei sitae* and *lex contractus* was invalidly transferred to the Deutsche Orient-Gesellschaft.[17] But, as so often, this claim under the German law of unjust enrichment is barred by the German statutes of limitations under which the claim had to be raised within thirty years after the donation to the Berlin Egyptian Museum. The statutes of limitations are not applied ex officio. They have to be pleaded, and Germany, as the defendant, in order to establish friendly

[16] Krauss (supra n. 10) at 93 *et seq.*; Gert v. Paszensky (supra n. 10) at 262 *et seq.*
[17] Another complication refers to the relation between the Deutsche Orient-Gesellschaft (DOG) and the sponsor James Simon. It seems to be unlikely that the DOG donated the bust to James Simon. The bust either was immediately transferred to Simon as the holder of the excavation permission or was a contracted consideration for his money paid to the DOG for the excavation campaign in Tell el-Amarna. But also in this case the DOG could not transfer title, which it did not have.

relations with the Egyptian antiquities authorities and Egyptian museums, should not plead them.

But this is not the end of the story. There are also problems of international law to be answered. International law may be the law of international conventions, customary international law, general principles of law recognized by civilized nations and, subsidiarily, judicial decisions and the teaching of the most highly qualified publicists of the various nations (Article 38 [1] of the Statute of the International Court of Justice). Today there are some international instruments on the protection and recovery of cultural property. In relation to Egypt as a non-European country the UNESCO Convention of 1970 on the Means of Prohibiting and Preventing the Illicit Import, Export, and Transfer of Ownership of Cultural Property[18] and the 1995 Unidroit Convention on Stolen or Illegally Exported Cultural Objects[19] might be helpful. But even if they were in force between Egypt and Germany, neither of them works retroactively to apply to irregularities of the past.

2. Cultural Treasures Lost in Times of Occupation or Dependence

It has to be admitted that no international convention governs the request for return of the bust of Nefertiti to Egypt. Therefore, the question is whether there are additional sources of international law supporting the attitude of the Egyptian government. In recent years issues of cultural property and the illegal export of cultural property have been discussed on the international, supranational and national levels.

a) *Return Claims of States of Origin*
The two most important international instruments on the return of illegally exported cultural property have already been mentioned.[20] Both of them subscribe to the same policy governed by the following principles:

- Every state may retain its own national heritage by prohibiting the export of pieces of the national heritage without government permission.
- If pieces of any national heritage have been illegally exported, the state to which the pieces have been imported shall return these pieces to the state of origin.

[18]   823 U.N.T.S. 231. This convention has been implemented by the United States: Cf. 19 U.S.C.A. §§ 2601 *et seq.* and 19 C.F.R. §§ 12.104–12.109.
[19]   34 I.L.M. 1330 (1995); 5 *International Journal of Cultural Property* 155 (1996).
[20]   Supra n. 18 and n. 19.

- If there had been a bona fide purchase of an illegally exported cultural object, the bona fide purchaser will be compensated but cannot prevent the return of the object to the state of origin.

This scheme is interesting insofar as it distinguishes carefully between title in the object and the right to decide the place where the object has to be located. This is evidenced by the principles mentioned *supra*. The state of origin need not have any title in the illegally exported cultural object. Even if the title holder removed the object across national borders, the state under its policy of preserving and retaining objects of national cultural importance has a claim to enforce this policy in foreign countries and require even the title holder to keep the art treasures in the country of origin and not in any other country. The same is true with respect to bona fide purchasers. They may have acquired good title under the respective *lex rei sitae* and they may even retain this title but they have to return the object to the state of origin. This may amount to a special kind of expropriation. But this is no objection. It is a matter of compensation and the amount of compensation to be paid by the state of origin claiming back the object as a piece of national cultural importance.

The same policy has also been adopted by the European Union. The Council Directive 93/7/EEC of 15 March 1993 on the return of cultural objects unlawfully removed from the territory of a Member State[21] obliges every Member State of the European Union and of the European Economic Area (Iceland, Liechtenstein and Norway) to implement this directive and provides that illegally removed cultural objects have to be returned to that Member State from which they had been illegally removed. The old eighteen member states of these supranational organizations have already enacted implementing legislation[22] and the new ten member states were required to do the same after 1 May 2004.[23] Also here the member states have a separate right to ask for the return of illegally removed cultural objects. This right has no basis whatsoever in national law. It is a right under international or supranational law given to sovereign states in order to enable them to protect their national cultural heritage.

---

[21] Official Journal EC 1993 No. L 74/74 as amended by the Directive 96/100/EC of 17 February 1997, *Official Journal EC* 1997 No. L 60/59.

[22] Cf. the list of national statutes in: 1999 *Aktuelle juristische Praxis* at 963 n. 14 and in: 8 *Uniform Law Review* at 556 n. 25 (2003).

[23] This has already been done by the Czech Republic: Sbírka zákon Česká republika of 12 June 2003, No. 63, pos. 180, p. 3439.

If international instruments or supranationally harmonized national laws do not apply – for example, between Egypt and Germany – the question is whether there is an unwritten right of the state of origin to ask for the return of illegally exported or wrongfully taken cultural property. In recent years courts in Italy and in the United Kingdom have declined to recognize the right of a state to recover illegally exported cultural objects. In the case *Attorney General of New Zealand v. Ortiz* the House of Lords, asked to order the return of illegally exported Maori carvings, declined to enforce the export prohibitions of a foreign country.[24] Because of this attitude the Kingdom of Spain as the state of origin of an illegally exported painting by Francisco de Goya did not ask the auction house Christie's to return the painting. It preferred to ask for a declaratory judgment that the painting had been illegally exported, thereby tainting the painting with an obscure and criminal provenance in an attempt to make it unmerchantable.[25] Italian courts shared that attitude and declined to return French tapestries stolen and illegally exported to Italy and sold to the bona fide purchaser De Contessini.[26]

There are, however, trends in the opposite direction. German and Swiss courts have applied the principles of the 1970 UNESCO Convention despite the fact that this convention has not yet entered into force in these countries. The German Bundesgerichtshof (Federal Supreme Court for Civil and Criminal Matters) had to decide about an insurance contract covering the transport risk of Nigerian statues illegally exported from Nigeria. The court declined to enforce this contract and stated, "The export of items of cultural interest contrary to a prohibition in the country of origin does not deserve to be protected under civil law, in the interest of maintaining propriety in international trade in *objets d'art*."[27] It is true that the German court was not asked to return the illegally exported Nigerian cultural objects that were lost en route during the voyage to European ports.

In the Swiss case, a painting stolen in France was located in Switzerland and the French owner asked the Swiss authorities to return the painting as the proceeds of a crime according to the 1959 European Convention on Mutual Assistance in Criminal Matters.[28] At the very end of the decision the

[24] [1984] 1 A.C. 1, 35 (H.L.).
[25] *Kingdom of Spain v. Christie, Manson & Woods Ltd.* [1986] 1 W.L.R. 1120 (Ch.D.).
[26] Tribunale di Roma 27 June 1987 (*Stato francese c. Ministero per i beni culturali e ambientali e De Contessini*), 71 *Rivista di diritto internazionale* 920 (1988); Corte di Cassazione 24 November 1995, n. 12166, 80 *Rivista di diritto internazionale* 515 (1997).
[27] Bundesgerichtshof 22 June 1972, 59 *Entscheidungen des Bundesgerichtshofs in Zivilsachen* (BHGZ) 82, 88, and in 73 *International Law Reports* 226, 229.
[28] *European Treaty Series* No. 30; 472 U.N.T.S. 185.

Swiss Federal Court added: "Lorsque, comme l'espèce, la demande porte sur la restitution d'un bien culturel, le juge de l'entraide doit veiller à prendre en compte l'intérêt public international, comme à la Suisse et à la France, lié à la protection de ces biens [citing the 1970 UNESCO Convention for France and the 1995 Unidroit Convention signed by France and Switzerland but not yet ratified by either country]. Ces normes, qui relèvent d'une commune inspiration, constituent autant d'expressions d'un ordre public international en vigueur ou en formation.... Ces normes, qui concrétisent l'impératif d'une lutte internationale efficace contre le trafic de biens culturels"[29] Although the Swiss Federal Court did not have to deal with illegally exported cultural property, it strongly supported the policy of the two international conventions and their intent to fight international smuggle with cultural objects protected by states of origin and illegally taken or exported for sale in the international market of objets d'art.[30]

In recent years there is a clear trend favoured by qualified publicists advocating a right of every state to protect its national cultural heritage and to enforce this right in foreign courts by asking for the return of illegally exported cultural objects. The most important contribution to this discussion is made by the Institute of International Law (IIL), the most prominent body of highly qualified publicists and conflicts scholars from all nations. At the 1991 session in Basel the institute adopted a resolution concerning "The international sale of works of art from the angle of the protection of the cultural heritage".[31] This resolution is designed as a conflict of laws instrument, whose Article 2 states, "The transfer of ownership of works of art belonging to the cultural heritage of the country of origin shall be governed by the law of that country." In Article 3 is added, "The provisions of the law of the country of origin governing the export of works of art

---

[29] Tribunal Fédéral Suisse 1 April 1997 (L. c. Chambre d'accusation du Canton de Genève), 123 II *Arrêts du Tribunal Fédéral Suisse* 134, 143–44. The English translation of the French original reads as follows: "If, as in the present case, the claim is for the restitution of cultural property, the judge of international legal assistance should pay regard to the international public interest which, in Switzerland as well as in France, is bound to protect these objects. These provisions [of the UNESCO and UNIDROIT Conventions], based on a common inspiration, express such an international public policy already in force or in the making.... These provisions demand for an effective international fight against the [illegal] trade of cultural objects..."

[30] Switzerland just ratified the UNESCO Convention of 1970 and implemented this instrument in the Federal Act of 20 June 2003 on the International Transfer of Cultural Objects (*Bundesblatt* 2003, p. 4475) to enter into force on 1 January 2005.

[31] 64 II *Yearbook of the Institute of International Law* at 403–407 (1992).

shall apply." The reason why these conflicts rules were advanced to replace the traditional rules of *lex rei sitae* and of non-application of foreign public law becomes clear when we recall the English and Italian cases *Ortiz*[32] and *De Contessin.i*[33] In the *Ortiz* case the English courts would, if they applied Article 3 of Resolution IIL, enforce the export prohibitions of New Zealand and the entailing obligation to return the illegally exported objects. Also in the Italian *De Contessini* case the French government as the plaintiff would be successful. The tapestries, part of the French unmerchantable *domaine public*, were stolen and illegally exported to Italy. The Italian courts would have to apply Article 2 of Resolution IIL and deny any bona fide purchase by the art dealer in *De Contessini* because the Italian *lex rei sitae* does not govern the transfer of ownership; rather the French *lex originis*, which prohibits any alienation of pieces qualifying as part of the French *domaine public*, does. Therefore, because De Contessini did not acquire good title under the governing French law, the tapestries would have to be returned.

The policy of Resolution IIL, adopted by twenty-four highly qualified publicists against three abstentions,[34] can be summarized as follows:[35]

- The principle of freedom of circulation of goods also applies to cultural property.
- Every country has the right and the duty to take measures to preserve its cultural heritage by restricting free trade with *objets d'art* and by enacting prohibitions to export these objects without government licence.
- These protective measures of the country of origin shall be recognized by every country.
- As most cases concerning the return of stolen and/or illegally exported cultural property are tried in state courts and not before international tribunals, the rules governing such return claims in state courts have to be revised and adjusted to the needs for the protection of cultural property.

---

[32] Supra n. 24.
[33] Supra n. 26.
[34] Cf. 64 II *Yearbook of the Institute of International Law* at 338 (1992).
[35] This summary is based on the final report of Antonio de Arruda Ferrer-Correia, "La vente internationale d'objets d'art, sous l'angle de la protection du patrimoine culturel", in: 64 I *Yearbook of the Institute of International Law* at. 90 *et seq.*, 140–186 (1991), and the Resolution itself (supra n. 31).

- Because the state of origin has the most interest in preserving its cultural heritage, the law of that state (the *lex originis*) should govern the transfer of ownership and the possibility of free export.
- The result of this change is that objects of cultural property have a special regime in private international law insofar as the *lex originis* governs and not the traditional conflicts rules of *lex rei sitae* and non-application of foreign export prohibitions.
- Under Resolution IIC of 1991 the right of every state to restitution of stolen or illegally exported cultural property is recognized. This right does not impair the obligation to compensate bona fide purchasers.

The 1991 resolution of eminent publicists of the Institute of International Law is a proposal *de lege ferenda* whose quality as an emerging rule has been accepted by the Belgian Statute of 2004 on private international law.[36] This is not the only manifestation of an already existing or still emerging rule of international law. Several younger scholars not yet members of the Institute of International Law have ascertained a clear trend in international law to establish a right of every nation to ask for restitution of cultural property that was removed without permission of the country of origin and has been located in a foreign country.[37] These scholars also do not exclude the obligation of the country of origin to compensate bona fide purchasers or other persons bona fide seized of the cultural object.

b) *Application to Situations of the Past*

The Institute of International Law, according to the preamble of the 1991 resolution, underlined that "this Resolution is without prejudice to situations which have occurred prior to its adoption."[38] This is correct for an international instrument to be submitted to a diplomatic conference and to be ratified by states. Further, the 1970 UNESCO Convention (Article 15)[39] and the 1995 International Institute for the Unification of Private Law (UNIDROIT)

---

[36] Moniteur belge 2004, p. 57344.
[37] Christiane Freytag, "'Cultural Heritage': Rückgabeansprüche von Ursprungsländern auf 'ihr' Kulturgut?" in: Frank Fechner/Thomas Oppermann/Lyndel V. Prott (eds.), *Prinzipien des Kulturgüterschutzes. Ansätze im deutschen, europäischen und internationalen Recht* (Berlin 1996) 175–200; Stefan Turner, *Das Restitutionsrecht des Staates nach illegaler Ausfuhr von Kulturgütern. Eigentumsordnung und völkerrechtliche Zuordnung* (Berlin/New York 2002) 9 *et seq.*; Martin Philipp Wyss, "Rückgabeansprüche für illegal ausgeführte Kulturgüter. Überlegungen zu einem kulturpolitischen Ordre public", in: Fechner/Oppermann/Prott (supra) at 201–223.
[38] 64 II *Yearbook of the Institute of International Law* at 405 (1992).
[39] Supra n. 18.

Convention (Article 10)[40] donot work retroactively. But what about general principles of customary international law? Do they apply to situations that originated in the past and continue to be unsolved in the present? With respect to the bust of Nefertiti it has to be asked whether Egypt's right to restitution of the bust (which does not question the title of the present title holder) can be enforced because after almost one hundred years since the removal of the bust from Egypt such a right of restitution has emerged. This is a problem of intertemporal public international law with regard to customary international law to be enforced *ex nunc* without retroactive effect questioning title or possession and exploitation of the bust by exhibiting it. There are no international treaties on the general problem of intertemporal international law. General principles also apply here. Without going into the details of a very complicated matter the basic principles may be summarized as follows:[41]

- A legal transaction is governed by the law at the time of the transaction. Any right acquired at this time is protected as a vested right.
- The exercise of any vested right is governed *ex nunc* by the law applying at the time of the respective exercise.
- If the law valid at the time of exercise devalues the vested right, the title holder has to be compensated by the party taking advantage of this devaluation.
- These principles are subject to the requirements of bona fides, public policy and estoppel.

c) *Obstacles to Restitution?*

According to the principles mentioned *supra* the right of Egypt to restitution also applies to the bust of Nefertiti. Any vested right will not be questioned. The title holder is, however, obliged to return the object and enjoy it while it is located in Egypt. Whether the Stiftung Preußischer Kulturbesitz will be compensated for such a loss of possession (in money or antiquities) may be

---

[40] Supra n. 19.

[41] This summary is based on the following studies: Anthony D'Amato, "International Law, Intertemporal Problems", in: Rudolf Bernhardt (ed.), 2 *Encyclopedia of Public International Law* 1234–1236 (1995); Hans Baade, "Intertemporales Völkerrecht", in: 7 *Jahrbuch für internationales Recht* p. 229–256 (1957); T. O. Elias. "The Doctrine of Intertemporal Law", 74 *American Journal of International Law* 285–307 (1980); Wolf-Dietrich Krause-Ablaß, *Intertemporales Völkerrecht* (Hamburg 1970); Max Sørensen, "Le problème dit du droit intertemporel dans l'ordre international", in: 55 *Annuaire de l'Institut de Droit International* 1–98 (1973).

doubtful because the foundation's predecessor received the bust as a gift from James Simon, who must have been aware of the irregularities that occurred at the division of finds in 1913. For the same reason the Stiftung is not allowed to decline to make restitution as an unfair and unreasonable reaction to events that happened almost one hundred years ago. The Stiftung would be estopped to plead these irregularities on the German side as a defence. In addition, lapse of time is no defence. There are no statutes of limitation in public international law. A claim, however, may be precluded because of extinctive prescription.[42] This general principle of international law applies if the creditor was inactive for a certain time so that the debtor relied on the extinction of the claim.[43] But Egypt never gave up any claim and insisted on the return of Nefertiti.[44] The only defence to be raised for a delay in returning it is the objection that the bust of Nefertiti will not be exhibited in Egypt and diligently preserved. Until adequate physical preservation of the bust is guaranteed, the Stiftung, according to a special kind of *ordre public culturel*, may postpone the restitution of the bust of Nefertiti.[45]

d) *Intermediate Summary*

Under the emerging principle of customary international law Egypt has a right to restitution of the bust of Nefertiti. Such a claim does not affect the title of the present title holder. Whether the title holder will be compensated (in money or antiquities) may be doubtful. But the title holder may insist that restitution must be postponed until the bust of Nefertiti will be safely and diligently preserved and exhibited in Egypt.

3. Protection of Cultural Property *Ensembles*

The bust of Nefertiti was discovered in the workshop of the Egyptian sculptor Thutmose of Amarna.[46] This was not the only object found in the excavation compound of houses P 47.1–47.3. Many other items were discovered,

---

[42] Carl-August Fleischhauer, "Prescription", in: Rudolf Bernhardt (ed.), 3 *Encyclopedia of Public International Law* 1105–1108 (1997); Roger Pinto, "La prescription en droit international", in: 87 *Recueil des Cours* at 387 *et seq.* (1955–I).

[43] Cf. Article I of Résolution concernant la prescription libératoire en Droit International public, in: 32 *Annuaire de l'Institut de Droit International* 558–560 (1925).

[44] Supra at I 3 text after n. 10.

[45] Cf. Kurt Siehr, "International Art Trade and the Law", in: 243 *Recueil des Cours* 9–292, at 278 (1993–VI).

[46] As to Thutmose cf. Arnold (supra n. 2); Rolf Krauss, "Der Bildhauer Thutmose in Amarna", in: 20 *Jahrbuch Preußischer Kulturbesitz* 119–132 (1983).

registered, analysed and finally preserved and exhibited. At the division of spoils on 20 January 1913 the responsible persons took care that correlated pieces should not be separated. Nevertheless many different items of Thutmose's workshop were dispersed to several museums and collectors.

It has long been recognized by archaeologists, art historians, museum curators and even politicians that objects of cultural property should not be dismembered and, if this had happened in the past, such a mutilation of objets d'art should be stopped and dispersed pieces of an *ensemble* should be reassembled. Such a policy has been supported in some international instruments. Under the Peace Treaty of Vienna of 3 October 1866 between Austria-Hungary and Italy,[47] which had joined Prussia in the German War of 1866 between Prussia and Austria, Austria had to give up the Kingdom of Lombardy-Venetia and to return certain pieces of cultural property to Italy. In execution of Article 18 of the Peace Treaty Austria delivered the cup of Queen Theodolinde († 627/28 A.D.) to the Cathedral of Monza (Italy) in order for it to be reunited with the Iron Crown of Lombardy, the traditional crown of the kings of Italy.[48] The same policy worked in favour of Austria in the Peace Treaty of St. Germain-en-Laye of 10 September 1919 between the Allied and Associated Powers of World War I.[49] According to Article 195 (1) of this Treaty a committee of three jurists appointed by the Reparation Commission were obliged to examine the conditions under which certain objects (i.e., the regalia of Norman kings in Palermo, Sicily) were carried off by the House of Hapsburg. In the Special Convention of 4 May 1920 Italy gave up all claims regarding the regalia of Palermo in order not to disperse the complete collection of Imperial Regalia exhibited to the present in the Imperial Treasury (Weltliche Schatzkammer) in Vienna.[50] Best known is Article 247 § 2 of the Peace Treaty of Versailles of 28 June 1919 between the Allied and Associated Powers of World War I and Germany.[51] Germany undertook to deliver to Belgium (1) the leaves of the *Mystic Lamb* triptych by the van Eyck brothers, formerly in the Church of St. Bavon at

---

[47] 133 *Consolidated Treaty Series* at 209.

[48] Cf. Article 7 of the Convention du 14 juillet 1868 entre l'Autriche et l'Italie, pour la restitution de certains documents et objets d'art, in: Martens (ed), *Nouveau Recueil Général de Traités* vol. XVIII (1868) 428–432.

[49] 226 *Consolidated Treaty Series* at 9 *et seq.*

[50] Article 4 (2) of the Convention spéciale du 4 mai 1920 afin de résoudre les controverses relatives au patrimoine historique et artistique de l'ancienne Monarchie austrohongroise, in: Martens (ed.), *Nouveau Recueil Général de Traités*, 3e sér., vol. 19 (1928) 682 *et seq.*

[51] 225 *Consolidated Treaty Series* at 189 *et seq*, at p. 304.

Ghent and then in the Berlin museums, and (2) the leaves *Last Supper* of the triptych by Dierick Bouts, formerly in the Church of St. Peter at Louvain and then in the Berlin museums and the Old Pinakothek at Munich. These leaves had been sold in former times by Belgian authorities and legally acquired by the German museums. The Peace Treaty of Versailles took the opportunity to "enable Belgium to reconstitute two great artistic works" (Article 247 § 2).

Even those scholars who are in favour of international art trade, international exchange and internationalism in the field of cultural property and who object to any policy of selfish and nationalistic retentionism are concerned about the integrity of work of art.[52] Of course, the main concern is to prevent any destruction of such works, but the restoration of dismembered masterpieces is also generally supported. The only questions are whether the dispersed parts of a sculptor's workshop as a kind of Gesamtkunstwerk can be reunited, whether it is a Gesamtkunstwerk at all and who is authorized to answer such questions. As there is no professional body of archaeologists authorized to solve these problems, it is arguable that the country of origin normally has the best information about *ensembles* of its culture and the principal interest in restoration of a dismembered masterpiece formerly located in this country. In the Nefertiti case it is Egypt that has to decide whether the workshop of Thutmose and the contents of the workshop (including the bust of Nefertiti) can be re-established in a museum. It can be anticipated that such a re-arrangement would be possible in the planned new Egyptian Museum to be built in Giza close to the pyramids.

4. Nationality or Home of Cultural Property

The basis of any national policy to preserve and retain cultural treasure is the unspoken conviction that there is some sort of a "genuine link" between art objects and a nation. Such a link may be called "nationality" of an objet d'art[53] or its "home". International instruments dealing with the return of

---

[52] John Henry Merryman, "Thinking about the Elgin Marbles", 83 *Michigan Law Review* 1880 *et seq.*, at 1918–1919 (1985); reprinted in: id., *Thinking about the Elgin Marbles. Critical Essays on Cultural Property, Art and Law* (The Hague/London/Boston 2000) 24 *et seq*; at 59; id, "The Retention of Cultural Property", 21 *University of California Davis Law Review* 477 *et seq.* (1988), reprinted in: id., *Thinking* (supra) p. 122 *et seq.*

[53] Erik Jayme, *Kunstwerk und Nation: Zuordnungsprobleme im internationalen Kulturgüterschutz* (Heidelberg 1991), and reprinted in: id., *Nationales Kunstwerk und Internationales Privatrecht* (Heidelberg 1999) 54–74; id., "Die Nationalität

illegally exported cultural objects do not use any specific term to designate the link between the object and the country asking for return. They assume that every art object that should not be exported without government permission is part of the cultural heritage of the protecting state and that this attribution should be respected and, upon application, enforced by state parties or member states.[54] There are good reasons to be very critical of the notion of nationality of an objet d'art and the attribution of a territorial home to works of art created for humankind and for a common cultural heritage.[55] Must every painting of Raffaello be in Italy, every masterwork of Dürer in Germany, every canvas of Goya in Spain and every portrait of Frans Hals in the Netherlands? There are also good arguments against the modern conventions designed to preserve the status quo rather than to encourage trade, exchange and internationalism in cultural policy.[56] And yet it makes sense to attribute to archaeological finds a special regime and a special link to the country of origin and excavation, for several reasons:

- Archaeological objects are more than any other pieces of cultural property attached to the *territory* of the country of origin.
- Most archaeological finds are *connected* with objects discovered on the same site or neighbouring sites.
- Many archaeological objects were *manufactured* in the country of origin, are the *expression* of the local culture and are evidence of the *history* of the country of origin.
- In order to fight *illegal excavations* and to preserve the *context* of archaeology, *preventive measures* have to be taken; this is done by recognizing a territorial link to the country of origin more than for any other piece of cultural property.

des Kunstwerks als Rechtsfrage", in: Gerte Reichelt (ed.), *Internationaler Kulturgüterschutz – Wiener Symposion 18./19. Oktober 1990* (Wien 1992) 7–29, and reprinted in: Erik Jayme, *Wiener Vorträge. Internationales Privat- und Verfahrensrecht, Rechtsvergleichung, Kunst- und Kulturrecht* (Wien 2001) 129–153; id., "Antonio Canova und das nationale Kunstwerk – Zur Ideengeschichte des europäischen Kulturgüterschutzes", in: id., *Nationales Kunstwerk* (supra) 1–15, and reprinted in: id., *Wiener Vorträge* (supra) 171–186.

54 Cf. Article 5 of the 1995 UNIDROIT Convention (supra n. 19) and Article 1 (1) of the 1993 EEC – Directive 93/7/EEC (supra n. 21).

55 Cf. John Henry Merryman, "The Nation and the Object" 3 *International Journal of Cultural Property* 61–76 (1994), reprinted in: id., *Thinking* (supra n. 51) 158–173.

56 Cf. the basic study of John Henry Merryman, "Two Ways of Thinking about Cultural Property", 80 *American Journal of International Law* 831–853 (1986), reprinted in: id., *Thinking* (supra n. 51) 66–91.

This special regime for archaeological objects is well recognized by
national legislation, by national courts and by international instruments on
the protection of cultural property. Many source states with a rich archaeological past provide in their domestic statutes on the protection of cultural
property that all archaeological finds are ipso facto and *ipso iure* state property.[57] This policy of state property has been recognized and enforced in
European countries[58] and recently in the United States as well.[59] The earliest
convention recognizing state property in archaeological finds is the German-
Greek Convention of 1874 on the German excavations in Olympia. Article 6
of this convention provides that Greece becomes the owner of all archaeological objects discovered in Olympia.[60] The result of this agreement is that
all important archaeological objects excavated in Olympia are exhibited in
Greece (Olympia and Athens). Almost one hundred years later the Council of
Europe prepared the European Convention of 6 May 1969 for the Protection
of the Archaeological Heritage,[61] revised in 1992.[62] Since enactment of the
convention on Cultural Property Implementation Act in 1983, the United
States has recognized the interest of several source countries to preserve
and retain their archaeological heritage. All nine agreements with foreign
state parties (Bolivia, Canada, Cyprus, El Salvador, Guatemala, Italy, Mali,

---

[57] Cf. the somewhat outdated list of national legislation in: Lyndel V. Prott and Patrick
J. O'Keefe, *Law and the Cultural Heritage*. Vol. 1: *Discovery and Excavation* (Abingdon,
Oxon. 1983) at 34 *et seq*. The most recent statute of this kind is the Greek Statute
No. 3028 of 28 June 2002 on the Protection of Antiquities and the Cultural Heritage
in General, 2002 *Ephimeris tis Kyberniseos* at 3003.

[58] Cf., e.g., Oberlandesgericht Schleswig 10 February 1989, 1989 *Neue Juristische Wochen-
schrift* at 3105 (return of ancient coins excavated in Greece from Germany to Greece);
Tribunale di Torino 25 March 1982, 18 *Rivista di diritto internazionale privato e proces-
suale* at 625 (1982) (the collector Danusso had to return pre-Columbian antiquities
to the Republic of Ecuador).

[59] *United States v. Schultz*, 178 F. Supp. 2d 445 (S.D.N.Y. 2002); affirmed by the U.S. Court
of Appeals on 25 June 2003 (return of Egyptian antiquities from New York to Egypt).
Cf. Martha B. G. Lufkin, "End of the Era of Denial for Buyers of State-Owned
Antiquities: *United States v. Schultz*", 11 *International Journal of Cultural Property*
305–322 (2002); id., "Criminal Liability for Receiving State-Claimed Antiquities in
the United States: The 'Schultz' Case", 8 *Art Antiquity and Law* 321–342 (2003).

[60] "La Grèce aura la propriété de tous les produits de l'art antique et de tout autre objet
dont les fouilles amèneront la découverte." Article 6, sentence 1, of the Convention du
13/25 avril 1874 relative à des fouilles archéologiques à entreprendre sur le territoire
de l'ancienne Olympie, *Reichs = Gesetzblatt* 1875 at 241 *et seq.*, at p. 243.

[61] *European Treaty Series* No. 66; 8 *International Legal Materials* at 736 (1969).

[62] European Convention of 16 January 1992 on the Protection of the Archaeological
Heritage, *European Treaty Series* No. 143.

Nicaragua and Peru) that impose American import restrictions on articles of cultural property refer to *archaeological* material of these foreign countries.[63] The latest special provision for archaeological objects is Article 3 (2) of the 1995 UNIDROIT Convention.[64] This rule provides that "for the purpose of this Convention, a cultural object which has been unlawfully excavated or lawfully excavated but unlawfully retained shall be considered stolen, when consistent with the law of the State where the excavation took place."[65] This qualification ensures that archaeological objects enjoy the more effective and less unsafe regime of "stolen cultural objects" under Chapter II of the 1995 UNIDROIT Convention.

Summarizing the present legal situation, it can be said that archaeological objects have their "home" in the country where they have been excavated and should stay in this country and, if removed without the expressly given consent of this country of origin, should return to this country.

5. Support of Countries Suffering from Imperialism

A basic principle of international law is that all states are treated equally and should not be subjected to discrimination.[66] All have equal rights and obligations under international law. Despite these principles of equal treatment and non-discrimination the question whether states that suffered under colonization, imperialism and dependence should be treated differently with respect to problems arising from decolonization and independence has yet to be answered. Egypt has been one of those states that suffered severely from Ottoman and European imperialism:[67]

- ∼1650–1551 B.C.: Invasion and rule of the Hyksos
- 525–404 B.C.: Province of Persia
- 332–30 B.C.: Macedonian and Ptolemaic rule
- 30 B.C.–642 A.D.: Roman and Byzantine rule
- 639–868: Arab and Turkish rule

---

[63] Cf. the list at 19 Code of Federal Regulations § 12.104g (a) (2003).

[64] Supra n. 19.

[65] As to this departure from the *Urtext* cf. John Henry Merryman, "The UNIDROIT Convention: Three Significant Departures from the *Urtext*", 5 *International Journal of Cultural Property* 11–18, at 13–15 (1996), reprined in: id., *Thinking* (supra n. 51) 270–277, at 273–275.

[66] Günther Jaenicke, "States, Equal Treatment and Non-Discrimination", in: Rudolf Bernhardt (ed.), 4 *Encyclopedia of Public International Law* at 660–669 (2000).

[67] This abbreviated chronology follows the history of Egypt as set out in 18 *The New Encyclopædia Britannica* 91 *et seq.*, at 104 *et seq.* (15th ed. Chicago 2003).

- 1517–1798: Rule by the Ottoman Empire
- 1798–1805: French occupation
- 1805–1882: Muhammed Ali and successors as viceroys of the Sublime Porte
- 1882–1922: British occupation and protectorate

The Egyptians were often not masters in their own house. For a long time the Egyptian Antiquities Authority was headed by French archaeologists (Maspero and Lefebvre, responsible for the 1913 division of spoils in Tell el-Amarna, were Frenchmen, and Borchardt was a member of the Comité d'Egyptologie in charge of giving advice to the Egyptian authorities) and even after 1922 the United Kingdom exercised certain rights with respect to the Suez Canal.

The status of decolonized nations succeeding the former colonial power is regulated either in bilateral agreements between the predecessor state and the successor state or in multilateral conventions. In bilateral agreements only bilateral problems can be solved.[68] The two multilateral conventions on state succession deal with problems in respect of treaties[69] and of state property, archives and debts.[70] There are no special provisions on cultural property in general and even fewer on cultural objects removed in times of occupation and dependence. The only conclusion to be drawn from these instruments is the general idea that the successor state should not be blamed for those acts, transactions and omissions for which the predecessor state is responsible. Therefore, it is not inconsistent that the Republic of Egypt is asking for the return of a cultural object that was removed to Germany at a time when Egypt was still under control of foreign powers and local authorities dominated by foreign personnel who, under dubious circumstances, gave permission for the export of important Egyptian cultural treasures.

Another conclusion to be drawn from these instruments is the well recognized policy to support successor states as newly independent states in their effort to become self-conscious and stable members of the international community with equal rights and obligations. Therefore it has been argued that the successor states may adjust their economy to new conditions and may even expropriate and compensate foreigners in order to

---

[68] Werner Morvay, "Decolonization: British Territories", in: Rudolf Bernhardt (ed.), 1 *Encyclopedia of Public International Law* at 976–983 (1992).

[69] Vienna Convention of 23 August 1978 on Succession of States in Respect of Treaties, 1946 U.N.T.S. 3; 17 *International Legal Materials* at 1488 (1978).

[70] Vienna Convention of 8 April 1983 on Succession of States in Respect of State Property, Archives and Debts, 22 *International Legal Materials* 306 (1983).

terminate their domination in the local economy.[71] Also in cultural affairs the newly independent states deserve a preferential status in order to establish or reestablish a new and distinct cultural identity. For this reason some international conventions on the return of stolen or illegally exported cultural property require only "just" or "reasonable" compensation because newly independent states and developing countries cannot afford to pay full compensation.[72] The United Nations and UNESCO have constantly encouraged and supported every effort to return cultural objects to the country of origin formerly governed by colonial powers.[73]

The general conclusion can be easily drawn. The newly independent states should be supported in their efforts to collect and recover their cultural heritage dispersed within their country and, in times of colonialism, removed to foreign countries. Against reasonable compensation on money or in kind the removed cultural objects should be returned and exhibited in the country of origin and thereby contribute to the cultural identity of these decolonized states.

III. SUMMARY

If Egypt decided to ask for the return of the bust of Nefertiti, it should plead and argue as follows:

1. The bust of Nefertiti should be returned to Egypt.
2. This return is supported by the emerging rule of international law that cultural treasures lost in times of occupation or dependence have to be

---

[71] Cf. Hans Dölle/Fritz Reichert-Facilides/Konrad Zweigert, *Internationalrechtliche Betrachtungen zur Dekolonisierung* (Tübingen 1964) at 21 *et seq.*

[72] Guido Carducci, *La restitution internationale des biens culturels et des objets d'art volés ou illicitement exportés. Droit commun, Directive CEE, Conventions de l'UNESCO et d'UNIDROIT* (Paris 1997) 425 *et seq.*, at 433 *et seq.*; *Diplomatic Conference for the Adoption of the Draft UNIDROIT Convention on the International Return of Stolen or Illegally Exported Cultural Objects. Acts and Proceedings* (Roma 1996) p. 39; Patrick J. O'Keefe, *Commentary on the UNESCO 1970 Convention on Illicit Traffic* (Leicester 2000) at 66; Lyndel V. Prott, *Commentary on the UNIDROIT Convention on Stolen and Illegally Exported Cultural Objects 1995* (Leicester 1997) at 42 at n. 12.

[73] Cf. the preliminary study of the UNESCO Intergovernmental Committee for Promoting the Return of Cultural Property to Its Countries of Origin or Its Restitution in Case of Illicit Appropriation in regard to three national situations (Bangladesh, Mali, Western Samoa), CC-79/CONF.206/5 of 14 March 1980, also reprinted in: Dorothee Schulze, *Die Restitution von Kunstwerken. Zur völkerrechtlichen Dimension der Restitutionsresolutionen der Generalversammlung der Vereinten Nationen* (Bremen 1983) at 199.

returned to the countries of origin. Such a claim is neither barred by time nor by any other exception.

3. This claim for restitution is strengthened by four additional arguments:

   a) The 1913 division of spoils was incorrect insofar as the Egyptian Antiquities Authority never consciously agreed to the removal of the bust of Nefertiti to Berlin.
   b) Cultural property *ensembles* should not be dismembered and, if dismembered, should be united.
   c) Archaeological finds have their "home" in the country of origin and should be preserved in at country.
   d) States that suffered under imperialism or colonialism should be supported in their efforts to collect their cultural treasures and to recover them from foreign states to which they had been removed in times of dependence.

4. Germany will be compensated in money or in kind with Egyptian antiquities.

7 THE BEAUTIFUL ONE HAS COME – TO STAY

Stephen K. Urice[1]

This chapter argues that the bust of Nefertiti[2] – her name translates as "The Beautiful One Is/Has Come"[3] – should remain in Germany, where it has

---

[1] The author wishes to acknowledge and thank individuals who assisted in the preparation of this chapter. Adrienne Fricke, J.D. (2004) University of Pennsylvania Law School, prepared new translations from French and Arabic of Egyptian laws and regulations in effect at the time of the discovery, partage, and export of the bust. Those translations (which are used throughout this chapter) are presented in Adrienne L. Fricke's appendix (see Appendix II). Tracy Musacchio, Ph.D. candidate, University of Pennsylvania, prepared the annotated bibliography on Nefertiti in Appendix I. Sung-Kee Kim, LL.M., University of Pennsylvania Law School, 2004, provided translations of Rolf Krauss, 1913–1988: 75 Jahre Büste der NofretEte/Nefret-iti in Berlin, 24 *Jahrbuch, Preussischer Kulturbesitz* 87 (1987) for this chapter. Megan Canter, J. D. candidate (2005), University of Pennsylvania Law School, prepared an insightful research paper on which the author relied greatly in Part III, *infra*. Laura Forman, J.D. (2004), University of Pennsylvania Law School, and Karen Tani, J.D., Ph.D. candidate, University of Pennsylvania, provided additional research assistance and help with citation formating. Alexander Bauer, associate director of the Project for Cultural Heritage Law and Policy and Ph.D. candidate, University of Pennsylvania, discussed with the author the issues presented by the bust of Nefertiti on numerous occasions, leading the author to new understandings. The author expresses gratitude to the University of Pennsylvania Law School for providing an opportunity to teach and engage in research during academic year 2004–5, when this chapter was prepared and presented in a shorter version at a symposium, *Imperialism, Art and Restitution*, March 26–27, 2004, at the Washington University School of Law, St. Louis, Missouri. The assistance of the staff of the University of Pennsylvania Law School's Biddle Law Library, especially Maria Smolka-Day, Merle Slyhoff, and Bill Draper, was indispensable and is deeply appreciated.
    The organizers of the St. Louis symposium requested that the author and Professor Kurt Siehr take opposing positions on the question whether the Bust of Nefertiti should remain in Berlin or be returned to Egypt. As lawyers, both of us might have argued either position.
    The views expressed in this chapter are solely those of the author and do not reflect the position of any institution with which the author is associated. Of course, errors in this article are entirely the responsibility of the author.

[2] Hereinafter referred to as the "bust."

[3] Arielle P. Kozloff, *Nefertiti, Beloved of the Living Disk*, 64 *Bull. Cleveland Museum Art* 287, 287 (1977). Kozloff notes: "[Nefertiti's] image is accompanied by a variety of

been located and cared for since 1913. The discussion is in five parts. Part I
provides the background and relevant facts. Part II analyzes whether Egypt
has a cognizable legal claim for return of the bust, and concludes that it
does not. Part III addresses nonlegal concerns in determining whether the
bust should, in the absence of an enforceable legal claim, nevertheless be
returned to Egypt. Part IV extends the argument of Part III, focusing on the
special interests of living artists and securing for them unfettered access to
works of art as sources for new creative expression. Finally, Part V concludes
that relevant nonlegal values and concerns argue strongly against returning
the bust to Egypt. In short, this chapter states why "The Beautiful One Has
Come" to Berlin to stay.

I. BACKGROUND AND RELEVANT FACTS

A. Historical Background

The bust of Nefertiti in Berlin's Ägyptisches Museum[4,5] was discovered
on December 6, 1912, at the site of Tel el-Amarna.[6] Amarna served for a
brief period as the Egyptian royal capital under Amenhotep IV (1350–1333
BCE),[7] who later took the name Akhenaten. Amenhotep IV was born to

flattering and romantic epithets: 'heiress of great favors, possessed of charm, sweet
[of love] . . .'; she 'soothe[s] [?] the king's heart in his house'; 'one is happy to hear
her voice.'" *Id.*

[4] The museum is one of sixteen museums forming the Staatliche Museen zu Berlin.
"Staatliche Museen zu Berlin," *at* http://www.smb.spk-berlin.de/e/index.html (last
visited March 9, 2004). The museum's full name is the Ägyptisches Museum und
Papyrussamlung. It is often loosely referred to as the "Charlottenburg" after the district in Berlin where it is located – opposite the Charlottenburg Palace (completed
1695). The Egyptian Museum building, formerly a component of the palace complex,
was designed by Friederich August Stüler and built in the 1850s. *See* "Charlottenburg
Palace," *at* http://www.berlin.de/stadttouren/en/chlbg.html (last visited February 17,
2004). For information on the museum, see "Ägyptisches Museum und Papyrussamlung," *at* http://www.smb.spk-berlin.de/amp/e/s.html (last visited March 9, 2004).

[5] The bust of Nefertiti, Ägyptisches Museum und Papyrussamlung, Accession # 21300.

[6] The literature on the Amarna period is vast. *See, e.g.,* Geoffrey Thorndike Martin, *A
Bibliography of the Amarna Period and Its Aftermath* (1991) (recording more than
2,000 bibliographic entries). The person, personality, and bust of Nefertiti form
but a small portion of the scholarly and popular writing on the subject. An annotated bibliography of sources relevant to Nefertiti, by Tracy Musacchio, appears at
Appendix I.

[7] The name *Amenhotep* is interchangeable in the Egyptological literature with
Amunhotpe and *Amenophis.* Dates in Egyptian history vary substantially from author
to author, with three principal chronologies in use, commonly called the "high,"

Amenhotep III and his wife, Tiye. As part of dramatic religious and political reforms, matched by a revolutionary change in Egyptian visual styles, imagery, and iconography,[8] Amenhotep IV moved the royal capital from Thebes to Amarna, known in antiquity as Akhetaten, meaning "horizon (or seat) of the Aten."[9] The Aten, "a heavenly father and kingly god, manifest in the sunlight,"[10] was represented as a solar disk in Amarna period art. As early as year 4 of his reign, Amenhotep IV chose Amarna as his new capital and construction began there immediately. By year 6 of Amenhotep IV's rule, fourteen boundary stelae demarcating the area of the new capital had been erected.[11] On these stelae Amenhotep IV changes his name to Akhenaten.[12] Akhenaten's primary wife was Nefertiti. By year 14 of Akhenaten's reign, Nefertiti disappears from the historical record: whether she died or whether we have absence of documentation indicating a longer life is not clear.[13] Akhenaten's death in 1333 ended a reign of approximately seventeen years. He was succeeded by the two-year reign of Smenkhare, who was succeeded by Tutanhkhamun, whose intact royal tomb was discovered to international fame in 1922.[14] With Tutankhamun's transfer of the court from Amarna back to Thebes, Amarna was effectively abandoned, presenting for modern archaeologists the rare opportunity of excavating a royal capital that was occupied only briefly and never built over.

B. Excavations at Amarna

The German Orient Society (Deutschen Orient-Gesellschaft, hereinafter referred to as the DOG) excavated at Amarna from 1911 to 1914.[15] The

---

"middle," and "low" or the "CAH [Cambridge Ancient History], conventional, and low." Amelie Kuhrt, *The Ancient Near East* 194 (1995). For purposes of this chapter, dates conform to those given in William W. Hallo, and William Kelly Simpson, *The Ancient Near East: A History* (2d ed. 1998).

[8] Some art historians and archaeologists recognize that the stylistic shifts that reached full expression in the Amarna period began prior to the reign of Amenhotep IV/Akhanaten. For a concise, insightful, and illustrated discussion, see William Stevenson Smith, *The Art and Architecture of Ancient Egypt* 170–180 (3d. ed. 1998), revised with additions by William Kelly Simpson.

[9] Cyril Aldred, *Akhenaten and Nefertiti* 22 (1973).

[10] Aldred, *supra* n. 9, at 11.

[11] Hallo and Simpson, *supra* n. 7, at 268.

[12] William Stevenson Smith, *supra* n. 8, at 173.

[13] Aldred, *supra* n. 9, at 25.

[14] Hallo and Simpson, *supra* n. 7, at 272.

[15] Rolf Krauss, 1913–1988: 75 Jahre Büste der NofretEte/Nefret-iti in Berlin, 24 *Jahrbuch, Preussischer Kulturbesitz* 87, 87 (1987).

excavation permit was held by James Simon, a merchant, museum patron, and funder of the DOG's expedition to Amarna.[16,17] The expedition was headed by Ludwig Borchardt (1863–1938), who served at the time as the director of the Imperial German Institute for Egyptian Archaeology in Cairo.[18] According to Rolf Krauss, who has written the most extensive, albeit tendentious, account of the finding of the bust and its subsequent history, "The purpose of the excavation was the extraction of finds which would be loaned [from the excavation permit holder] to the Egyptian department of the Royal Museums in Berlin for exhibition purposes."[19,20] It is clear, however, from the DOG's published excavation reports[21] and from other Egyptologists' interpretive reports of those publications, which began as early as 1916,[22] that Krauss substantially understates the expedition's scientific purposes. While Egyptian law defining the sharing of finds from the site – referred to as *partage* – indeed provided for an equal division, the DOG publications make clear that the archaeological effort was aimed primarily at learning

---

[16]   Krauss, *supra* n. 15, at 87–92. Simon is also described as the "founder and originator of the [DOG]." Rudolph Anthes, *The Head of Queen Nofretete* 5 (Kathleen Bauer, trans., 1954).

[17]   Krauss, *supra* n. 15, at 87.

[18]   *Id.*

[19]   *Id.*

[20]   Krauss, citing Borchardt, notes that stimulus to mount an expedition to Amarna arose from the availability on the open market of antiquities of the period, providing yet another example of legitimate excavations that follow from the appearance of illicit excavations. *Id.* A more recent example is that of Sipan in Peru, where the sudden appearance of important objects of Moche civilization in the hands of dealers and tomb robbers led archaeologists to the site that has yielded the most significant scientific excavations of Moche culture. *See* Brian Alexander, Archeology and Looting Make a Volatile Mix, 250 *Science* 1074 (1990).

[21]   Ludwig Borchardt, *Die Wohnhäuser in Tell el-Amarna* (1980); Ludwig Borchardt, *Excavations at tell-el-Amarna, Egypt, in 1913–1914* (1921); Ludwig Borchardt, *Porträts der Königin Nofret-ete, Ausgrabungen der Deutschen Orient-Gesellschaft in tell el-Amarna* III (1923); Ludwig Borchardt, Ausgrabungen in Tell el-Amarna 1911: vorläufiger Bericht, 46 *Mitteilungen der Deutschen Orient-Gesellschaft zu Berlin* [*MDOG*] 1 (1911); Ludwig Borchardt, Ausgrabungen in Tell el-Amarna 1911/12: vorläufiger Bericht, 50 *MDOG* 1 (1912); Ludwig Borchardt, Ausgrabungen in Tell el-Amarna 1912/13: vorläufiger Bericht, 52 *MDOG* 1 (1913); Ludwig Borchardt, Ausgrabungen in Tell el-Amarna 1913/14: vorläufiger Bericht, 55 *MDOG* 3 (1914).

[22]   *See*, e.g., James Henry Breasted, Studio of an Egyptian Portrait Sculptor in the Fourteenth Century B.C. 4 *Art and Archaeology* 233 (1916). For other examples, see Appendix I.

as much as possible about the site through scientific methods. Put another way, the German expedition to Amarna was no treasure hunt, although remarkable finds were discovered.

The bust was discovered in what was identified as the complex of a sculptor named Thutmose. Part of the complex contained Thutmose's living areas and sculpture studio; an internal wall separated these functions from the living quarters for Thutmose's assistants and apprentices.[23] Ten years later Borchardt described the finding of the bust as follows:

After my lunch break on December 6, 1912, I found a note by Prof. Ranke[24] who was the supervisor, in which he asked me to come to House 47, 2 [the Thutmose complex]. . . . I went there and saw the pieces of Amenhopis IV's life-size bust, which had just been discovered right behind the door in room 19. Soon after and close to the same place in room 19, very delicate and fragile pieces [of sculpture] were found. It seemed wise to call the most diligent worker, Mohammed Ahmed es-Snussi, and let him do the work alone, and order one of the younger men to record the work in writing. Slowly but surely we worked our way through the debris, which was only about 1.10 m. high, towards the east wall of room 19. We found more pieces with high artistic value, but which need not be mentioned individually. About 0.2 m. from the east wall and 0.35 m. from the north wall, on a level with our knees, a flesh colored neck with painted red straps appeared. "Life-size colorful bust of Queen" was recorded. The tools were put aside and the hands were now used. The following minutes confirmed what appeared to be a bust: above the neck, the lower part of the bust was uncovered, and underneath it, the back part of the Queen's wig appeared. It took a considerable amount of time until the whole piece was completely freed from all the dirt and rubble. This was due to the fact that a portrait head of the king, which lay close to the bust, had to be recovered first. After that, we concentrated on the bust, and we held the most lively (*lebensvollste*) piece of Egyptian art in our hands. It was almost complete. Parts of the ears were missing, and there was no inlay in the left eye. The dirt was searched and in part sieved. Some pieces of the ears were found, but not the eye inlay. Much later I realized that there had never been an inlay."[25]

---

[23] Breasted, *supra* n. 22, at 235–237. Breasted reports that the walls of Thutmose's complex "in the best preserved places, are standing to a level probably a little less than half-way up to the ceiling." *Id.* at 237.

[24] Hermann Ranke (1878–1953). For a review of his distinguished career, see the obituary notice published by Rudolf Anthes, Hermann Ranke, 1878–1953, 17 *U. Bull* (Philadelphia) 57, 57–59 (1953).

[25] Krauss, *supra* n. 15, at 88–89 (quoting Ludwig Borchardt, Porträts der Königin Nofret-ete, *Ausgrabungen der Deutschen Orient-Gesellschaft im Tell el-Amarna* III 30–31 (1923).

The division of finds from the excavations that occurred in the winter of 1912/13 took place on January 20, 1913.[26] The *partage* was overseen by Gustave Lefebvre, an Egyptologist serving as an inspector of the Egyptian Antiquities Service, acting as agent for Gaston Maspero, director of both the Egyptian Antiquities Service and the Egyptian Museum in Cairo.[27] As provided for in Egyptian law,[28] title to the objects that the Antiquities Service did not claim was transferred to James Simon as holder of the excavation permit. I have discovered no information on Simon's subsequent export of his share, but no question has been raised that it was not entirely in accordance with Egyptian law.

Krauss documents that Simon placed some of the finds – including the bust – in his home, but the majority he lent to the Egyptian Museum in Berlin. Krauss further suggests that Simon lent the bust (and other pieces) to the museum in 1914 prior to the war. On July 7, 1920, Simon made an inter vivos transfer of the Amarna finds to the museum, legally transferring his title to the objects to the Prussian state.

Krauss incorrectly states that Borchardt did not publish the bust until 1923/24 and did so then involuntarily.[29] In fact, Borchardt published a black and white photograph of the bust in October 1913, within ten months of its discovery, in an academic journal that would have been widely read and circulated among Egyptologists.[30] Although the image is only partial, it sufficiently demonstrates the quality and significance of the bust. With that publication the Egyptian Antiquities Service and the entire Egyptological community was on notice that the bust was in Germany. At the time, Egypt made no complaint about the allocation of finds from the excavation and made no demand for the bust's return; Egypt waited until ten years later, when the bust was placed on exhibition in the Egyptian Museum in Berlin, to ask for its return.[31]

---

[26] Krauss, *supra* n. 15, at 93.
[27] Gustave Lefebvre (1879–1957). Lefebvre was no mere functionary but a distinguished Egyptologist. See his obituary, Étienne Drioton, 13 *Revue d'Égyptologie* 19 (1961), including a four-page bibliography of Lefebvre's publications.
[28] Antiquities Law, no. 14, art. 11 (1912) (Egypt), *translated in* Adrienne L. Fricke, in Appendix II.
[29] Krauss, *supra* n. 15, at 88 ("Borchardt veröffentlichte die Büste erst 1923/24 und dies unfreiwillig."). Later in his article, Krauss mentions the 1913 publication of a photograph of the bust. *Id.* At 99.
[30] 52 *Mitteilungen der Deutschen Orient-Gesellschaft zu Berlin* 43 illus. 19 (1913).
[31] Krauss, *supra* n. 15, at 102.

II. THE LAW[32]

A. Egyptian Law in Effect at Time of Discovery/*Partage*

As early as 1883 Egypt enacted a vesting statute stating: "All the monuments and objects of antiquity, recognized as such by the Regulation governing the

---

[32] A concise history of the development of Egyptian antiquities legislation is provided by Patrick J. O'Keefe and Lyndel V. Prott: "Egypt, because of its visible monuments, had long been of interest to European travelers: Wortham dates the beginning of British Egyptology to 1549. Napoleon's Egyptian expedition (1798–1801) intensified interest in ancient Egyptian civilization. The French Emperor established in Cairo the French Egyptian Institute which conducted a survey of Egyptian antiquities The decipherment of Egyptian hieroglyphics, attributed in the main to the French-man Champollion (1822), inspired further excavations and a second survey in 1828 in which Champollion participated. In 1858 there was created an Egyptian Service of Antiquities with the French excavator Mariette as its Director. Despite the apathy of the Khedive he managed not only to build up a collection for the National Museum but also to prevent in Egypt much of the looting and undignified rivalry between nationalities which was then taking place in Mesopotamia. He also strenuously opposed the export of antiquities from Egypt and some time before 1879 the export of antiquities was banned by law. After Mariette's death in 1881, Maspero, head of the French Institute in Cairo, became the new Director of Antiquities and head of the Museum and in 1884 he persuaded the Egyptian Government to modify its regulations and allow antiquities not required by the museum to be exported by the finders, provided that everything was first submitted to the authorities for inspection. At this period the likelihood of being able to take home at least some finds of the excavation had direct effect on the enthusiasm and also the funding of excavators by European institutions. Concern about vandalism and neglect of Egypt's monuments led to an official survey in 1888 and funds were raised in England the 'Society for the Preservation of the Monuments of Ancient Egypt.' In 1889 the British Egypt Exploration Society established the archaeological Survey (still in existence) to record the great monuments of Egypt, their inscriptions and paintings, before the record was destroyed. This record of foreign concern for the archaeological heritage of Egypt has continued to the present day, marked by the great international campaign led by UNESCO to map and preserve as many as possible of the Nubian monuments threatened by the Aswan High Dam. In 1897 Egypt took legislative action to control all excavations. New legislation followed in 1912. The present law is the Protection of Antiquities Act 1951. The Egyptian legislation uses a system of registration not unlike the French system. In view of the strong French influence in the history of the Egyptian Department of Antiquities (the Directors throughout the nineteenth century were French) this is hardly surprising. Though some antiquities may be privately owned and some may be assigned to excavating teams, there are restrictions on dealing with them and registered antiquities may not be exported. Finds must be reported and all excavations must be licensed." Patrick J. O'Keefe and Lyndel V. Prott, *Law and the Cultural Heritage* 1: 45–46 (1984).

matter, shall . . . be declared property of the Public Domain of the State."[33] Exceptions would develop under Egyptian law for excavations conducted under governmental approval.

The Decree of November 17, 1891,[34] addresses the conditions under which permits for excavations are granted. Article I provides that excavations by "private individuals" require a permit from the Director General of Museums and Excavations. Article 2 pronounces that excavation finds belong to the state. Article 3, however, states that "in consideration of the expenses made by the excavator, the government shall cede to him a part of the antiquities found." Articles 4 and 5 set out the method by which that division of finds (or *partage*) is accomplished. In essence, Article 4 requires that the Antiquities Service and the excavator shall partition the objects in two shares of equal value. If the two parties cannot agree on a selection of the shares, they are to be selected by lot. Important for the current case are the provisions of Article 5, which reserves to the Antiquities Service the right to re-purchase any piece of the share allocated to the excavator.

Several other laws follow the Decree of November 17, 1891, but have no bearing on the situation presented by the bust. The next applicable statute is Law No. 14 of June 12, 1912,[35] effective as of July 1, 1912 – six months prior to the discovery of the bust and seven months prior to the division of finds from that season's excavations at Amarna.

Article 1 of Law No. 14 reiterates previous law vesting title in the national government to every antiquity found on or in the ground. Article 12 reiterates previous law requiring excavators to have a permit granted by the Minister of Public Works on the recommendation of the Director General of the Antiquities Service. Article 12 states also that finds from an excavation shall be divided by a partition into two shares of equal value in the same manner provided in Article 11 of the law (applicable to partage between the state and an individual who has made a find other than in an illicit excavation). Article 11 requires that the shares be divided *by the Antiquities Service* and gives to the *discoverer* the right to choose between the two shares. Crucially, Article 11 gives a right of preemption to the service to acquire an object by paying a negotiated price to the discoverer. Article 14 provides that the

New English translations of early Egyptian antiquities laws appear as Appendix II to this chapter.

[33] Decree of May 16, 1883, Bulletin de Législation et de Jurisprudence Égyptienne, Répertoire Permanent de Législation Égyptienne 1944, 1 (Egypt) (hereinafter "Répertoire Permanent"), *translated in* Fricke, Appendix II.

[34] Répertoire Permanent, *supra* n. 33, at 1, *translated in* Fricke, Appendix II.

[35] Répertoire Permanent, *supra* n. 33, at 2, *translated in* Fricke, Appendix II.

exportation of antiquities is prohibited unless the Antiquities Service has granted permission. Regulations pertaining to Law No. 14 of June 12, 1912, were promulgated on December 8, 1912.[36] Paragraph 11, addressing partage, refers to and reiterates the substance of Article 11 of Law No. 14, described above.

Thus, Egyptian law at the time of discovery, partage, and export of the finds from the winter season of 1912/13 was clear. Nothing in the factual record suggests that the Antiquities Service and the DOG engaged in anything less than complete compliance with all applicable Egyptian laws and regulations. Although the Antiquities Service could have pre-empted the allocation of the bust to the DOG's share of the finds, it did not do so. Accordingly, title to the bust, originally in the Egyptian government (by virtue of Article 1 of the law of 1912) was transferred to Simon (by virtue of the partage accomplished on January 20, 1913) as holder of the excavation permit for the DOG's expedition. Subsequently, on July 7, 1920, Simon transferred title to the bust to the Prussian state by inter vivos gift.[37] In 1957 Germany enacted a statute[38] establishing the Stiftung Preussischer Kulturbesitz (Prussian Cultural Heritage Foundation [SPK]) and transferring title to all cultural assets owned by the Prussian state prior to 1945 to the SPK. Accordingly, good title to the bust is, today, and has been since 1957, in the SPK.

Although Egypt has regretted Lefebvre's selection, there is no question that the partage accomplished on January 20, 1913, comported entirely with Egyptian law. That Egypt subsequently would have preferred another result is irrelevant to the *legal* issue: a partage and subsequent export of the DOG's share of finds from the 1912/13 season at Amarna, including the bust, occurred in compliance with Egyptian law. The bust's owner, Simon, permitted the excavator, Borchardt, to publish a black and white image of the bust in October 1913 in a scholarly journal that doubtless would have been read by members of the Antiquities Service in Egypt. In short, Egypt, through the Antiquities Service and its agent Gustave Lefebvre had one, perhaps two, opportunities in 1913 to demand title to and possession of the bust: at the time of *partage* and, possibly, on publication of the bust nine months later. Egypt took no such action.

---

[36] Répertoire Permanent, *supra* n. 33, at 5. *translated in* Fricke, Appendix II.
[37] Krauss, *supra* n. 15, at 94.
[38] Gesetz zur Errichtung einer Stiftung "Preussischer Kulturbesitz" und zur Übertragung von Vermögenswerten des ehemaligen Landes Preussen auf die Stiftung v. 25.7.1957 (BGBl. I S. 841).

B. Outcome of Any Current Legal Claim for Return of the Bust

A proper analysis of any legal claim that Egypt might bring today for return of the bust presents exceptionally complex issues of international law, and these are discussed thoroughly in Professor Kurt Siehr's chapter in this volume.[39] For purposes here, only two issues are relevant. First, Egypt has never asserted, nor has it at any recent time stated that it might assert, a legal claim for return of the bust. Second, regardless of how Egypt might attempt to assert a legal claim for return of the bust, the timeliness of any such claim would have expired decades ago. The purposes of statutes of limitations are well served in this instance. As the United States Supreme Court put it succinctly:

Statutes of limitations, which "are found and approved in all systems of enlightened jurisprudence [citation omitted]," represent a pervasive legislative judgment that it is unjust to fail to put the adversary on notice to defend within a specified period of time and that "the right to be free of stale claims in time comes to prevail over the right to prosecute them" [citation omitted]. These enactments are statutes of repose; and although affording plaintiffs what the legislature deems a reasonable time to present their claims, they protect defendants and the courts from having to deal with cases in which the search for truth may be seriously impaired by the loss of evidence, whether by death or disappearance of witnesses, fading memories, disappearance of documents, or otherwise.[40]

III. NON-LEGAL ISSUES

As with all disputes over cultural property, the legal analysis is only a beginning. There is perhaps no better example of the law's impotence to resolve competing claims to cultural property than the Parthenon/Elgin Marbles. In 1985, John Henry Merryman conclusively demonstrated that on known evidence Greece has no *legal* claim for return of the Marbles.[41] Nevertheless, the controversy over the Marbles continues unabated,[42] and some writers believe the Marbles should and eventually will be transferred from London to Athens.[43] In the case of the Marbles and in many other cases, the law

---

[39] See Chapter 6.

[40] *U.S. v. Kubrick*, 444 U.S. 111, 117 (1979).

[41] John Henry Merryman, Thinking about the Elgin Marbles, 83 *Mich. L. Rev.* 1880 (1985).

[42] See the Introduction and Chapter 5 by Professor Merryman and Chapter 4 by William St Clair.

[43] See, e.g., Michael J. Reppas II, The Deflowering of the Parthenon: A Legal and Moral Analysis on Why the "Elgin Marbles" Must Be Returned to Greece, 9 *Fordham Intel. Prop. Media & Ent. L.J.* 911 (1999).

is ill suited to address either the passions aroused by competing claims to cultural property or the moral and ethical issues implicated in such claims. If the law cannot adequately resolve these issues, what extra-legal concerns might assist in balancing and ultimately determine competing claims?

In 1983 Paul Bator presented a values-based approach to regulating the international trade in art,[44] identifying five fundamental categories (several of which he subcategorized).[45] Bator's publication developed a reasoned and balanced rubric for analyzing competing arguments regarding the international trade in cultural property. His work applies not only to the international trade but also to cultural property disputes of the kind presented by the bust: situations in which no enforceable legal claim exists but ethical, moral, or practical considerations might nevertheless call for return of a disputed object to its country of origin.[46] Since Bator's seminal work, a substantial literature on the topic has developed.[47] Bator's analysis and subsequent scholarship have developed a group of measures – values and theories – providing a mechanism to determine whether sufficient moral, ethical, or practical arguments exist to justify return of an object to its nation of origin in the absence of an enforceable legal claim. In the following discussion, the

---

[44] Paul Bator, An Essay on the International Trade in Art, 34 *Stanford L. Rev.* 275 (1982). Bator's article subsequently appeared as a monograph, Paul Bator, *The International Trade in Art* 18–34 (1983), and references in this chapter are to the later publication.

[45] The values Bator describes are the preservation of works of art and the associated values of integrity and visibility: the preservation of art against destruction and mutilation; the preservation of artistic entities, sets, and collections; Making art known, visible, and accessible; the preservation of archaeological evidence; preserving the national patrimony; the nationalistic perspective: art as part of the national wealth; the reciprocal perspective: preserving each country's cultural inheritance; the values promoted by international trade in art; the exporting country's interest in export: art as a good ambassador; the importing country's interest in import: enriching the national patrimony; the general interest in the breakdown of parochialism (international trade in the work of living artists). Bator (1983), *supra* n. 44, 18–34.

[46] An extremely clear and concise summary of the arguments for and against the return of cultural property to its country of origin appears in Lyndel V. Prott and P.J. O'Keefe, *Law and the Cultural Heritage*, Volume 3, *Movement*, 838–855 (1989).

[47] The author does not review that literature here but, instead, refers readers to the most recent printed bibliography, Wilfried Fiedler and Stefan Turner, *Bibliographie zum Recht des Internationalen Kulturgüterschutzes/Bibliography on the Law of the International Protection of Cultural Property* (2003), and the largest on-line cultural heritage bibliography, Patrick J. O'Keefe and Lyndel V. Prott, *Heritage Law Bibliography* (2002), *at* http://daryl.chin.gc.ca:8000/BASIS/herb/user/www/sf (last visited April 27, 2002).

more pertinent of these measures will be described and applied to the circumstances of the bust's presence in Berlin. Part IV presents a new measure
that develops from a recent controversy in which the bust played a central
role.

The Preservation Value. As Bator correctly and succinctly stated, "The
preservation of art constitutes our fundamental value."[48] Modern interpretations of the preservation value place an emphasis on the requesting
country's obligation and ability to preserve a returned object.[49] Institutions
that hold and have cared for works, often for decades, take the position that
their curators would "feel that they would be abrogating their responsibility
for the objects [whose return is requested] if they released them from good
conditions of security to instable situations where their safety could not
be assured."[50] Of course, this argument can be and has been made disin-
genuously.[51] Applying the preservation value to the bust provides neither
Germany nor Egypt with an advantageous argument: both nations have
museums and museum professionals of international caliber, assuring the
safety and preservation of the bust in either nation.

---

[48] Bator, *supra* n. 44, at 19.
[49] For example, an Ad Hoc Committee appointed by the Executive Council of ICOM
      at UNESCO's request prepared Study on the Principles, Conditions and Means for
      the Restitution or Return of Cultural Property in View of Reconstituting Dispersed
      Heritages, 31 *Museum* 62, 63–64 (1979), explicitly placing "Primacy of the object"
      as a principal concern. Typical of scholarly concern in this area is the comment
      that a requesting country "ensure that the recovered property will be protected
      by conservation, safety and security measures that meet international standards,
      and that the object will be adequately displayed and, normally, accessible to the
      public." James A. R. Nafziger, The New International Legal Framework for the Return,
      Restitution or Forfeiture of Cultural Property, 15 *N.Y.U. J. Intl L. and Pol.* 789, 808
      (1982–83).
[50] Thurstan Shaw, Whose Heritage? 38 *Museum* 46, 47 (1986).
[51] See, e.g., Andromache Gazi, Museums and National Cultural Property, 9 *Museum
      Mgm't & Curatorship* 121, 132 (1990) (arguing that whereas "in some cases removal
      has saved objects from dispersal, the opposite has occurred" in other cases, and that it
      is "cynical to say that 'you cannot guarantee stability anywhere outside the West.'");
      Karen Goepfert, The Decapitation of Ramesses II, 13 *B.U. Intl L.J.* 503 (1995) (arguing
      that the argument that holding institutions are more able to perform the safekeeping
      function of objects "originally held some credence, [but] the development of many
      requesting countries has substantially lessened the potential for possible neglect
      due to insufficient resources"); Allen Wardwell, Repatriation of Artworks: An Old
      Problem Resurfaces, 68 *Art In America* 13 (1980) (noting that the argument that "only
      some museums and countries can and will provide the only safe repository for the
      great works of man" is "inflammatory").

Correcting Historical Wrongs. After the universal concern with preservation, the next most frequently emphasized factor in evaluating a demand for return[52] are the circumstances under which an object left its place of origin. Certain situations present clear solutions. For example, a work acquired by sale or by agreement between two parties of equal bargaining power and subsequently exported in compliance with the laws of the country of origin is presumptively held legitimately by the acquiring party. A work stolen from a public or private collection, whether legally or illegally exported, remains a stolen work, and the theft victim's claim for return, even if no longer actionable on account of repose statues, procedural issues, or other reasons, may carry a moral imperative for return. Difficulties arise, of course, in the gray zone between these clear poles. Works acquired during periods of colonial occupation, wartime, or periods of civil unrest, for example, demand special scrutiny.

There is no question that Egyptian law provided for the legal transfer of title to the bust from the Egyptian government to the holder of the excavation permit. No question has ever been raised to suggest that the bust's subsequent export contravened Egyptian law in any way. Indeed the *partage* system created under Egyptian law benefited both Germany and Egypt exactly as intended: by offering tangible rewards for the risky investment in an archaeological expedition, Egypt gained knowledge of its own history and collections of antiquities acquired through scientific excavation. Germany gained prestige for discovery, valuable objects for its museums, and standing within the international archaeological community. Accordingly, it is difficult, if not impossible, to find any historical wrong that would be "righted" by return of the bust.

The Set Value.[53] Some objects of cultural property were intended to be independent works; others were intended to be components of a complex

---

[52] See, e.g., Gazi, *supra* n. 51 (providing an informative consideration of the importance of various historical contexts surrounding the taking of cultural property); Goepfert, *supra* n. 51, at 503 ("one cannot help but consider the circumstances under which the museum or host country acquired these timeless objects"); Jeanette Greenfield, The Return of Cultural Property, 60 *Antiquity* 29, 35 ("The issue of return should be determined on the basis of two main criteria: (1) the means of acquisition"). For an example of how some entities have adopted consideration of this factor into their process of evaluating claims for return, see Norman Palmer, Sending Them Home: Some Observations on the Relocation of Cultural Objects from UK Museum Collections, 5 *Art Antiquity & L.* 9, 13 (2000) (noting that the Glasgow City Council's Repatriation Committee lists among its criteria "[h]ow the object/s have been acquired").

[53] *Cf.* Bator, *supra* n. 44, at 22.

work. In situations in which an object of cultural property derives from a complex work or is part of a series or set, this set value is a relevant consideration in weighing a demand for return. Thus, for example, had the Treaty of Versailles not commanded it, Belgium would have an argument under this theory for the return from the Kaiser-Friederich-Museum in Berlin of the side panels of van Eyck's *Ghent Altarpiece*.

The bust was discovered in the remains of the house/studio of a sculptor identified as Thutmose.[54] Significant portions of the objects excavated from that find spot are in Berlin, and others remain in Egypt. Thus, an argument exists that all the finds from Thutmose's house/studio should be gathered in one location to provide a complete picture of the sculptor's workshop. However, it is highly doubtful that a museum in either nation would choose to exhibit *all* of those archaeological finds for the general public: too many of them are of interest only to specialists, and scholars already have easy access to the finds by visiting Berlin and Cairo and by referring to published sources.

A strict reading of the set value would argue for unification of all the finds from the Thutmose complex but would not resolve whether that unification should occur in Berlin or Cairo. More significantly, the bust is an independent work, not part of a complex work or a series requiring reunification to achieve full meaning. Additionally, it is unlikely that a work that has achieved iconic status such as the bust would be exhibited in close proximity to the other finds from Thutmose's house/studio: public visitorship is simply too large (currently in Berlin or potentially in Cairo) to permit the bust to be exhibited in any manner other than as it is now in Berlin: independently with sufficient gallery space to accommodate tourist groups. On balance, then, there is no compelling argument for return based on the set value.

Making Art Known, Visible, and Accessible.[55] The aesthetic, educational, and scientific value of cultural property is universally acknowledged, and providing access to cultural property represents an important value.[56] At its core, the access value asserts that a work should exist where it is most easily available to the largest interested audience. As Bator rightly noted, however, there are situations in which access threatens the very work itself, putting access it into conflict with the preservation value discussed previously.

---

54 *See* discussion *supra* at Part I.B
55 Bator, *supra* n. 44, at 23.
56 There are, of course, exceptions, such as cultural objects whose significance to a living culture requires that access be limited to certain members of the community.

Examples, include the exclusion of visitors to the cave at Lascaux, France,[57] and the rotating closure of the pyramids at Giza.[58]

Further, as the Louvre's *Mona Lisa* makes obvious[59] or the 1996 Vermeer exhibition at the National Gallery of Art in Washington, D.C., demonstrated,[60] an iconic work or group of works can attract so many visitors as to make contemplating the works on display virtually impossible. Bator put it succinctly: "Like the wilderness, some art spoils in a mob scene."[61]

[57] André Malraux, as Minister of Culture, ordered the cave closed in April 1963. Norbert Aujoulet, *The Cave of Lascaux*, at http://www.culture.gouv.fr/culture/arcnat/lascaux/en/ (last visited June 26, 2004).

[58] The *Chicago Tribune* reported: "The visitor head-count has climbed to the point that the Pyramids have to be closed on a rotating basis – each year, one of the three Giza Pyramids is given a rest – so their interiors can be routinely cleaned of the byproducts of human visitation. [An official of the Egyptian Antiquities Service] reports that each person who enters the pyramids leaves behind an average 20 grams of water in breath and perspiration. When Khufu's Pyramid was closed for cleaning in 1998, the humidity level inside was 80 percent, and the walls of the Grand Gallery had salt deposits as thick as 2 centimeters in places.... [Egypt has] also limited the number of people allowed in: only 300 people a day inside the Great Pyramid." Toni Stroud, The Great Survivors; Like the Mysteries That Surround Them, the Pyramids Outlast Time – and Defeat All Foes, *Chi. Trib.* Mar. 2, 2003, at C1.

Another recent example involves Egyptian tomb paintings that had been on view in the Metropolitan Museum of Art for nearly a century behind protective glass shields. During the recent reinstallation of the museum's Egyptian collections, delivery of new glass barriers was delayed, and the museum permitted a small number of visitors to enter the reconstructed tombs to view the wall paintings without the distorting lens of the old glass. Yet several days after announcing this rare opportunity, the museum closed access: the museum said that it had "'never anticipated that the response would be so huge'... [and the] crush of visitors near the 4,000-year-old limestone carvings 'ha[d] put the humidity at unacceptable limits.'" Citing the museum's primary responsibility to preserve the works, the museum blocked access after two weeks. Glenn Collins, Don't Touch, Don't Push, Don't Push, Don't Delay: Tombs Closing, *N.Y. Times*, Feb. 18, 2004, at B3. *See also* Glenn Collins, The Mummy's Tomb, Unwrapped; Glass Will Be Removed, Temporarily, at Met, *N.Y. Times*, Jan. 28, 2004, at B1.

[59] For an interesting discussion of how *Mona Lisa* became the world's most recognizable work of art (and the most difficult painting to see given the crowds around it at the Louvre), see Donald Sassoon, *Becoming Mona Lisa: The Making of a Global Icon* (2003).

[60] The huge demand for the exhibition "Johannes Vermeer" (November 12, 1995–February 11, 1996), is discussed on the National Gallery's Web page: "Past Exhibitions: Johannes Vermeer," at http://www.nga.gov/past/data/exh707.htm (last visited March 22, 2004).

[61] Bator, *supra* n. 44, at 24.

Institutions have asserted modern interpretations of the access value to justify retention of cultural objects in their collections.[62] Such institutions may say that a particular object is better studied, more accessible to the scholarly community, or more readily viewed by a larger public in its current location. These arguments can be disingenuous and, given the significance of collections in European museums, have even been labeled Eurocentric.[63]

Applying the access value presents a difficult analysis: In Berlin, the bust is easily accessible to Germans and tourists, including Egyptian visitors; in Cairo, the work would be easily accessible to Egyptians and tourists, including German visitors. However, the disparity in wealth between Germany and Egypt[64] results in the greater likelihood that more German visitors would see the bust in Cairo than Egyptian visitors would see it in Berlin. But the economic argument is not conclusive; a political one has equal measure – the impact of terrorist attacks (or the threat of such attacks) on tourism. In the current environment, Germany's stable political situation may well encourage greater tourism to Germany than Egypt's political situation can encourage tourism to Egypt.[65] Thus, one might argue that a larger audience is more likely to visit the bust in Berlin than in Cairo. More importantly, Egypt already holds an abundance of Amarna period art in its museums, thereby assuring that Egyptians (and tourists to Egypt) know about and can appreciate the stylistic shifts and achievements of that age. Put another way,

[62] Gazi, *supra* n. 51.
[63] Shaw, *supra* n. 50, at 48.
[64] Germany's purchasing power is estimated at $2.2 trillion, whereas Egypt's, is $268 billion; Germany's revenues are approximately $802 billion, Egypt's, $21.5 billion. All statistics reported as of 2002; to compare country reports, see Emulate Me, *Egypt*, *in* countryreports.org (2004), *at* http://www.countryreports.org/content/egypt.htm (last visited March 22, 2004) and Emulate Me, *Germany*, *in* countryreports.org (2004), *at* http://www.countryreports.org/content/germany.htm (last visited Mar. 22, 2004).
[65] *See*, e.g., Gil Bindlegas, Egyptian Artifacts and Tourism, 1 *TED Case Studies* (1992), *at* http://gurukul.ucc.american.edu/ted/egypt.htm (last visited March 22, 2004) (noting in 1992 that "the tourist trade is highly vulnerable to regional conflicts and terrorism, as is evident now [recent outbreaks of terrorism have greatly reduced the tourist activity in Egypt]"). But cf. Bomb Blast Fails to Deter Tourists, *L.A. Times*, Sept. 20, 1997, at A6; Egypt Attracts More Tourists, *London Fin. Times*, Aug. 5, 1996, at O2 (both reporting that tourism was not impacted by specific incidents of terrorism in Egypt). A contrary position is taken by a reporter for the *Los Angeles Times* who reported in 2003: "Tourist flow to Egypt dwindled drastically after the triple blows of September 11, the 1997 massacre of dozens of tourists in Luxor by Islamic militants, and the war in Iraq. The falloff is a serious problem for Egypt, whose economy depends heavily on tourism." Megan K. Stack, Big Daddy of the Mummies, *L. A. Times*, Sept. 26, 2003, at A1.

the bust is not necessary to demonstrate to Egyptians or visitors to Egypt the significance of the Amarna period; Germany has fewer such examples, meaning that the bust's continued presence in Berlin assures that Germans and tourists to Berlin have easy access to a great example of Amarna period Egyptian art.

National Wealth. As Bator observed:

The claim that a country's artistic patrimony should be preserved may simply be part of a broader nationalistic claim that a country's wealth not be dissipated. From this perspective the national patrimony consists of all works of art within the borders of a country . . . that are subject to that country's power or jurisdiction. . . . All such works of art are part of the national capital; They generate income (by attracting tourists, etc.) and they can produce social and psychological benefits for a country and its inhabitants.[66]

Cultural property forms a component of a nation's economic and cultural capital.[67] Accordingly a nation possessing a work as important as the bust reaps many benefits from its presence. The question is not one of who needs the benefits the more but whether the benefits to the country in possession derive from a fair transfer from the place of origin.

The bust's contribution to Germany's and especially Berlin's economic and cultural capital is obvious. Tourists are attracted to the city and to the Egyptian Museum on account of the bust's presence there, the bust appears in most touristic advertisements for the city, and replicas of the bust are sold

---

[66] Bator, *supra* n. 44, at 27–30. In recent years, a large literature has developed addressing the "value" of culture. See, e.g., Michael Hutter and Ilde Rizzo, *Economic Perspectives on Cultural Heritage* (1997); Ståle Navrud and Richard C. Ready, *Valuing Cultural Heritage* (2002); Bruno S. Frey, Evaluating Cultural Property: The Economic Approach, 6 *Int'l. J. Cultural Prop.* 231 (1997); Massimiliano Mazzanti, Cultural Heritage a Multi-Dimensional, Multi-Value and Multi-Attribute Economic Good: Toward a New Framework for Economic Analysis and Valuation, 31 *J. Socio-Economics* 529 (2002).

[67] Perhaps the best recent discussion of the term *cultural capital* is given in David Throsby, *Economics and Culture* (2001). Throsby observes that "cultural capital gives rise to both cultural and economic value [while] 'ordinary' capital provides only economic value." Throsby defines cultural *capital* as "an asset which embodies, stores or provides cultural value in addition to whatever economic value it may possess." *Id.* at 46. Throsby states further: "[C]ultural capital exists in two forms. First, it may be *tangible*, occurring in the form of buildings, locations, sties, precincts, artworks such as paintings and sculptures, artifacts and so on. . . . Secondly, cultural capital may be *intangible*, occurring as intellectual capital in the form of ideas, practices, beliefs and values which are shared by a group." *Id.*

in novelty shops wherever tourist busses congregate. Were the bust in Egypt, Egypt would gain these benefits. The historical circumstances of the bust's export from Egypt (described above) offer no suggestion that Germany has been unjustly enriched. Indeed Article 3 of Egypt's Decree of November 17, 1891,[68] states explicitly that *partage* is predicated on and is justified "in consideration of the expenses made by the excavator." Germany's investment in excavations at Amarna, prompt publication of the expedition's results, and the resulting contribution to the archaeological record in addition to Germany's continued preservation and exhibition of the bust to the broadest possible audiences for decades constitute more than adequate consideration for Germany's continued possession.

Inalienable National Identity Value. Certain objects are of signal importance to national identity: the Crown of St. Stephen to Hungary,[69] the Declaration of Independence to the United States, the Stone of Scone to Scotland,[70] and the Imperial regalia to Japan.[71] Many writers have identified cultural property as having a unique status, believing it to be a "basic element of a people's cultural identity."[72] This inalienable national identity value has been well described by, among others, Merryman,[73] and some scholars have adopted relatively extreme expressions of it, advocating the return of all cultural property to its place of origin, no matter what the particular circumstances.[74] Balanced approaches to the very real connection between

[68]   See, Appendix II.
[69]   The Crown of St. Stephen was returned to Hungary in 1977 by President Jimmy Carter of the United States; the crown had been entrusted to the United States at the end of World War II. Efforts by a United States Senator, Robert Dole, to retain the Crown until a democratic government was installed in Hungary failed. *See Dole v. Carter*, 569 F.2d 1109 (10th Cir. 1977).
[70]   The Stone of Scone was returned from England to Scotland in 1996. Among many reports, see Richard Blystone, *Scotland's 'Stone of Scone' Finds Its Way Home*, *cnn.com*, Nov. 15, 1996, *at* http://www.cnn.com/WORLD/9611/15/stone.of.scone/ (last visited March 8, 2004).
[71]   These are said to consist of carved jewels, a sacred mirror, and a sacred sword. The regalia are a necessary part of the accession of a new emperor. Sanshu No Jingi, Imperial Regalia, *Kodansha Encyclopedia of Japan*, *at* http://www.ency-japan.com (last visited March 10, 2004).
[72]   *See*, e.g., Luis Monreal, Problems and Possibilities in Recovering Dispersed Cultural Heritage, 31 *Museum* 49, 53 (1979).
[73]   John Henry Merryman, Two Ways of Thinking about Cultural Property, 80 *Am. J. Int'l L.* 831 (1986).
[74]   *See*, e.g., Karl Becher, On the Obligation of Subjects of International Law to Return Cultural Property to Its Permanent Place, 44 *Annuaire de l' A.A.A.* 96 (1974).

cultural property and national identity recognize that certain objects have a "symbolic nature" and "high emotion attached" to them.[75] These symbolic and emotional connections can lead to a justification for return.[76]

It is difficult to see how Egypt can maintain a legitimate argument that the bust is of fundamental significance to Egypt's national identity: the cultural connection between Nefertiti's Egypt and contemporary Egypt is attenuated at best. The former was pagan; the latter is predominately Muslim; the former was a monarchy, the latter is a democratic state; and so on. Nefertiti's historical place as a short-lived queen of ancient Egypt hardly makes a persuasive argument that the bust's presence is required for current Egyptian national identity. There are no cultural, religious, political, social, or economic values of the eighteen Dynasty that find resonance in modern Egypt. Moreover, Egypt already possesses a plethora of portraits of pharaonic kings and queens. Thus there is no evidence that the bust is essential for contemporary Egyptians to understand who they are and the values their culture currently holds in esteem.

Essential Propinquity. In an important article addressing how the United States might formulate a unified and appropriate policy regarding the treatment of other nation's cultural property,[77] Merryman introduced the concept of "essential propinquity" – a near, but distinct, relative to the inalienable national identity value described above. Essential propinquity provides a justification for cultural property retention (and by extension an imperative for return).[78] Merryman identified two criteria for establishing essential propinquity: "First, the culture that gave the object its cultural significance must be alive. Second, the object must be actively employed for the religious

---

[75] Daniel Shapiro, Repatriation: A Modest Proposal, 31 *N.Y.U. J. Int'l L. & Pol.* 95, 98 (1998).

[76] Shapiro writes: "What is sought to be repatriated is said to 'belong' to a people, essentially or inherently connected to them in some inalienable way ... if critically important cultural heritage is not currently in a people's ... control, it should – self-evidently to them – be repatriated and returned. This deep, emotional connection is the bedrock of repatriation. As something self-defining, it is an elemental intuition, axiomatic and difficult to explain without being circular. Moreover, as something linked to one's identity, it presumably could not mean as much or be as highly valued by others as by those who claim it as their heritage." *Id.* at 96–97.

[77] John Henry Merryman, The Retention of Cultural Property, 21 *U. C. Davis L. Rev.* 477 (1988). *Reprinted in Thinking about the Elgin Marbles: Critical Essays on Cultural Property, Art and Law* 122, 142–43 (2000).

[78] *Id.* at 139–142.

or ceremonial or communal purposes for which it was made."[79] Objects meeting these criteria constitute a special category and require the highest level of sensitivity and scrutiny in cultural property disputes. Given the previous section's conclusion that the bust does not hold sufficient significance to modern Egypt to justify a return based on national identity, the same result is reached, a fortiori, under Merryman's theory of essential propinquity.

Art as Good Ambassador.[80] Many writers have recognized the importance of an equitable distribution of examples from culturally rich nations. A typical formulation states that cultural property from a foreign nation "bring[s] knowledge and appreciation of [that culture] to other peoples."[81] Bator summarized the theory this way: "Countries that allow their art to spread abroad derive both obvious and subtle advantages. Art is a good ambassador. It stimulates interest in, understanding of, and sympathy and admiration for that country."[82] As Bator and others[83] have observed, an equitable distribution of a nation's cultural property also contributes to a breakdown in parochialism and builds mutual respect and admiration for other cultural traditions. This value is especially significant at a time of cultural globalization: it promotes recognition of the world's many, distinct cultural traditions. The bust's presence in Berlin has permitted generations of German and international visitors the opportunity to view an exceptional example of pre-Islamic, Egyptian culture and to gain in appreciation for that culture. Return of the bust would eliminate that opportunity. On balance, this value is best supported by the bust's remaining in Berlin.

The Floodgates Concern.[84] Given increasing demands in recent years for the return of objects long held in museum collections, especially from

---

[79]   *Id.* at 141.

[80]   Bator, *supra* n. 44, at 30.

[81]   Wardwell, *supra* n. at 15.

[82]   Bator, *supra* n. 44, at 30.

[83]   Bator, *supra* n. 44, at 31–32; *see*, e.g., Shapiro, *supra* n. 75, at 103 (arguing that "[h]onoring repatriation claims can further the emphasis on cultural exclusivity, reinforce nationalism, and support hostility to ethnic and other forms of cultural differentiation," from which we can obviously infer that the distribution of a nation's cultural property does the opposite, contributing to the breakdown of parochialism); Wardwell, *supra* n. 51, at 15 (acknowledging that cultural property from a foreign nation "bring[s] knowledge and appreciation of [that culture] to other peoples").

[84]   Shapiro, *supra* n. 75, at 103–04, uses the name "Pandora's Box" in referring to this concern, and Reppas, *supra* n. 75, at 917, refers to it as the "domino effect."

collections in Western Europe and the United States, some scholars[85] have argued that acquiescing to such demands not only will generally diminish public access to such objects but also set a dangerous precedent.[86] They argue that the return of even one object will lead to an uncontrolled and uncontrollable set of demands for return. This concern has been rejected by other scholars,[87] who note that even since the United Nations Educational, Scientific, and Cultural Organization (UNESCO) 1970 recommendation and the growing international acceptance of the idea that return is appropriate in situations in certain circumstances even where no enforceable legal claim exists, the number of documented instances of return has been extremely limited.[88]

The floodgates/Pandora's box theory is an appropriate concern in assessing whether the bust should remain in Berlin or be returned to Egypt. In recent years, Egypt has aggressively pursued the return even of antiquities that have been held and exhibited in public collections for decades and that raise no issue of recent illicit excavation or illegal export.[89] Egypt has backed its efforts with threats of retribution for archaeologists from countries whose museums do not cooperate with Egypt's repatriation efforts.[90] These threats are inimical to Egypt's best interests (collaborating with foreign archaeologists assists Egypt in developing its own

---

[85] *See*, e.g., Shapiro, *supra* n. 75, at 101: "To recognize a special claim to an object by the culture that created it could balkanize humankind's heritage, empty the world's museums, and undo what has been presumed to be a universal cultural goal [– the study of such objects]."

[86] *See*, e.g., Wardwell, *supra* n. 51, at 13 ("Fears persist that to give any ground on the matter [of restitution] would mean entire collections might be lost").

[87] *See*, e.g., Lyndel V. Prott, The Experience of UNESCO with the Return of Cultural Objects, 89 *ASIL Proceedings* 443, 447 (1995) ("[S]uch a record hardly justifies claims by some museums that responding to such requests would provide dangerous precedents and result in 'emptying the museums of Europe.'").

[88] Wardwell, *supra* n. 51, at 13: "In actuality, formal repatriation requests have concerned only a small number of objects."

[89] For example, in 2002 Zahi Hawass, general director of the Supreme Council on Antiquities in Egypt, threatened legal action against the Virginia Museum of Fine Arts in Richmond for return of an Egyptian relief acquired by the museum from a dealer in New York in 1963 with a documented provenance going back to 1944. *See* Ariel Hart, A Journey Back to Egypt for a Mummy Thought to Be a Pharaoh, *N.Y. Times*, Oct. 25, 2003, at A20; Associated Press, The Nation Today/Virginia: Egypt Claims Artifact in Museum Is Stolen, *Boston Globe*, July 13, 2002, at A2.

[90] Among many news reports, see Gretel C. Kovah, The "Curse of the Mummies" Has a New Way to Strike, *Newsweek*, Sept. 2, 2002, at 40; Mike Toner, Egypt Reclaims Stolen Heritage, *Atlanta J.-Const.*, May 3, 2003, at 1 A; Paul Vallely, Stonewalled: Things

corps of archaeologists, increases the scientifically recovered historical record, lowers the cost to Egypt of archaeological excavation in Egypt, and continues to expand the field of Egyptology internationally, etc.) and presents a simplistic (though mediagenic), approach to exceedingly complex issues.[91]

IV. CONSIDERING A NEW VALUE: PROTECTING THE STREAM OF CREATIVE EXPRESSION

Living artists rely on and react to their predecessors; they create new works in the context of the creative expressions. As the individuals who maintain the ancient tradition of creating cultural heritage, they have interests that are entitled to special consideration in cultural property discussions. In the context of the international movement of works of art, Bator rightly observed: "Rules regulating the trade in art should not narrow the potential audience and market for new art, discouraging its creation. There is, therefore, a special argument against restricting the movement of art by living artists"[92] In determining who should possess a disputed work, especially one that has gained iconic significance, there is a special argument against restricting access to that work by living artists and a special argument that the work remain a participant in the stream of creative expression. A recent work of art that appropriated[93] and recontextualized[94] the bust, *The Body of Nefertiti*,[95] demonstrates the significance of this new value.

The practice of artists' drawing inspiration from their predecessors is a fundamental component of all of the world's artistic traditions; as H. W. Janson observed: "originality is always relative: there is no such thing as a completely original work of art."[96] Examples abound: Roman

---

are Looking Decidedly Rocky at the British Museum, *The Independent* (London), July 24, 2003, at 2–3.

[91] For a discussion of Egypt's reliance on foreign archaeological expertise and funding, see Katie Leishman, The Future of the Past, *The Atlantic*, Jan. 1985, at 21.

[92] Bator, *supra* n. 44, at 32.

[93] On appropriation art, see *infra*.

[94] On recontextualization, see *infra*.

[95] See *infra*.

[96] H. W. Janson, *History of Art* (2d. ed.) at 14 (1977). Another observer has commented: "Copying, faking, plagiarism, borrowing, reproduction and other practices that involve appropriation in one way or another have been central practices in the

artists copied and modified Greek works;[97] Renaissance artists constantly turned to classical models in sculpture, architecture, and painting;[98] Manet followed Goya's *Majas on a Balcony* for his *Two Women on a Balcony*.[99] In 1955 Picasso reinterpreted and even used the same name of Delacroix's 1834 *Women of Algiers*,[100] and in a series of works done in 1957, Picasso did the same with Velasquez's *Las Meninas* of 1656.[101] Chinese art has a five-millennium history of stylistic evolution with artists' relying directly on their predecessors' iconography, forms, and expressions.[102] When Buddhism arrived in Korea, Korean sculptors followed Chinese models – for centuries.[103] Australian aboriginal art has been adapted for use on contemporary textiles for the mass market.[104] The examples could be multiplied by the hundreds.

In the twentieth century, this long history of artists' drawing inspiration from and following earlier models continued and developed what is often

arts for as long as the arts have existed. No artist starts from scratch; every artist derives material from the past." Crispin Sartwell, Appropriation in Michael Kelly (ed.) *Encyclopedia of Aesthetics*, Vol. I at 68 (1998).

For a recent treatment see The Ancient Art of Emulation, *Studies in Artistic Originality and Tradition from the Present to Classical Antiquity* (Elaine K. Gazda ed., 2002).

[97] Among many sources, see, for example, B. S. Ridgway, *Roman Copies of Greek Sculpture: The Problem of the Originals* (1984).

[98] Among many sources, see, for example, Leonard Barkan, *Unearthing the Past: Archaeology and Aesthetics in Renaissance Culture* (1999); Luba Freedman, *The Revival of the Olympian Gods in Renaissance Art* (2003); F. Haskell and N. Penny, *Taste and the Antique: The Lure of Classical Sculpture* 1500–1900 (1981).

[99] For French artists' reliance on Spanish precedent, see Gary Tinterow and Genéviè Lacambre, *Manet/Velázquez: The French Taste for Spanish Painting* (2003).

[100] Timothy Anglin Burgard, Picasso and Appropriation, 73 *Art Bull.* 479, 490 (1991).

[101] *Id.* at 491.

[102] Howard Rogers (ed.), *China 5,000 Years: Innovation and Transformation in the Arts* (1998).

[103] Junghee Lee, Korea, The Grove Dictionary of Art Online at §III, 1, http://www.groveart.com (last visited June 30, 2004).

[104] *See*, e.g., *Bulun Bulun v. R & T Textiles Pty. Ltd.* (1998) 157 A.L.R. 193 (Federal Court, Austl.) (holding that R & T Textiles Pty. Ltd. infringed John Bulun Bulun's copyright in his painting that reflected indigenous knowledge of the Ganalbingu people and although the Ganalbingu people did not have a communal copyright interest in Bulun Bulun's painting, Bulun Bulun had a fiduciary obligation to the Ganalbingu people to preserve the integrity of their culture and ritual knowledge, which fiduciary obligation he fulfilled by enforcing his copyright in the painting against the infringing use).

referred to as "appropriation art."[105],[106] Appropriation artists do not merely draw inspiration from earlier works but rather incorporate existing objects

[105]   There is no single definition of *appropriation art*, but a few examples provide context: "In the parlance of the art world of the late twentieth century, *appropriation* refers to the conscious use of material (images, for example, in the case of the visual arts, sounds, in the case of music) that derives from a source outside the work. To appropriate an image in this sense is to incorporate it intentionally into the context of one's own body of work." Sartwell, *supra* n. 96, at 68. "Over the course of history, artists have frequently borrowed from previous works and have thus acknowledged the viability of their cultural quotations. These appropriations, far from being whimsical, usually had some serious sociopolitical connections with the era in which they were used. In the current postmodern period, art appropriation continues, and painters, sculptors, and architects who borrow from previous styles or images thus comment on contemporary issues in the arts. Appropriations may be taken from popular culture, but frequently there are derivations from revered monuments in the history of art or from works by modern masters. Artists who appropriate address concepts of creativity and intentionality, as well as encouraging a crucial reading of the history of art." Joan Marter, The Art of Appropriation, *Arts Mag.*, Dec. 1985, at 106. "The appropriation of imagery from mass media and other sources is, of course, a strategy central to postmodern art." Martha Buskirk, Appropriation Under the Gun, *Art Am.*, June 1992, at 38.

[106]   The bibliography on appropriation art is large; it includes discussions not only of appropriations of visual art, but also of music, literature, performance art, and culture. *See generally* Martha Buskirk and Mignon Nixon, *The Duchamp Effect* (1996); Barbara Kruger, Ann Goldstein, and Rosalyn Deutsche, *Barbara Kruger* (1999); Barbara Kruger and Kate Linker, *Love for Sale: The Words and Pictures of Barbara Kruger* (1996); Barbara Kruger, *Remote Control: Power, Cultures, and The World of Appearances* (1994); Barbara Kruger, *We Won't Play Nature to Your Culture* (1983); Timothy Anglin Burgard, Picasso and Appropriation, 73 *Art. Bull.* 479 (1991); Dan Cameron, A Conversation, 143 *Flashart* 76 (1988); Karl Erickson and Andrew Falkowski, A Manifesto for Reconstruction, 26 *New Art Examiner* 30 (1999); Lauri Firstenberg, Notes on Renewed Appropriationisms / Notizen zum Wiederaufleben von Appropriationsgesten, 67 *Parkett* 170 (2003); Thomas Heyd, Rock Art Aesthetics and Cultural Appropriation, 61 *J. Aesthetics & Art Criticism* 37 (2003); Gerardo Mosquera, Stealing from the Global Pie: Globalization, Difference, and Cultural Appropriation, 21 *Art Papers* 12 (1997); David Mura, Cultural Claims & Appropriations (e.g. Who Owns the Internment Camps?), 21 *Art Papers* (1997); Lillian Schwartz, Computers and Appropriation Art: The Transformation of a Work or Idea for a New Creation, 29 *Leonardo* 43 (1996); Ann-Sargent Wooster, Censorship v. Appropriation at the Whitney, 12 *High Performance* 14 (1989); Gregory M. Lamb, Spin Cycle, *Christian Sci. Monitor*, July 18, 2003, *available at* http://www.csmonitor.com/2003/0718/p13s02-almp.html (last visited March 10, 2004); Marter, supra n. 105, at 106; Catherine Moschou Abrams, History of Art Appropriation and the Appropriated Art Works of Sherrie Levine (1991) (unpublished Ph.D. dissertation, New York University); Jeff Koons, *The Banality Work* (ART/New York 1990); Rick Prelinger, Remarks on

(artistic or commercial) in their pieces. Duchamp's "ready mades" are often cited as the origin of appropriation art. Among these "ready mades" none perhaps is more famous than his *Fountain* of 1917, which consisted of a single standard urinal.[107] Later in the twentieth century artists such as Andy Warhol appropriated ubiquitous images from commercial media, providing insights into how visual images function in contemporary society. Warhol's paintings of Campbell's soup cans or his sculptures of Brillo boxes are among the best-known of these works.[108] Appropriation art has been said to have peaked in the 1980s in the hands of artists such as Sherrie Levine, Elaine Sturevant, Goerge Condo, Mike Bidlo, Gretchen Bender, Philip Taafe, and Jeff Koons.[109] The cultural landscape – at least in the West – has been enriched by appropriation artists: their works at their best force viewers to reconsider fundamental notions of what creativity is, to question the meaning of originality, and to remember that artistic creation depends on access to existing images.

At a time when the public domain from which artists can derive models and source material is shrinking,[110] copyright periods in the United States have been extended,[111] and lawsuits against artists working in an appropriation mode threaten to chill such activity,[112] there is cause for concern

Appropriation Art, Remarks at the Illegal Art Panel, San Francisco Art Institute (July 7, 2003), *in Otherzine*, *at* http://www.othercinema.com/ozframe.html.

[107] For an image, see http://www.beatmuseum.org/duchamp/fountain.html (last visited June 30, 2004). For Duchamp's continuing influence on current artists, see Martha Buskirk, Interviews with Sherrie Levine, Louis Lawler, and Fred Wilson, 70 *October* 98 (1994).

[108] Marco Livingstone, Andy Warhol, *Grove Art Online* (2004), *at* http://www. groveart.com (last visited June 30, 2004). For an image of Warhol's *100 Cans* (1962) in the Albright-Knox Art Gallery, see http://168.169.71.120/c1 online/ details.html?mkey=2018 (last visited June 30, 2004).

[109] Sartwell, *supra* n. 105, at 68–69.

[110] *See*, e.g., Lawrence Lessig, *How Big Media Uses Technology to Lock Down Culture and Control Creativity* (2004); Lawrence Lessig, *The Future of Ideas: The Fate of the Commons in a Connected World* (2001); Adam Cohen, The Intellectual Imperialists, *N.Y. Times Book Rev.*, Apr. 4, 2004, at 12.

[111] *See Eldred v. Ashcroft*, 537 U.S. 186 (2003) (upholding the 1998 Copyright Extension Act, which [inter alia] extended the duration of copyright protection not only to works created after the act became effective but also to works under copyright protection prior to the act).

[112] See, e.g., *Rogers v. Koons*, 960 F.2d 301, 308–09 (2d. Cir. 1992) (holding that artist Jeff Koons's sculpture *String of Puppies* infringed artist Art Rogers's photograph *Puppies* because an "ordinary observer" would find that Koons's expression of Rogers's idea was "substantially similar" to the original and because Koons's profit-making motive

that the practice of artists' learning, deriving inspiration, and taking from other artists' work – a practice that has been fundamental to creative activity throughout history – is at risk. That history argues that artists should have the greatest possible access to and use of existing works. Are there exceptions to this presumption of unfettered access? Of course. Sensitivity to religious beliefs would require that works that are venerated or used in religious practice (for example, Michelangelo's *Pieta* in the Vatican or the image of Shakyamuni at Hōryū-ji near Nara, Japan) be treated with special respect. Works that continue to have fundamental, unique (and often secret) significance in forming the identity of a people, such as the aboriginal textile pattern at issue in the Bulun Bulun case mentioned above,[113] form another

and lack of parodic purpose, combined with the creative nature of *Puppies* and the substantial amount of the work that Koons used, precluded him from claiming a "fair use" defense); *Hoepker v. Kruger*, 200 F.Supp. 2d 340, 345–47 (S.D.N.Y. 2002) (grounding dismissal of Edward Hoepker's complaint against Barbara Kruger for her 1990 appropriation of a photograph he created in 1960 solely on the fact that Kruger's "infringing act" occurred during a six-year window when his foreign work fell outside copyright protection in the United States). *But see Campbell v. Acuff-Rose Music, Inc.*, 510 U.S. 569 (1994) (holding that the rap group 2 Live Crew's appropriation of Roy Orbison's rock ballad "Pretty Woman" merited protection under the "fair use" doctrine because the derivative work's use of the copyrighted work was not excessive in relation to 2 Live Crew's parodic purpose, despite the derivative work's commercial nature). For a useful discussion of *Campbell*'s bearing on appropriation art, see Roxana Badin, Comment, An Appropriate(d) Place in Transformative Value: Appropriation Art's Exclusion from *Campbell v. Acuff-Rose Music, Inc., 60 Brook. L. Rev.* 1653 (1995). For further commentary on the legal parameters within which appropriation artists function, see, for example, Jane Gaines, *Contested Culture: The Image, the Voice, and the Law* (1991); Gloria Phares, Appropriation Art and Copyright, in 1 *Encyclopedia of Aesthetics* 70 (Michael Kelly ed., 1998); Laura Arici, Reality as Forgery / Wirklichkeit als Fälschung?, 39 *Parkett* 161 (1994); John Carlin, Culture Vultures: Artistic Appropriation and Intellectual Property Law, 13 *Colum.-VLA J.L. & Arts* 103 (1988); Lynne A. Greenberg, The Art of Appropriation: Puppies, Piracy, and Post-Modernism, 11 *Cardozo Arts & Ent. L.J.* 1 (1992); William M. Landes, Copyright, Borrowed Images, and Appropriation Art: An Economic Approach, 9 *Geo. Mason L. Rev.* 1 (2000); Dawn M. Leach, Art World Thinking versus Legal Thinking, 18 *Visual Resources* 205 (2002); Richard T. Pfohl, The Key to the (Digital) Salon: Copyright and the Control of Creative Expression, 16 *Visual Resources* 185 (2000); Julie Van Camp, Creating Works of Art from Works of Art: The Problem of Derivative Works, 24 *J. Arts Mgmt. L. & Soc'y* 209 (1994); Naomi Abe Voegtli, Rethinking Derivative Rights, 63 *Brook. L. Rev.* 1213 (1997); Martha Lufkin, Art Trumps Right to Privacy, *Art Newspaper*, Oct. 2002, at 1; Helen Razer, Copycat Commandos, *The Age*, Sept. 25, 2003, *at* http://www.theage.com.au/articles/2003/09/24/1064083041326.html (last visited July 4, 2004).

[113]   *Bulun Bulun v. R&T Textiles Pty. Ltd.*, *supra* n. 104.

set of exceptions. But the history of creative work argues powerfully in favor of a policy of providing artists the broadest possible access to the works of their predecessors.

In addition to appropriation, the past two decades have seen the development of efforts by some artists to recontextualize works in museum collections. The leading figure in the field is the American artist Fred Wilson.[114] In his landmark 1992 exhibition, *Mining the Museum*, at the Maryland Historical Society, Baltimore, Maryland, Wilson reinterpreted objects in the society's collection, exhibiting them in new contexts and in powerful juxtapositions.[115] For example, Wilson installed slave shackles alongside fine silver of the same period,[116] placed a Ku Klux Klan hood into a fancy perambulator,[117] and organized a group of distinguished nineteenth-century chairs in a semi-circle around a whipping post.[118] By recontextualizing the museum's collections, Wilson forced museum professionals to reconsider how they accomplish their mission of interpreting collections for the public, provided the opportunity for museum visitors to reconsider the objects

[114] For a survey of Wilson's work see Maurice Berger, *Fred Wilson Objects and Installations 1979–2000* (2001). *See also* Fred Wilson, The Silent Message of the Museum, in *Global Visions: Towards a New Internationalism in the Visual Arts* (Jean Fisher ed., 1994); Martha Buskirk, Fred Wilson, 70 *October* 109 (1994); Donald Garfield, Making the Museum Mine: An Interview with Fred Wilson, 72 *Museum News* 46 (1993); Judith E. Stein, Sins of Omission, 81 *Art Am.* 110 (1993); Fred Wilson, Silent Messages (Museological Installations by Artist Fred Wilson), 95 *Museums J.* 27 (1995); Fred Wilson, Remarks at the 2004 Annual Conference of the College Art Association (Feb. 18, 2004), *in* 2004 Annual Conference Wrap-up, *CAA News* (College Art Association, New York, N.Y.), *at* http://www.collegeart.org/caa/news/2004/May/Convocation.html (last visited July 4, 2004).

[115] *See* Fred Wilson, *Mining the Museum: An Installation* (Lisa G. Corrin ed., 1994). *Mining the Museum* is one among many recontextualization projects. Others include installations at the 2003 Venice Biennale, the Seattle Museum of Art, the Museum of Contemporary Art in Chicago, the de Young Memorial Museum, the Indianapolis Museum of Art, the Richard L. Nelson Gallery at UC Davis, the Berkeley Museum of Art, the Ian Potter Museum of Art at the University of Melbourne, and the Centre for Contemporary Art at Warsaw's Ujadowski Castle. *See* Fred Wilson, *The Spiral of Art History* (1993); Fred Wilson and Rachel Kent, *Viewing the Invisible: An Installation by Fred Wilson* (1998); Fred Wilson and Patterson Sims, *The Museum: Mixed Metaphors* (1993); Allan M. Gordon, Fred Wilson at UC Davis, 28 *Artweek* 21 (1997); Pamela Newkirk, Object Lessons, 99 *Art News* 156 (2000); James Putnam, The Quest for Othello, 16 *Modern Painters* 94 (2003); Putnam, Fred Wilson, 14 *Sculpture* 47 (1995).

[116] Berger, *supra* n. 114, at 69.

[117] *Id.* at 70–71.

[118] *Id.* at 71–72.

themselves (and the way the society had traditionally exhibited and interpreted them), and offered critics a new avenue to explore the many lives
of an object. In several of his works, Wilson has used antiquities, including
the bust. For example, in his installation *Re-Claiming Egypt* of 1993 at the
Whitney Museum of American Art, New York, Wilson mounted on wooden
shelves in a series five plaster copies of the bust ranging in color from pure
white to dark black.[119] Read from left to right, the bust gradually darkened;
read from right to left, the Bust transformed from black to white. The piece
compels a viewer to consider the debate whether pharaoronic Egypt was an
African civilization or a civilization that had been "caucasionized" by generations of Western European Egyptologists. Wilson's efforts to take original
works and place them in new contexts or take copies of well-known works
and to install them in ways that give them new meanings have been groundbreaking. His interest in combining the dual strategies of appropriation and
contextualization is not isolated.

In *The Body of Nefertiti*, two Hungarian artists, Balint Havas (b. 1971)
and András Gálik (b. 1970), who work collaboratively under the name Little
Warsaw,[120] created their country's contribution to the 2003 Venice Biennale,
the world's most important venue for contemporary visual arts. For *The
Body of Nefertiti*, Little Warsaw created a bronze, naked, headless torso, the
dimensions of which were based on the proportions of the bust. They took
their sculpture to the Egyptian Museum in Berlin, where it was positioned
adjacent to the display case in which the bust is normally on view. On May
26, 2003, the director of the Egyptian Museum and a conservator removed
the bust from its case and mounted it on the torso. Shortly thereafter the bust
was returned, safely, to its case. The transfer was recorded on video tape.

The short journey from its isolation in a glass case into the world of
contemporary art effected a dramatic set of visual images (Figure 7.1). For
a brief moment in the Egyptian Museum, Little Warsaw created a brilliant,
complex installation piece: while mounted on a contemporary torso, the bust
is reflected in the glass case where it normally resides in solitary confinement.
Simultaneously seeing the bust as an active participant in a twenty-first-
century work of art and as a reflection in the case that segregates it from other
objects and viewers raises a host of serious questions. It also demonstrates
how Little Warsaw breathed life into the bust by the simple act of releasing it
from a glass cage and joining it to an elegant body. In short, Little Warsaw's

---

[119]   *Id.* at 83.
[120]   For examples of Little Warsaw's oeuvre, see Lívia Páldi and Anna Gács, *Little Warsaw*
        (2003).

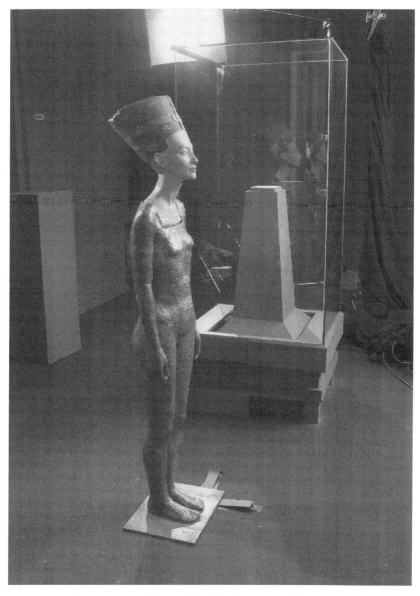

Figure 7.1. Little Warsaw / András Gálik and Bálint Havas, *The Body of Nefertiti*, 2003. Life-size bronze with the limestone bust of Nefertiti (1340 B.C.), May 26, 2003, Ägyptisches Museum und Papyrussammlung, Berlin-Charlottenburg. © Little Warsaw. Courtesy of Little Warsaw (provided by the artists).

appropriation and recontextualization of the bust, transforming it from an isolated icon to an integral part of a new work of art, provided an opportunity for the bust to convey new meanings four thousand years after Thutmose created it.

At the Venice Biennale, Little Warsaw created a second installation by exhibiting its headless bronze torso adjacent to a screen on which a video displayed the bust's transfer and brief unification with the torso in the Egyptian Museum. The Biennale installation demonstrated yet again that even iconic images, in the hands of creative artists, can achieve new dimensions, new meaning, and new vitality.[121] *The Body of Nefertiti* provides a clear example of the value of permitting working artists the broadest possible access to existing works of art. It also demonstrates how an iconic work, introduced into the stream of creative expression, develops new meaning. Despite (or perhaps because of) the ingenuity of *The Body of Nefertiti*, Egyptian officials were quick to respond harshly.[122]

Egypt's Ambassador to Germany, Mohammed al-Orabi, characterized Little Warsaw's piece as "not even silly; it is nothing. I mean, the project is nothing."[123] He also mistakenly stated about pharaonic art that Little Warsaw's piece "contradicts Egyptian manners and traditions. The body is almost naked, and Egyptian civilization never displays a woman naked."[124,125] Zahi Hawass, head of Egypt's Supreme Council of Antiquities,

---

[121] Little Warsaw's *The Bust of Nefertiti* was widely reported in the press. See, for example, Jeevan Vasagar, Turning Heads: Egypt Angered at Artists' Use of Nefertiti Bust, *The Guardian*, June 12, 2003, at 13; Hugh Eakin, Nefertiti's Bust Gets a Body, Offending Egyptians, *N.Y. Times*, June 21, 2003 at B14; John Ydstie and Emily Harris, Nefertiti Bust at the Center of an International Artistic Dispute, National Public Radio, Weekend Edition Sunday, July 6, 2003 at http://www.npr.org/features/feature.php?wfId=1321471; Marcia E. Vetrocq, Venice Biennale, *Art in America* 76 (September 2003).

[122] Whether Egypt's position on *The Body of Nefertiti* reflects genuine outrage; forms part of Egypt's newly vigorous efforts under Zahi Hawass, head of Egypt's Supreme Council of Antiquities, to repatriate significant works from Western museums (see *supra* n. 89); or is merely the most recent expression of Egypt's long-standing regret at having lost the bust to Germany through entirely legal means (see, *supra*, Parts I and II), is difficult to determine.

[123] National Public Radio, Weekend Edition Sunday, July 6, 2004. al-Orabi described the project as "silly" again in Hugh Eakin, Nefertiti's Bust Gets a Body, Offending Egyptians, *The New York Times*, June 21, 2003, § B, p. 1, Col. 1.

[124] Hugh Eakin, *supra* n. 123.

[125] For an especially beautiful sculptural representation of an Egyptian princess clad in a transparent dress from the same period and place as the bust, see Dorothea Arnold, *The Royal Women of Amarna* (1996) Figs. 21 and 22.

was even more blunt, calling Little Warsaw's piece a "degradation" of the bust, created in "wanton disrespect."[126] Hawass wasted no time in serving as witness, judge, and jury, proclaiming that the director of the Berlin Museum *and his wife* were to be "denied permission to excavate in Egypt in the future" and directing that "no Egyptian official should cooperate with them in any capacity."[127]

What Egypt's reaction to *The Body of Nefertiti* makes clear is that a return of the bust to Egypt would place it beyond the reach of contemporary artists such as Little Warsaw. The bust holds absolutely no place in current Egyptian religious practice and no appreciable use in developing or maintaining current Egyptian national identity. Were it to be returned to Egypt, it would likely be isolated from the stream of creative expression to which it can contribute and from which it can derive new meaning. To condemn the bust to such an existence is, to twist Clemency Coggins's famous observation, to assure that the bust remain forevermore beautiful but dead.[128]

V. CONCLUSION

The calculus of determining whether cultural property for which a source nation has no enforceable legal claim should, nevertheless, be returned for moral, ethical, practical, or other reasons is complex. The various factors – the values and issues described in Part III above – are never easy to apply. To those factors, this chapter adds a new consideration: protecting living artists' access to such works and maintaining such works' participation in the continuing stream of human creativity. In the case of the bust, Little Warsaw's appropriation and recontextualization demonstrate the significance of this new factor: *The Body of Nefertiti* forces critical viewers to think carefully about how museums isolate great works, reconsider who Nefertiti was and how she might have looked, recognize the continuing power of Thutmose's genius, and appreciate that even iconic works can be effectively (and in this case, literally) removed from their pedestals to their and their audiences' benefit.

---

[126]   Hawass, *supra* n. 122.

[127]   Id.

[128]   "An art object which has been excavated by *huaqueros* can rarely be traced to its place of origin even by experts. With no clear historical significance, therefore, the object can only be, forevermore, beautiful but dumb." Clemency Coggins, The Maya Scandal: How Thieves Strip Sites of Past Cultures, *Smithsonian*, October 1970, 8 at 10.

The analysis in Part III, on balance, favors the argument that the bust should remain in Berlin. Applying the value that this part has attempted to define resolves any uncertainty. Egypt's official reaction to *The Body of Nefertiti* makes clear that the bust will be more accessible to living artists and more likely to remain where all great works of art belong – at the heart of the creative enterprises – if it remains in Berlin. Accordingly, this chapter concludes that The Beautiful One Has Come to Berlin – to stay.

APPENDIX I

THE BUST OF NEFERTITI: AN ANNOTATED BIBLIOGRAPHY

Tracy Musacchio

The Amarna period in general and Nefertiti specifically have long been a source of intense interest. As the capital city of the pharaoh Akhenaten, Amarna caught the interest of biblical scholars, Egyptologists, and the public alike. Biblical scholars wanted to see the reforms of Akhenaten as monotheistic; Egyptologists were attracted to the archaeological potential of the briefly inhabited city (abandoned in the second millennium and untouched until its nineteenth-century rediscovery); and the popular community was captivated by the discovery of the bust of Akhenaten's queen, Nefertiti.

The bust of Nefertiti was discovered at the site of Amarna during the 1912/13 season by the Deutsche Orient-Gesellschaft, led by Ludwig Borchardt. It was found in the house of the sculptor Thutmose in the area of the South Suburb/ Main City. Thutmose's home and studio were immediately of interest. Egyptian portraiture is characterized by its rigid and formulaic nature, and Thutmose's workroom contained several striking and lifelike pieces exhibiting a realism typically lacking in Egyptian art. Although the excavators were quite prompt with their excavation publications, no proper photos of the bust were published until 1923. The revelation of the bust caused immediate scholarly interest, due both to the legal issues it raised concerning the division of finds in Egypt and to the intense beauty of the statue. The bust remains in the collection of the Staatliche Museum in Berlin, where it was taken after leaving Egypt.

The written material dealing with the Amarna period reflects the strong interest it has provoked. Several attempts have been made to document the bibliography surrounding the Amarna period; Geoffrey Martin's *Bibliography of the Amarna Period and Its Aftermath* stands as one of the most recent (published in 1991) and most comprehensive (with just over two thousand entries).

The bibliography below does not purport to be complete but instead features some of the sources most directly relevant to the historical person of Nefertiti, the physical bust, its discovery, its interpretation, and its subsequent fate.

SOURCES

Aldred, Cyril. *Akhenaten, King of Egypt.* London: Thames & Hudson, 1988. Revision of: Aldred Cyril. *Akhenaten, Pharaoh of Egypt: A New Study.* London, 1968.
> Commonly used introduction to Akhenaten and the Amarna period, covering the life and reign of the pharaoh including his religious reforms.

Anthes, R. *Die Büste der Königin Nofret Ete.* Berlin: Verlag Gebr. Mann, 1954. Also: Anthes, R. *The Head of Queen Nefertiti,* trans. Kathleen Bauer. Berlin: Verlag Gebrunder Mann, 1954.
> An art historical look at the bust of Nefertiti and its place as one of the peaks in Egyptian art history. Also recounts the discovery of the piece in the context of the workhouse of the sculptor Thutmose with speculation concerning the intended destination of the piece. Asserts that the bust was intended to be a model for a series of statues.

Arnold, Dorothea. *The Royal Women of Amarna.* New York: Metropolitan Museum, 1996.
> Exhibition catalogue from 1996–1997 exhibit "Queen Nefertiti and the Royal Women: Images of Beauty from Ancient Egypt" in the Metropolitan Museum of Art. Includes a discussion on women in Amarna art, an essay on the workshop of the sculptor Thutmose, and illustrations of the fifty-four exhibited pieces.

Borchardt, Ludwig. "Ausgrabungen in Tell el-Armarna 1912/13: Vorläufiger Bericht." *Mitteilungen der Deutschen Orient-Gesellschaft zu Berlin [MDOG]* 52 (Oct. 1913), pp. 1–55.
> DOG excavation reports were promptly published in *MDOG.* This report includes the excavation of the workshop of sculptor Thutmose, pp. 29–50. The first image of bust is also published here, although not easily identifiable and cropped, obscuring its full beauty, on p. 43.

Borchardt, Ludwig. *Porträts der Königin Nofret-ete.* Ausgrabungen der Deutschen Orient-Gesellschaft in tell el-Amarna III. Leipzig: J. C. Hinrichs'sche Buchhandlung, 1923.
> The first full publication of the bust, appearing ten years after its discovery. Volume includes full-color pictures and extensive descriptions of images of Nefertit, especially the bust.

Borchardt, Ludwig, and Ricke, Herbert. *Die Wohnhäuser in Tell el-Amarna.* Berlin: Verlag Gebrunder Mann, 1980.
> Final publication from the DOG excavations. Each house is detailed with its plan and construction technique and a list of noninscribed finds (treated in an appendix). House of Thutmose (P47.1–47.3) featured on pp. 87–100, with a detail in plan 27 and photos on plates 5 and 6.

Breasted, J. H. "Studio of an Egyptian Portrait Sculptor in the Fourteenth Century B.C." *Art and Archaeology* 4 (1916), pp. 232–242.
> Discussion of Thutmose's home/studio. Bust is alluded to but not explicitly mentioned (p. 241: "A wonderful portrait of the queen, not quite completed, bears marks made by the sculptor in ink, to show where the flesh forms were too heavy and were to be reduced. A finished replica shows clearly just what modifications the sculptor intended to introduce at the places marked. I am not able to illustrate here these two remarkable works.")

Brunner-Traut, E. "Nofretete." In Wolfgang, Helck, and Otto Eberhard, eds., *Lexikon der Ägyptologie*, vol. 4, col. 519–521.
> Biographic encyclopedia entry concerning the historical queen Nefertiti and her life.

Bulletin de Législation et de Jurisprudence Égyptiennes, U. Pace and V. Sisto, annotaters, "Antiquties." In *Répertoire Permanent de Législation Égyptienne*, Alexandria, 1944.
> Language of the statutes that deal with Egyptian antiquities. Specific laws include those enacted May 16, 1883 (concerning the Museum at Bulaq); November 17, 1891 (concerning permission for excavation); August 12, 1897 (taking measures to protect antiquities); June 12, 1912 (Law No. 14 concerning antiquities); December 8, 1912 (concerning the sale of antiquities; regulating the exporting of antiquities; and regulating excavations).

Capart, J. "Dans le studio d'un artiste." *Chronique d'Égypte* 32 (1957), pp. 199–217. Discussion of all of the artistic pieces from the house of the sculptor Thutmose.

Chamberlin, Russell. *Loot! The Heritage of Plunder.* London: Thames and Hudson, 1983.

Reviews: Seton Lloyd, *Antiquity* 58 (1984), 76–77; Ellen Herscher, *Archaeology* 37, No. 4 (July/August 1984), 74.
> History and overview of plundering done by modern, Western civilization. The book is divided into four main parts, each of which discusses plundering from a slightly different angle. Part I deals with the plundering of Greece (in particular the Elgin Marbles) and Egypt (pp. 62–65 are devoted to the bust of Nefertiti, with a brief overview of its finding and subsequent controversy); Part II gives

examples taken from plundering of royalty, including the Ashanti and St. Stephen of Hungary; Part III deals with Napoléon and Hitler (the so-called Warlords); and Part IV deals with the plundering of the (modern) Third World.

Charlton, N. "The Berlin Head of Nefertiti." *Journal of Egyptian Archaeology* 62 (1976). p. 184.
Brief communication regarding the missing eye of the bust (response to *Journal of Egyptian Archaeology* [*JEA*] 60, p. 200). Theorizes that the eye was broken later rather than unfinished.

Crabitès, P. "The Bust of Queen Nefertete." *Catholic World* 139 (1934), pp. 207–212.
Review of the discovery of the bust, Nefertiti's lineage, and the circumstances surrounding the bust's being allotted to the Germans in the division of finds. Maintains that finds were divided fairly and that Berlin hid the bust out of fear of Lord Kitchener. Also details the attempts since to return the bust and their implications for other collections (notably London).

de Wit, C. *La Statuaire de Tell el Amarna.* Brussels: Aux Editions "Erasme," 1950.

Review: A. Calderini, *Aegyptus* 31 (1951), p. 73.
A catalogue of Amarna art, including photographs, descriptions, and bibliography for statuary (mostly royal) from Amarna.

Dodson, A. "Nefertiti's Regality: A Comment." *Journal of Egyptian Archaeology* 67 (1981), p. 179.
Disputation of Samson's ideas concerning Nefertiti's sole reign (see Samson, *JEA* 63, below).

Eaton-Krauss, Marianne. "Akhenaten vs. Akhenaten." *Biblioteca Orientalis* 47 (1990), pp. 541–559.
Joint review of Aldred and Redford's volumes on the Amarna period, comparing and contrasting their subjective theories against the objective evidence.

Ertman, E. L. "The Cap-Crown of Nefertiti: Its Function and Probably Origin." *Newsletter of the American Research Center in Egypt* 91 (Fall 1974), pp. 26–27.
Abstract from a 1974 American Research Center in Egypt (ARCE) conference paper concerning the unusual crown the bust of Nefertiti wears.

Girardet, Cells- Margaretha, "Die Dame vom Nil." *Art. Das Kunstmagazin,* No. 9 (September 1982), 44–55.
Review of the discovery of the bust and its subsequent transport to Berlin.

Harris, J. R. "Nefernefruaten." *Göttinger Miszellen* 4 (1973), pp. 15–17.
The first paper to assert the idea of an independent reign by Queen Nefertiti.

Harris, J. R. "Neferitit Rediviva." *Acta Orientalis* 35 (1973), pp. 5–13.
Discussion of a stela in Berlin with three empty cartouches, which the author
says were reserved for Nefertiti. Along with art historical evidence concerning
neck curvature in Amarna art, the author argues in favor of Nefertiti's prominent
status (which supports his belief that she ruled independently).

Harris, J. R. "Akhenaten or Nefertiti?" *Acta Orientalis* 38 (1977), pp. 5–10.
A study of a colossal statue from the temple of Karnak that the author suggests is
not Akhenaten as often thought but instead Nefertiti. Such a grandiose and royal
portrayal would give further support to his theory about Nefertiti's independent
reign.

Hornung, Erik. *Echnaton: Die Religion des Lichtes.* Düsseldorf: Artemis &
Winkler Verlag, 1995.

Also: Hornung, Erik. *Akhenaten and the Religion of Light*, trans. David Lorton.
Ithaca N.Y.: Cornell University Press, 1999.
Balanced overview of the history of the Amarna period focusing on religious
innovation.

Kemp, B. J. "Tell el-Amarna." In Wolfgang, Helck, and Otto Eberhard, eds.
Lexikon der Ägyptologie, vol. 6. col. 309–315.
The current excavator at Amarna gives a brief archaeological overview of the city
history, layout, and excavation history. Note: House of Thutmose is situated in
South Suburb/Main City area.

Khater, Antoine. *Le Régime Juridique des Fouilles et des Antiquités en Egypte.*
Cairo: Insitut Français d'Archéologie Orientale, 1960.
Review of the relevant laws governing excavation in Egypt from August 15, 1835,
through November 5, 1953. The book is divided into two main parts: Part One
is an overview of the history of excavation and the earliest attempts to control it
(including three chapters that deal with the history of plundering from antiquity
through the Middle Ages, a discussion of the 1835 ordinance, and the inauguration
of the Service des Antiquités); Part Two is a critical study of the implemented
laws, their implementation, and their interpretation (including a definition of
antiquities, specific discussions of the laws, and obligations and rights of the
excavators). A general conclusion is following by an appendix containing the
specific language of the statutes.

Kozloff, A. P. "Nefertiti, Beloved of the Living Disk." *Bulletin of the Cleveland
Museum of Art* 64, No. 9 (Nov. 1977), pp. 287–298.
Discussion of Nefertiti in relation to new *talatat* blocks purchased by the Cleveland
Museum.

Krauss, Rolf. "1913–1988: 75 Jahre Büste der NofretEte/Nefret-iti im Berlin."
Jahrbuch. Preussischer Kulturbesitz 24 (1987), pp. 87–124.
An account of the controversy that surrounded the excavation, publication, and
exhibition of the bust of Nefertiti, including the possibility of an art exchange

with the Egyptian government that would have returned the piece to Egypt but was vetoed by Adolf Hitler.

Krauss, Rolf. "Der Bildhauer Thutmose in Amarna. Mit einem Beitrag von Heinrich Newesely." *Jahrbuch Preussicher Kulturbesitz* 20 (1983), pp. 119–132.
Publication of the ivory fragment bearing the name of the sculptor Thutmose that has been used as evidence that the bust of Nefertiti was his work (the two were found in proximity during excavation). The fragment is of interest not only because of its relationship with the famous queen and sculptor, but also because of its uniqueness as an inscribed ivory horse blinker.

Krauss, Rolf. "Nofretete – eine Schönheit vom Reissbrett?" *Museums Journal, Berichte aus den Museen, Schlössern und Sammlungen im Land Berlin, zuglecih "Berliner Museen,"* 5. Folge 3, No. 11 (April 1989), pp. 25–27.
Analysis of the bust of Nefertiti shows that the artist created it with a mind to creating proper proportions.

Krauss, Rolf. "Nefretitis Ende." *Mitteilungen des Deutschen Archäologischen Instituts Abteilung Kairo* 53 (1997), pp. 209–219.
Krauss's contribution to the arguments surrounding the date of the death of Nefertiti is the publication of a hieratic docket from Amarna that makes mention of the estate of an unnamed queen during year 11 of the reign of Akhenaten. This estate was also attested in years 14–17 of Akhenaten's reign, thereby supporting the idea that Nefertiti outlived her husband.

Martin, Geoffrey Thorndike. *A Bibliography of the Amarna Period and Its Aftermath.* Studies in Egyptology. New York: Kegan Paul International, 1991.
Extensive bibliography (not annotated) of Amarna with special attention paid to Akhenaton, Smenkhare, Tutankhaten/Tutankhamun, and Ay. Heavy focus is on Egyptian history of the time period; includes excavation reports.

Matthieu, M. "Portret caricy Nefertiti" [The portrait head of Queen Nefertiti] *Xudožink* 4 (1961), pp. 45–51.
Treatment of the bust of Nefertiti in light of the art of the Amarna period.

Matthieu, M. *Vo vremena Nefertiti.* Leningrad: Izdatel'stvo "Iskusstvo," 1965.
Volume dedicated to the art of the Amarna period, featuring the bust of Nefertiti.

Meier-Graefe, Julius. "Die Büste der Königin Nofretete." *Kunst und Künstler* 28 (1930), pp. 479–481.

Mode, Markus. "Nofretete – Ein Nachspiel ze den Ausgrabungen der Deutschen Orient-Gesellschaft in Tell el-Amarna." *Hallesche Beiträge zur Orientwissenschaft,* 6 (1984), pp. 37–45.
Another review of the excavation of the bust of Nefertiti and the controversy surrounding its ending up in the Berlin Museum.

Mussgnug, R. *Wem gehört Nofretete?* Schriftenreihe der Juristischen Gesellschaft, 52. Berlin, 1977.

Title is an allusion to a post–World War II pamphlet published by the German Federal Republic claiming West German ownership of the bust.

Paczensky, Gert von, und Herbert Ganslmayr. *Nofretete will nach Hause. Europa – Schatzhaus der "Dritten Welt."* Munich: C. Bertelsmann, 1984.

Although the book features Nefertiti in its title and on its dust jacket, only a small section of this book discusses the bust of Nefertiti (and its acquisition by Germany). The rest of the book discusses European collections that include art originating from the Third World.

Redford, Donald B. *Akhenaten: The Heretic King.* Princeton, N.J.: American University in Cairo Press, 1984.

Commonly used introduction to Akhenaten and the Amarna period. Relevant discussions of Nefertiti include Nefertiti and her prominence in reliefs, pp. 78ff.; Kiya and her relationship with Nefertiti, pp. 150ff.; Nefertiti's demise/independent reign, pp. 190–193 (seems to discount the theory of an independent reign). Note: Stands in opposition to Aldred's opinion.

Ricke, H. *Der Grundriss des Amarna-Wohnhauses.* Deutsche Ortient-Gesellschaft. Wissenschaftliche Veröffentlichungen, 56. Leipzig: J. C. Hinrichs'sche Buchhandlung, 1932.

Publication of the DOG work at Amarna, focusing on the workhouses. The house of Thutmose is drawn on p. 41. Extensive plates.

Samson, Julia. *Amarna: City of Akhenaten and Nefertiti. Nefertiti as Pharaoh.* Warminster, England: Aris & Phillips, 1972.

Illustrated discussion of the collection of Amarna artifacts from the Petrie Museum (London). Discussion of different art historical aspects of traditional representations of Nefertiti. Extensive second part ("Nefertiti as Pharaoh") uses the Petrie collection to further her assertion that Nefertiti had an independent reign (see Samson, *JEA* 63).

Samson, Julia. "Nefertiti's Regality." *Journal of Egyptian Archaeology* 63 (1977), pp. 88–97.

Samson's initial expression of theory that Nefertiti succeeded Akhenaten as pharaoh.

Samson, Julia. "Royal Names in Amarna History. The Historical Development of Nefertiti's Names and Titles." *Chronique d'Égypte* 51, No. 101 (1976), pp. 30–38.

A chronological examination of the names of Nefertiti and their development, used to support the idea that Nefertiti and Smenkhare are the same person.

Samson, Julia. *Nefertiti and Cleopatra*. London: The Rubicon Press, 1985.
Popular comparison of the two queens that uses Amarna reliefs and vivid writing in a romantic attempt to bring Nefertiti to life.

Schlögl, Hermann Alexander. *Echnaton-Tutanchamon: Daten, Fakten, Literatur*. Wiesbaden: Harrassowitz Verlag, 1993.

Also: Schlögl, Hermann Alexander. *Echnaton-Tutanchamon: Fakten und Text*. Wiesbaden: Otto Harrassowitz, 1983.
Detailed study of Egyptian politics (only internal; study does not deal with foreign affairs) leading up to and including the Amarna period. Includes art history and major Egyptian texts.

Sirry, Ismaïl. "La Nouvelle Loi sur les Antiquités de l'Égypte et ses Annexes." *Annales du Service des Antiquités de l'Égypte* 12 (1912), pp. 245–263.
Publication of the Laws enacted in 1912 governing antiquities. Included are Law No. 14, which defines antiquities and specifies how they are to be treated in excavation (licit and illicit) and sale including penalties; Ministerial Order No. 50, which concerns the sale of antiquities; Ministerial Order No. 51, concerning the exportation of antiquities; and Ministerial Order No. 52, which governs (legal) excavation in Egypt.

Tyldesley, Joyce. *Nefertiti: Egypt's Sun Queen*. New York: Viking Penguin, 1998.
A trained Egyptologist contributes a recent popular biography of the queen.

Vandenberg, P. *Nofretete: Ein Archäologische Biographie*. Munich: Berne, 1975. Also: Vandenberg, P. trans. Ruth Hein. *Nefertiti: An Archaeological Biography*. London, 1978.
A popular survey of the Amarna period. The author reviews both the scholarly and sensationalized theories on the history of Akhenaten and Nefertiti.

Wells, Evelyn. *Nefertiti*. London: Robert Hale, 1965.
One of the first popular biographies of the queen.

Werner, Edward K. "The Amarna Period of Eighteenth Dynasty Egypt, Bibliography: 1965–1974." *Bulletin of the American Research Center in Egypt* 95 (1975), pp. 15–36.

———. "The Amarna Period of Eighteenth Dynasty Egypt, Bibliography Supplement 1975." *BARCE* 97/98 (1975), pp. 29–40.

———. "The Amarna Period of Eighteenth Dynasty Egypt, Bibliography Supplement 1976." *BARCE* 101/102 (1977), pp. 41–65.

———. "The Amarna Period of Eighteenth Dynasty Egypt, Bibliography Supplement 1977." *BARCE* 106 (1977), pp. 41–60.

————."The Amarna Period of Eighteenth Dynasty Egypt, Bibliography Supplement 1978." *BARCE* 110 (1978), pp. 24–39.

————."The Amarna Period of Eighteenth Dynasty Egypt, Bibliography Supplement 1979." *BARCE* 114 (1979), pp. 18–34.
Early attempt at a comprehensive bibliography of the Amarna period, sub-sumed by Martin's work. Divides material into categories as follows: A) Akhen-aten, Smenkhare, and the Amarna Revolution (changes to History in 1978 Supplement); B) Religion; C) the Role of Nefertiti; D) Pathological Studies; E) Art; F) Excavations and the Akhenaten Temple Project; G) Language and Writing.

Wiedemann, H. G., and G. Bayer. "The Bust of Nefertiti: The Analytical Approach." *Analytical Chemistry* 54 (April 1982), pp. 619A–628A.
Chemical analysis of the composition of colors used to paint the bust, which included red (ferric oxide), green (possible acetate of copper), black (coal), and blue (Egyptian blue).

Wildung, Dietrich. "Zerstörungsfreie Untersuchungen an altägyptischen Objekten." *Jahrbuch Preussischer Kulturbesitz*, 29 (1992), pp. 133–156.
Results of x-ray and Computed Tomograpy (CT) scan tests on several famous pieces in the Berlin Museum, including the head of Queen Teye, an Old Kingdom reserve head, and the bust of Nefertiti. The results of the test show that the bust is a stone core with considerable gypsum layering.

Worms, René. "Nefretîti." *Journal Asiatique* 11, No. 7 (1916), pp. 469–491.
Analysis of the information available on the historical person of Nefertiti. Exami-nation of the titulary of Aye and Tiye (whom he refers to as Ej and Tj). Speculates that Aye was the father of Nefertiti but married Tiye (who was not Nefertiti's mother) in a second marriage later in life.

A NEW TRANSLATION OF SELECTED EGYPTIAN ANTIQUITIES
LAWS (1881–1912) CONTAINED IN ANTOINE KHATER'S
*LE RÉGIME JURIDIQUE DES FOUILLES ET DES ANTIQUITÉS
EN ÉGYPTE.*[129]

Adrienne L. Fricke

Decree[130] of December 18, 1881, Instituting a Committee Charged with the Conservation of Monuments of Arab Art (L. & D. 407)[131]

1. A committee for the conservation of Arab art is instituted under the chairmanship of the Minister of Wakfs.[132]
2. The committee's functions are as follows:
    2.1. To proceed with an inventory of Arab monuments of historic or artistic value,
    2.2. To attend to the maintenance and conservation of these monuments, advising the Minister of Wakfs of the work to be done, drawing his attention to those that are most urgent,

---

[129] Khater, Antoine. *Le régime juridique des fouilles et des antiquités en Égypte.* Cairo: Imprimérie de l'institut français d'archéologie orientale, 1960.

[130] The French version of the document states that it is a "décret" (decree); however, until World War I, all legislation in Egypt was promulgated under Ottoman authority, and was available in two languages: French and either Ottoman Turkish or Arabic. A "décret" issued by the Ottoman Sultan (the Sublime Porte), as opposed to the Egyptian ruler, would have been a *firman*, or grant, which carries different legal weight than a decree.

[131] L. & D. is likely the legal recorder Loi et Decrets. Khater's footnote cites Ph. Gélat, *Receuil de Législation Égyptienne.* This translator was unable to locate a citation for the title; however it is likely that one of the two publications is Khater's source for the official French text of many of these laws: Philippe Gélat, Corp Author Egypt, *Répertoire Général Annoté de la Législation et de l'administration Égyptiennes.* Alexandrie: Impr. J.C. Lagoudakis, 1906; *Répertoire de la Législation et de l'administration Égyptiennes.* Alexandrie: Type-Lithographie "Serapis", 1888. (Including Treaties).

[132] The word *wakf* in Islamic law has two meanings: (i) inalienable lands belonging to the Government which are charitable and (ii) pious endowments with reference to the subject matter of trusts. This is an unusual attempt to enforce laws protecting un-Islamic aspects of Egypt's past through a venerated Islamic legal institution.

©Adrienne L. Fricke 2004.

2.3. To study and approve projects and plans for repair of these monuments, overseeing their strict execution,

2.4. To insure the conservation of the plans of all the works undertaken in the archives of the Ministry of Wakfs, and to report to the Ministry on monumental remains which should be transferred to the National Museum in order to conserve them.

Decree of May 16, 1883, Holding That the Bulaq Museum[133] and All the Objects It Contains or May Contain in the Future Are Declared to Be the Property of the Public Domain of the State

We, the Khedive[134] of Egypt,
On the proposal of Our Council of Ministers;
Administrative Order:

Art. 1. The Museum of Egyptian Antiquities, prior to the Arab conquest, known by the name "Bulaq Museum," as well as all the objects it contains or may contain in the future, are declared the property of the Public Domain of the State, and consequently are inalienable, unassignable, and indefeasible.

Art. 2. The new museums and warehouses which may be created in the future, as well as all of the objects they may contain, are also declared property of the Public Domain of the State.

Art. 3. All the monuments and objects of antiquity, recognized as such by the Regulation governing the matter, shall also be declared property of the Public Domain of the State.

Art. 4. Our Minister of Public Works is charged with the execution of the present decree.

Done at the Palace of Ismailiyya, 9 Rajab 1300,[135] May 16, 1883.

---

[133]   The Bulaq collection eventually formed the basis of the Egyptian Museum, located in Midan al-Tahrir. Opened in 1863, the Bulaq Museum was initially conceived by the French Egyptologist Auguste Mariette. In 1890, the collection was moved to Giza, then eventually to the site of the new Egyptian Museum, which officially opened on November 15, 1902. see http://www.sca.gov.eg/f/egy-museum/100.html (last visited June 20, 2004).

[134]   French *khédive*, from Turkish *hidiv*, from Old Persian *khedv, khidv* meaning "prince, sovereign." It became the new title of the viceroy or ruler of Egypt under Ismail Pasha in 1867. It remained the title of the ruler of Egypt from 1867 to 1914, theoretically governing under the sultan of Turkey.

[135]   Dating in the Muslim calendar is in Annum Hijri (A.H.), counting from the date of the Prophet's flight to Medina in 622.

Decree of June 27, 1883, Holding That the Monuments of Arab Art Are Not Subject to Servitudes d' Alignment[136] (L. & D. 205)[137]

1. The monuments of Arab Art, inventoried as stated in Article 2 of our Decree of December 18, 1881, are not subject to *servitudes d'alignment*. It shall be the same for all other historic monuments designated and classified by the Administrative Order of the Minister of Public Works.

2. Authorizations for executing all works of reparation or any sort of consolidation recognized as necessary by the Committee for the Conservation of Arab Art to assure the conservation of these monuments shall be accorded by the Minister of Public Works in the forms indicated in the decree and in the Tanzim Law.[138] These authorizations are exempted from payment of Road Works Duties regardless of their nature.

3. All orders contrary to the present decree which may have been contained in our decree of March 12, 1881, and in the Tanzim Law of December 25, 1882, are revoked.[139]

Decree of November 17, 1891, Outlining the Conditions under Which Excavation Permits May Be Granted

On the proposal of Our Minister of Public Works and with the assent of Our Council of Ministers:

Art. 1. Excavations may not be made by private individuals without a permit delivered by proposition of the Director General of Museums and Excavations, after examination by the Permanent Egyptology Committee, under the terms of Article 6 of its Interior Regulation of March 9, 1889. The permit shall become valid only after the sanction of the Minister of Public Works. It will be delivered by the Director General of excavations.

---

[136] This is a French legal concept governing urban planning. A *servitude of alignment* is defined as an "obligation upon landowners to observe the building line (of a street, etc). *Heath's Standard French and English Dictionary* Bath: Pitman Press, 1934 at 27.

[137] See footnote 2, *supra*.

[138] The reforms initiated within the Ottoman Empire in the late 19th century were based on Tanzim law (pl. *Tanzimat*).

[139] The reference to Turkish legal reforms is unusual, given that the Khedive technically had discretion to issue and implement laws interpreting Ottoman prerogatives. This highlights the tension in pre-nationalist Egyptian legislation between the Ottoman regime and the emerging elites.

Art. 2. All of the objects found in excavations belong by right to the State and must be placed in the Giza Museum.

Art. 3. Regardless, in consideration of the expenses made by the excavator, the government shall cede to him a part of the antiquities found, in conformance with the following sections.

Art. 4. The Administration of the Antiquities Service and the excavator shall together divide these objects into two shares of equal value.[140] The Administration and the excavator shall draw lots for the two shares if they prefer this method to a negotiated assignment of the shares.[141]

Art. 5. The Administration reserves the right to re-purchase any piece of the share which falls to the excavator. The Administration will make its offer; if the excavator refuses it, he will indicate his price. The Administration will have the power either to take the object at the price indicated by the excavator, or to relinquish the object to the excavator, for which he will pay the price previously offered by the Administration. In all cases, the Administration may appropriate the objects it wants to re-purchase, compensating the excavator by a sum which shall never surpass the costs of the excavation incurred in their discovery.

Art. 6. Articles 3, 4, and 5 above are not applicable:

1. to monuments fixed to the ground, regardless of their state, which in the judgment of the Administration must be conserved in place, as well as the detached fragments which it wants to put back into place;
2. to pieces which are entirely turned over, which in the judgment of the Administration must be set right or conserved in place;
3. to pieces too heavy which the excavator refuses to transport at his own cost.

Art. 7. All provisions contrary to the present decree are hereby abrogated.

Art. 8. Our Ministries of the Interior and of Public Works are charged, inasmuch as each is concerned, with the execution of the present decree.

Decree of August 12, 1897, Supporting Protection of Antiquities (Approved by the Mixed Court of Appeals on June 19, 1897).

1. They shall be punished with a fine of 50 to 100 P.E. and imprisonment of 3 days to one week:
   1.1. those who, without being authorized, make excavations in terrain belonging to the Government;

---

[140] The system referred to as *partage* is based on this principle.
[141] Lit., "si ceux-ci ne prefèrent une attribution à l'amiable."

1.2. those who appropriate, or displace with the goal of appropriating, an antiquity belonging to the Government, outside of all objects found in the museums or buildings of the State;

1.3. those who by their actions destroy or degrade an antique monument, or cause the ruin of all or part of an antique construction, or have mutilated bas-reliefs, statues, inscriptions on the same constructions, or have written names or inscriptions on these same monuments;[142]

1.4. those who remove sebakh[143] from a prohibited place.

Order of September 10, 1905, Relating to the Transport of Antiquities by Railway

The Minister of Public Works,
Considering article 3 of the decree of December 10, 1878;
Considering the ministerial order No. 486, dated July 31, 1902;
On the proposal of the Administrative Council for State Railways;
Administrative Orders:

Art. 1. No antiquities shipment shall be admitted for transport, unless accompanied by an official authorization of the Cairo Antiquities Service which shall be permanently joined to the objects in the shipment, and may never be returned to either the shipper or the recipient.

Art. 2. In order to enjoy the preferential tariff [5th class instead of 1st],[144] the shipper must moreover produce a certificate from the same Service attesting that the expedition is destined for a public museum, be it Egyptian or Foreign.

Alexandria, September 10, 1905.

The Minister of Public Works, H. Fakhry.

Ministerial Order of December 7, 1909, No. 43, Relating to the Collection of Sebakh[145]

The Minister of Public Works,

---

[142] The inclusion of this early antigraffiti law gives insight into the social context and concerns of legislators.

[143] *Sebakh* (from the Arabic *s-b-kh*, meaning manure) here refers to soil from ancient burial sites containing a high percentage of decomposed human and animal remains, thus making it highly prized for fertilizer. Khater notes, "It is an Arabic word meaning manure, and has a specific sense for Egyptologists." The collection of sebakh was first regulated under the first Inspector of Antiquities, Youssef Zia Effendi, in the administrative order of November 1835. Khater, n. 4, at 43.

[144] Parenthetical contained in the original.

[145] *See* n. 14, *supra*.

Considering article 3 of the Decree of May 16, 1883, declaring monuments and objects of antiquity to be property of the of the Public Domain of the State; Considering the Decree of August 12, 1897, setting forth the penalties for certain infractions of interest to the Antiquities Service; Considering the approval of the Ministries of the Interior and of Finance; Administrative Order:

1. The extraction of sebakh accumulated on the tells[146] and ancient grounds may not take place except upon authorization of the Antiquities Service and upon the conditions which shall be prescribed in order to assure effective monitoring.
2. In order to exercise effective monitoring during the extraction of sebakh, the Antiquities Service, should it believe necessary, may name provisional guards: the salary of the guards mentioned shall be paid by the sebakh collectors, and may not exceed 5 piastres daily per man.

Those that collect sebakh shall provide in advance the approximate amount they intend to take, appraised by the Antiquities Service in accordance with the local authorities.

3. The ruins of stone or brick buildings, columns, stelae, inscriptions, statues, figurines, amulets, beads, jewels, copper, gold, and silver coins, papyri, parchments, sarcophagi, coffins, mummies of men and animals and all archeological objects of any value and of any epoch, which may be brought to light as a result of the sebakh operations, belong, under the term of article 3 of the Decree of May 16, 1883, already prescribed, to the Public Domain of the State and shall be reported to or given to the guard.
   Bricks, shards, glass debris, cut stones, cement, homra[147] and in general all ancient materials found dispersed in the sebakh shall be left in place at the determination of the Antiquities Service.
4. Whoever removes sebakh without authorization or outside of the limits and conditions of the authorization shall be considered as having removed sebakh from a prohibited place; consequently, the already prescribed Decree of August 12 shall be applied, without prejudicing the application of the most serious penal provisions, if it is necessary.
5. The extraction of sebakh from tells and grounds belonging to the State situated between Ain El-Sira[148] and the Mosque of Amru[149] shall continue to be governed by the Administrative Order of November 4, 1901.

[146]   A tell is a hill or ancient mound composed of remains of successive settlements.
[147]   Homra is brick rubble, which is sometimes used for building.
[148]   A neighborhood of Cairo near the Nile in which there is a Roman aqueduct.
[149]   This is the first mosque in Africa, in Fustat, the oldest part of modern Cairo.

6. The present administrative order is applicable to all tells and koms[150] of sebakh enumerated in the appendix hereby attached (this list has been published in the *Journal Officiel*).[151]

An administrative order of the Minister of Public Works shall suffice in order to add to the list any other tell or kom which it shall designate.

7. Mr. Director General of the Antiquities Service is charged with the execution of the present administrative order.

Cairo, December 7, 1909.
The Minister of Public Works,
(Signed): Ismail Sirry

Law No. 14 of 1912 on Antiquities

We, the Khedive of Egypt,
On the proposal of Our Minister of Public Works and with the assent of Our Council of Ministers;
The Legislative Council agreeing,
We decree:
Antiquities in General

Art. 1. Subject to the provisions of the present law, every antiquity found on, or in the ground, shall belong to the Public Domain of the State.

Art. 2. Legally, antiquities are deemed to be all manifestations and all products of the arts, sciences, literature, religion, manners, industries of Pharaonic, Greek, Roman, Byzantine and Coptic Egypt, pagan temples, what is abandoned and disused, chapels, basilisks and monasteries, as well as fortresses and city walls, houses, baths, nilometers, stone wells, cisterns, causeways, ancient quarries, obelisks, pyramids, mastabas,[152] funerary hypogea,[153] with or without above-ground structures, sarcophagi, all manner of coffins, decorated or not, mummy wrappings, mummies of men or animals, painted or gilded portraits and masks, stelae, naoi,[154] statues and statuettes, with or without inscriptions, inscriptions on rocks, ostraca,[155] manuscripts on skins, fabric, or papyrus, worked flints, arms, utensils, vases, glasswork, boxes and objects of offering, fabric and pieces

---

[150] Arabic, "refuse heap."
[151] Parenthetical contained in the original.
[152] Underground stone-lined burial vaults.
[153] Underground tombs or catacombs.
[154] Greek temples or shrines (sing. *naos*).
[155] Inscribed potsherds.

of clothing, ornaments, rings, jewels, scarabs and amulets of every form and manner, weights, coins, engraved stones and shells.

Art. 3. Equally deemed antiquities are the remains of walls and houses in stone or in terracotta or mud-brick, blocks of stone and sparse brick, fragments of stone, glass, or wood, shards, sand, homra,[156] and sebakh, which are found on or in the grounds belonging to the State and declared ancient by the Government.

Art. 4. However, antiquities belonging to the discoverer, by virtue of either Article 11 which follows, or by the terms of an excavation permit, as well as antiquities belonging to good faith private owners, may enter into the trade.

Art. 5. For the purposes of the present law, movable antiquities which are attached to the ground or are difficult to transport are assimilated with immovable antiquities.

Art. 6. All grounds belonging to the State, which are now or may be declared ancient by the Government, shall be part of the Public Domain.

Art. 7. All antiquities which are now or may be conserved in the museums of the State shall also be part of the Public Domain.

Immovable Antiquities

Art. 8. The Government may either proceed with the removal at any time of an immovable antiquity found on private property, or conserve it in place by expropriating the portion of the land on or in which it is found, conforming to laws in force on expropriation for the cause of public use.

In evaluating the indemnity for expropriation to be paid by the State, neither the existence nor the value of the antiquities found therein either in or on the ground shall be taken into account.

However, an indemnity fixed in this manner shall be increased by ten percent.

In the case where the Government proceeds with the removal of the antiquity, it shall be required to pay the owner of the land an indemnity equal to ten percent of the real value of the portion of the land taken up by the antiquity.

Art. 9. Every discoverer of an immovable antiquity, every owner, renter, or holder of land where an immovable antiquity has been discovered shall be held to give immediate notice, either to the nearest authority, or to local agents of the Antiquities Service.

For six weeks after the day of the declaration, the Antiquities Service may proceed with every measure of surveillance and with any useful investigation to determine the nature of the discovery, provided that things are returned to their normal state at the end of this time.

[156] *See* n. 18 *supra*.

Movable Antiquities

Art. 10. Whoever has found a movable antiquity on or in whatsoever land throughout the expanse of the Egyptian territory shall be held responsible, except where he is carrying a normally issued excavation permit, to report and present it within six days time to the closest administrative Authority or to the agents of the Antiquities Service, who will give him a receipt.

Art. 11. Whoever discovers a movable antiquity, except in the course of an illicit excavation, and who is in conformity with the regulations in the preceding article, shall receive as a bonus half of the objects found, or half of their value. Absent an agreement on amiable partition, the Antiquities Service shall take the objects it intends to keep. For the other objects, the partition into two shares of equal value shall be made by the Service, and the discoverer will have the right to choose between the two lots.

The two parties each shall set a price on the value of each object taken by the Service. If the discoverer does not accept half of the of price set by the Service, the Service shall have the power to take the object and pay the price designated by the discoverer, or to leave to the discoverer the object,[157] receiving from the discoverer half of the price which he himself had set on the object.[158]

Excavations

Art. 12. No one may carry out surveys, excavations, or clearings with the purpose of searching for antiquities, even on land belong to him, without preliminary authorization granted by the Minister of Public Works on the proposal of the Director General of the Antiquities Service.

This authorization shall fix the locality where the excavations may take place and the period in which they shall be valid.

The discoverer shall be granted a part of the antiquities found, or the value of that part, in conformance with the preceding article.

The following shall not be considered as having the goal of searching for antiquities: surveys, excavations and the removal of earth, if the person who

---

[157]   The Arabic translation of the text, provided below, is slightly clearer than the French,

"يكون عندها الحق بان اتاخد الاثر او تركه و ذلك بان تدفع نصف الثمن الذي بعين المكتشف."

al-Waqa'i' al-Misriyya. (Official Egyptian Gazette) Number 70, 29 Gamad II, 1330 (June 15, 1912) Cairo: 1913: 1675–77.

[158]   For the sake of clarity, translator has added subjects to the various verbs in this sentence based on pronoun analysis. The formula would be applied as follows for any and all objects which the Service has preemptively set aside: the Service will value the object at X and the discoverer will value it at Y. If the discoverer refuses to accept $\frac{1}{2}$ (X) in exchange for relinquishing his claim on the object, then the Service has two options. First, it can take the object and pay the discoverer his stated price Y; second, it can relinquish the object to the discoverer and receive $\frac{1}{2}$ (Y) in consideration for ceding the piece to him.

proceeded with this work had no reason to believe that the land could contain antiquities.

Sale of Antiquities

Art. 13. Every antiquities merchant must be provided with an authorization, which the Antiquities Service alone may grant or deny.

The Ministry of Public Works is charged with regulating the conditions for bringing antiquities into the trade, and in particular with setting their manner of certification as antiquities placed for sale.

Exportation of Antiquities

Art. 14. Exportation of antiquities is prohibited without a special authorization which the Antiquities Service alone may grant or deny.

Every antiquity attempted to be taken out of Egypt without authorization shall be seized and confiscated for the profit of the State.

Collection of Sebakh

Art. 15. The Antiquities Service may authorize the collection of sebakh in places and conditions which it shall determine.

Every antiquity found in the course of collecting sebakh shall be declared and handed over immediately to the guards supervising the removal.

Penalties

Art. 16. {The following} shall be punished with imprisonment not to exceed one year and a fine not to exceed 100 Egyptian Pounds, or only one of these two sentences:

1. Those who have displaced, battered, mutilated or destroyed in any way immovable antiquities.
2. Those who have seized, without the special authorization of the Government, materials originating in the total or partial destruction of immovable antiquities.
3. Those who have transformed hypogea, roadways, temples, and in general, all buildings or remains of ancient buildings, into dwellings for people or animals, depositories, tombs, or cemeteries, in addition to the sentence for the amount of damage caused thereby.

Art. 17. Further punishments with the same sentences:

1. Every infraction of the provisions of articles 9, 10, and 12 above.
2. Every sale or offer of sale of antiquities made outside of the conditions dictated in articles 4 and 13.

Art 18. {The following} shall be punished with imprisonment not to exceed one week and a fine not to exceed 1 Egyptian Pound, or only one of the two sentences:

1. Any collection of sebakh in a prohibited place, or outside of the regulatory conditions, as well as every infraction of the provisions of article 15.
2. The act of drawing names or inscriptions on immovable antiquities.

Art. 19. Every movable antiquity which has been the object of an infraction of the provisions of the present law may be seized and confiscated for the profit of the state.

Miscellaneous Provisions

Art. 20. Conservators, inspectors and sub-inspectors of the Antiquities Service, as well as the agents through whom they function shall be considered officers of the Criminal Investigation Department, inasmuch as concerns the duties with which they are charged.

Art. 21. The decrees mentioned in the appendix of the present law are abrogated in regards to those answerable to whom this law applies.

Art. 22. Our Ministers of Public Works are charged each inasmuch as he is concerned, with the execution of the present law, which shall enter into effect on July 12, 1912.

Done in Alexandria, 26 Gamad II 1330 (June 12, 1912).

Ministerial Order No. 50, December 8, 1912, Containing Regulations of Authorizations for Trading in Antiquities.

The Minister of Public Works,
In light of article 13 of Antiquities Law No. 14 of 1912;
Decree:

Art. 1. There are two types of authorizations of trading in antiquities:

1. Authorization for a merchant with an antiquities shop.
2. Authorization for a stall-keeper.[159]

Only duly authorized, first-class merchants may be authorized to open and maintain a shop; on the other hand, they may not deal in antiquities outside of the shop, or another, similar establishment mentioned in their authorizations.

The stall-keeper may be authorized to trade only in minor objects, the price of which may never exceed 5 Egyptian pounds, displaying them at the place, or at one of the places, mentioned in his permit.

---

[159]   "Vendeurs à l'étalage."

Art. 2. Authorizations for store merchants shall be granted by the Directorate-General of the Antiquities Service; those of the stall-keepers shall be granted by the local directorate of the aforementioned Service, after having obtained the opinion of the local authority.

All authorizations shall be strictly personal.

Art. 3. Requests for store merchant authorizations shall be addressed by interested parties to the Directorate-General of the Antiquities Service on paper with 3 piastres worth of stamps.

They shall contain:

1. The last name, first name, and domicile of the requesting party.
2. Indication of the premises where he would like to do business.
3. A certificate of the requesting party's criminal record.

Art. 5. Every shop merchant must keep a register, following the model approved by the Antiquities Service, where he shall keep a daily record, in numerical sequence, of the antiquities which he has acquired, with all the details of dimensions, material, color, etc., necessary for the identification of the object as well as the indications of provenance sufficient to establish that it has come into the trade.

When an object entered in the register is sold, mention shall be made in the register indicating, to the extent possible, the name and authority of the buyer.

Before being put to use, each page of the register must be initialed or sealed by an Inspector of the Antiquities Service.

The only articles for sale which shall be exempt from the present article are those whose worth does not exceed 5 Egyptian pounds.

Art. 6. None of the objects available for sale by the merchant shall be kept outside of the premises where he is authorized to conduct his business.

Art. 7. No antiquity shall be transported inside the country by the merchant without the written authorization of the Antiquities Service.

When a merchant owns more than one shop, transport from one to another shall be recorded in the registers of both establishments, as though for a sale or purchase.

Art. 8. The inspector of the Antiquities Service, either accompanied or unaccompanied by the Criminal Investigation Department, may enter, at any moment and in every part, premises assigned to the trading of antiquities, in order to inspect the register described in article 5, and to control for regular conduct, and to verify the merchant's stock. The merchant as well as the personnel of his establishment must facilitate the inspection as needed. At the end of the inspection, the inspector shall stamp the establishment's register and record in it any and all useful observations.

Art. 9. Without prejudice to the sentences stated above in article 17 of the aforementioned Law, the unauthorized pursuit of the occupation of merchant or seller of antiquities shall be punished by imprisonment not exceeding 7 days and a fine not exceeding 1 Egyptian pound, or only one of the two sentences.

Art. 10. In the case of conviction for infraction of the provisions of the present regulation, the judge may always order the withdrawal of the authorization. In the event of a second conviction committed in the same year as the first, withdrawal of authorization shall be mandatory.

The authorization may always be withdrawn by the Antiquities Service, in case of conviction for one of the infractions of the aforementioned Law.

Art. 11. The present regulation shall enter into effect on January 1, 1913.

Cairo, December 8, 1912.
The Minister of Public Works,
(Signed): Ismail Sirry

Ministerial Order No. 5 of December 8, 1912, Containing Regulations for the Exportation of Antiquities

The Minister of Public Works,
In light of article 14 of Antiquities Law 14 of 1912;

Art. 1. All persons wishing to export antiquities by sea or land shall request written authorization on plain paper to the Antiquities Service General Supervisory Administration, to obtain the authorization required by article 14 of Antiquities Law 14 of 1912.

Art. 2. The request shall contain the first and last name, authority and nationality of the requestor, as well as indication of the port or point of exit. At the same time, the objects and the parcels or cases containing them shall be presented for examination by the Supervisory Administration, with a list indicating the number of pieces, their nature, their dimensions and their purchase or commercial value. The parcels or cases shall contain only Egyptian objects from Pharaonic, Greco-Roman, Byzantine or Coptic times; the presence of an object from any other epoch shall cause refusal of authorization.

Art. 3. In cases where the examination does not reveal the presence of any object of suspect origin, authorization shall be issued without delay. If the presence of any object of suspect origin is revealed, and the explanations furnished by the requestor are not recognized as satisfactory by the Service, these objects shall be removed; otherwise authorization shall be refused for all.

Art. 4. The parcels or cases containing the objects for which exit has been authorized shall be wrapped in wire held in place by one or more seals; the requestor shall pay, for each parcel or case, a fee of 4 piastres to be used to cover the cost of operation.[160] He must at the same time pay an export fee of 1.5%[161] on the declared value of the objects, from which the amount shall be turned over to the Customs Duty Administration by the General Administration of the Service.

Art. 5. After the completion of the formalities and the payment of related fees, the General Administration shall issue to the requestor:

1. A certificate addressed to the Administration of State Railways, which shall be issued by it[162] or its representative to the authorities of the station from which it shall send the parcels or cases containing the objects.
2. A certificate addressed in duplicate to the Customs Duty Administration certifying that the export fees have been paid. One of the two copies shall rest in the possession of the requestor or his representative, the other shall be sent by care of the Service to the customs duty of the city or the port of exit.

Art. 6. The same examination formalities shall be required for parcels sent by post. However, parcels containing objects must be fixed securely with a string, the two ends of which shall be held by a seal in wax or metal. A printed pass, taken from a stock book and signed by a representative of the Service, shall be affixed to the parcel.

No fee other than that of sealing shall be required for parcels sent by post in this way.[163]

Art. 7. Parcels or boxes shall be presented to the railway bureaus, to customs, and the post with seals intact, on pain of being seized and returned to the Antiquities Service for investigation.

Art. 8. The present regulation shall enter into effect after January 1, 1913.

Cairo, December 8, 1912.
The Minister of Public Works,
(Signed): Ismail Sirry.

---

[160] Khater's footnote: The sealing duty had been set at 6 piastres after January 27, 1916, as indicated in Ministerial Order No. 8 dated February 10, 1921, published in the *Journal Officiel* No. 16, February 17, 1921.
[161] Khater's footnote: The export duty had been seat at $2^1/_2$% after January 27, 1916.
[162] The General Administration of the Antiquities Service.
[163] Khater's footnote: Ministerial Order No. 8 of February 1921 appended the following to Article 6: Apart from the sealing fee, the requestor must at the same time pay an export duty of 2.5% of the declared value of the objects, which shall be collected by the Antiquities Service which shall carry out the transfer to the Customs Duty Administration.

Ministerial Order No. 52 of December 8, 1912, Concerning the Regulation of Excavations

The Minister of Public Works,
In light of article 14 of Antiquities Law No. 14 of 1912;
Decides:

Art. 1. Authorizations for excavations shall be granted by the Minister of Public Works on the proposal of the Director-General of the Antiquities Service after a favorable opinion from the Egyptology Committee.

Provisional authorizations for excavations or preliminary studies may be given by the Director-General for a period which may not exceed one month, on the condition that he refer the matter to the Minister, and to the Egyptology Committee in its first useful meeting.

Art. 2. Authorization shall be granted only to scientists in charge of a mission or recommended officially by governments, universities, academies, scientific societies, and to individuals who appear to present sufficient guaranties. These latter must, if they are not already known for their field work, secure the aid of a scientist reputed as having the necessary experience to direct their undertaking.

Art. 3. Authorizations shall be granted solely for one entire season or for any unspecified part of a season, without detriment to the provisions of article 16 hereafter. The entire season includes the time that passes between November 15 of a year and November 14 of the following year.

Art. 4. Authorizations may not be granted for more than two sites at once for the same individual, nor for representatives of the same government, university, society, or academy.

Art. 5. Requests for authorizations shall be addressed, as often as possible before October 25 of each year, to the Directorate-General of the Antiquities Service in Cairo.

They must contain:

1. The first and last name, rank or posts, domicile, and nationality of the requestor.
2. In the case of official mission or recommendation, mention of the Government, University, Academy, or Scientific Society which gave them, with supporting documents.
3. In the case of a private individual not possessing the desired experience to direct the work in person, the first and last name, positions, and nationality of the scientist with whom he intends to be associated.
4. The exact indication, with map or supporting sketch, of the site, and the limits of the site or sites which he proposes to exploit.

5. A summary exposition of the goal of the excavations and the program of work to be carried out.

6. Authorizations may hold only for one part of the site or sites requested.

Art. 7. Every agent shall be held accountable for paying out to the Secretariat of the Antiquities Service, at the end of each campaign, and for each day which passes between the beginning and the ending of the work, the sum of 10 piastres, which shall be allocated to defray the cost of guarding the site or sites granted to him. However, where he likes, he may be accompanied throughout the duration of the work by a delegate of the Service, to whom he shall pay the sum of 20 piastres a day by way of compensation, in addition to round-trip travel costs. He must declare his course of action upon being given authorization.

Art. 8. Every authorization shall entail the obligation to continue work, on the site or on each of the sites granted, for at least 60 days over the course of the period for which it was granted.

Art. 9. The agent shall be held to leave [the following things] in place and to put them back into their original state, if their displacement or temporary deposition were authorized by the terms of his permit:

1. Monuments fixed on the ground, whatever their state, which in the judgment of the General Administration must be kept in place, as well as detached fragments that it wishes to have put back into position,

2. Entirely shifted objects that the General Administration shall judge must be removed, or kept as they are, in place.

3. Heavy objects which the agent refuses to carry away at his own cost.

Art. 10. It shall be prohibited to make wet-process rubbings on monuments, or to expose them to any maneuver that would risk damaging them.

Art. 11. The movable objects found by the agent in the course of excavations carried out in conformity with the provisions of his permit, shall be divided between him and the Government, as provided in article 11 of Antiquities Law No. 14 of 1912. The *partage*[164] will be performed on the spot, or at the Museum, according to whether the excavator, or the Director-General, or his representative, have requested it; in either case, the transportation of the pieces which have been subjected to *partage* to the Museum shall be made at the excavator's expense.

---

[164] An elaborate process for dividing up excavated objects between the Egyptian government and the excavators. *See* Decree of November 17, 1891, *supra*, for description.

Art. 12. The agent shall receive, upon written request to the Service, the necessary permits for internal transportation and for exportation of movable objects which he has found.

Moreover, it shall be possible for him to be issued certificates noting the entry into the trade of each important piece due to him from the *partage*.

Art. 13. At the end of the excavation, the permit holder must fill the trenches and wells, bury the fragments of mummies or coffins, and, in a general fashion, put the grounds on which they have been operating back into place to the satisfaction of the Antiquities Service. He shall not be authorized to export his portion of the objects found until the Antiquities Service has certified the satisfactory state of the grounds.

However, the excavator who has been strictly in conformance with the conditions of his authorization, and who wishes to resume his work the following year, may be authorized, if the nature of the places permits it, to leave them in the state in which they were found at the end of the campaign. He must, in this case, make human bones and debris of the same genre disappear, as their presence might shock visitors or passers-by.

Art. 14. He shall give to the General Administration, at the end of each campaign:

1. A map, or at least a sketch, of the field of excavations, with a legend indicating the position of objects and monuments discovered.
2. A list of all these objects and monuments, including among the latter those which are due to him from the *partage*.
3. A summary report containing a work history and indication of the principal results obtained, with references to the map and the list.

Art. 15. Agents as well as the universities, academies, and societies they represent, must deposit in the Museum library and in the Khedival Library[165] a copy of the works, samples, [and] collected engravings published through their care on the facts revealed and objects discovered in the course of their excavations.

Art. 16. When the agent who has been strictly in conformance with the conditions of his authorization and who, before the end of his campaign, has addressed a request tendering the renewal of his authorization for the next season to the General Administration, this renewal shall be granted to him, unless the Minister, on reasoned opinion of the Egyptology Committee, supported by the Director-General, decides otherwise.

---

[165]   The Viceroy's Library. The Viceroy was the ruler of Egypt, later known as the Khedive.

However, if it has been noted that he is not able to maintain all the work sites open at the points of a site at the same time, the renewal shall be granted solely for a portion of the site.

Art. 17. In the event of infraction of any of the conditions of the authorization, work may be suspended by the Director-General or by all agents of the Service authorized to do so, until the state of infraction has ceased. The authorization may even be withdrawn, in the case of a serious infraction, by order of the Minister of Public Works, taken on reasoned opinion of the Egyptology Committee, supported by the Director-General.

Art. 18. In addition to the clauses having the goal of giving effect to the provisions of the present regulation, excavation authorizations may contain all technical conditions which, proposed by the Director-General, shall be approved by the Egyptology Committee.

Art. 19. The present regulation shall come into effect as of January 1, 1913.

Cairo, December 8, 1912.
Minister of Public Works,
(Signed): Ismail Sirry

8 NAGPRA FROM THE MIDDLE DISTANCE

Legal Puzzles and Unintended Consequences

Michael F. Brown and Margaret M. Bruchac[1]

The global decolonization movement that gathered strength after World War II began to shake the genteel world of museums and cultural repositories in the 1980s. Works of art acquired by warriors, explorers, and, in more recent times, professional looters became the focus of concerted diplomatic efforts by countries determined to see the restitution of their national patrimony. Many improperly acquired items have been returned to their original private owners or national museums; countless cases involving more ambiguous provenance await final resolution. It is safe to say that mere possession of art objects no longer guarantees that museums will be able to retain title to them indefinitely.

This same trend has sparked a revolution among institutions that manage material collected among the world's indigenous peoples. The scope of collections under dispute encompasses not just works of aesthetic value but human remains, religious objects, and in some cases even the raw archaeological or ethnographic information associated with them. If the complexities of Western fine-art repatriation cases seem formidable, these are eclipsed by the legal puzzles associated with the repatriation of museum holdings to indigenous communities. European governments may disagree about who should hold title to specific cultural treasures, but at least they share a general understanding of the objects' significance and the kinds of evidence that can disprove or substantiate claims to them. When museum curators sit across

---

[1] For help in understanding the complexities of repatriation, we wish to thank James Bradley, C. Wesley Cowan, T. J. Ferguson, Martha Graham, Robert L. Kelly, William L. Merrill, Donna Moody, John Moody, David Hurst Thomas, and Joe E. Watkins, among others. The opinions expressed here, however, are ours alone. For their memorable hospitality at the Imperialism, Art and Restitution conference at Washington University-St Louis, Michael Brown wishes to thank John O. Haley, John Henry Merryman, and Steven J. Gunn.

a negotiating table from a delegation of indigenous people, in contrast, they are likely to find themselves confronted by unfamiliar ways of thinking and talking about cultural property, a gulf that greatly complicates efforts to resolve contesting views.

In the United States, the principal force behind the return of cultural property to indigenous peoples is the Native American Graves Protection and Repatriation Act (Public Law 101-601), better known as NAGPRA, a measure enacted in 1990. The implementation of NAGPRA prompted anthropologists to examine their profession with a critical eye, to weigh the thoughtless and sometimes shameful behavior of anthropology's intellectual ancestors against more recent efforts to set matters right. For some, the discipline's role in the systematic collection of human skeletal materials and religious objects has summoned emotions that approach professional self-loathing. Anthropology, they charge, was a willing partner in acts of colonial oppression. Others evince little sympathy for such self-criticism, opting instead to defend science against what they scornfully dismiss as the emotionalism and science hatred of the repatriation movement. Our own informal queries suggest that a solid majority of anthropologists support NAGPRA but remain uneasy about its implications for future anthropological research and the management of ethnographic and archaeological collections.

Among Native peoples in the United States, NAGPRA is heralded as landmark legislation, a restoration of respect to ancestors whose remains have long been considered the property of non-Native others.[2] On the surface, NAGPRA is about intercultural reparations. The legislation was grounded in recognition that alienation of human remains and items of cultural patrimony violated Native religious traditions and common-law rights to protect the dead.[3] The impassioned nature of repatriation debate makes finding uncontested ground from which one can both assess the direction of relevant policies and make constructive suggestions about how to pursue them fairly difficult. This situation is not helped by the insistence of some of the movement's most respected proponents that repatriation must be seen primarily

[2] Since the NAGPRA legislation defines *Indian*, and *tribe* as terms exclusive to federally recognized tribes, in this chapter we have chosen to use the term *Native* as an inclusive generic for all of the indigenous peoples of the United States, whether or not they are acknowledged as sovereign peoples by the United States government.

[3] Jack E. Trope and Walter R. Echo-Hawk, "The Native American Graves Protection and Repatriation Act: Background and Legislative History." In *Repatriation Reader: Who Owns American Indian Remains,* ed. Devon A. Mihesuah. Lincoln and London: University of Nebraska Press, 2000, pp. 123–168 (essay originally published in 1992).

as a human-rights issue.[4] Although repatriation has a human-rights dimension primarily relating to the free exercise of religion, the discourse of human rights gravitates toward an absolutism that inhibits necessary discussion about how repatriation claims can best be framed and adjudicated in a multicultural and intertribal context. The discourse of property, also invoked in repatriation talk, has flaws of its own. Clearly, repatriation demands a synthetic approach that blends principles of human rights and property law with emerging ideas about how intercultural justice can best be achieved in postcolonial situations.

Rather than approaching the repatriation movement as a vast exercise in moral indemnification and cultural reclamation, which of course it is, we propose to examine it as an administrative puzzle whose contours are more visible now – the "middle distance" of our title – than they were in 1990. How does this important legislation deal with the cultural differences and distinctive histories that mark the nation's hundreds of Native societies? Given the varied survival strategies of Native people, does the law accommodate groups whose legal statuses may differ significantly? What kinds of evidence should be accepted in repatriation decisions? By imposing an Anglo-American legal framework on issues of cultural property, is NAGPRA yet another tool of colonialism? Because NAGPRA has now been in effect for a decade and half, its social consequences – both intended and unintended – have much to teach us about the possibilities and limitations of public efforts to make adequate reparations for historical wrongs.

BACKGROUND: NAGPRA'S LOGISTICS AND SCALE

In broad strokes, NAGPRA can be described as a federal law that gives federally recognized Native tribes, Native Hawaiian organizations, and Native individuals the right to petition for return of human remains and certain categories of artifacts for which these individuals and groups can establish lineal descent or prior ownership. Federal agencies, as well as all public or private institutions that receive any form of federal support, are required to inventory items in their collections that the law defines as potentially subject to repatriation. This information must be distributed to those federally recognized Indian tribes that, in the opinion of the repository, might

---

4   "[T]he bill before us is not about the validity of museums or the validity of scientific inquiry. Rather, it is about human rights": Senator Daniel Inouye. In 136 Congressional Record S17174, October 26, 1990. Quoted in Jack E. Trope and Walter R. Echo-Hawk, op. cit., p. 127.

conceivably come forward with repatriation requests. Similar rules for disclosure, consultation, and possible repatriation also apply to new discoveries on federal and tribal lands.[5]

The challenges of complying with the law cannot be fully grasped without first considering the scale of the repatriation enterprise in the United States. Estimates of the total number of Native American individuals whose remains are held in U.S. museums vary widely, the most credible falling in the neighborhood of 200,000.[6] Whatever the actual number, we know that the remains are numerous, that many are not well curated, and that the records associated with them are highly variable in their completeness and accuracy. At Harvard's Peabody Museum alone, the staff has had to review the status of 8 million archaeological items, including skeletal materials from approximately 12,000 individuals, to meet NAGPRA's reporting requirements.[7] One can immediately see how complex an undertaking it is to identify these materials and determine whether they can be affiliated with existing Indian tribes.

On the Native side of the equation, many federally recognized tribes have found themselves inundated by NAGPRA summaries and inventories that they were ill equipped to evaluate because of a lack of trained staff. NAGPRA is a classic instance of an underfunded federal mandate that imposes substantial burdens on agencies, museums, and tribes alike. The government disbursed approximately $22 million in NAGPRA implementation grants to tribes and institutions in the ten-year period between 1994 and 2003. This represents only a small fraction of the actual cost of repatriation – a cost that some observers contend is disproportionately shouldered by Native tribes. The availability of funding often determines the level of participation of the 562 federally recognized tribes and approximately

[5]   On NAGPRA's legislative history, see Trope and Echo-Hawk, op. cit. For an engaging overview of the history that made NAGPRA necessary, see David Hurst Thomas, *Skull Wars: Kennewick Man, Archaeology, and the Battle for Native American Identity*, New York: Basic Books, 2000. Space considerations prevent us from discussing the National Museum of the American Indian Act (Public Law 101–185, passed in 1989), companion legislation that provides for the repatriation of remains and artifacts held by the museums of the Smithsonian Institution.

[6]   For estimates of the number of individuals represented by American skeletal collections, see, among others, Jerome C. Rose, Thomas J. Green, and Victoria D. Green, "NAGPRA Is Forever: Osteology and the Repatriation of Skeletons," *Annual Review of Anthropology* (1996) 25: 84.

[7]   Barbara Isaac, "Implementation of NAGPRA: The Peabody Museum of Archaeology and Ethnology, Harvard," In Cressida Fforde, Jane Hubert, and Paul Turnbull, eds., *The Dead and Their Possessions: Repatriation in Principle, Policy and Practice*, New York: Routledge, 2002, pp. 160–170.

300 unrecognized tribes who have an interest in the NAGPRA process.[8] Particularly hard to measure is the impact of NAGPRA on museums that have had to curtail normal activities in order to ramp up the research and record keeping necessary to comply with the law. At some institutions, including the Smithsonian's National Museum of Natural History, almost all new hiring through the 1990s was focused on repatriation staff rather than on employees supporting normal curatorial and educational operations. This doubtless affected the institution's ability to pursue other programs closer to its core mission.

The National Park Service has been assigned the task of administering NAGPRA and monitoring compliance efforts.[9] Its May 2003 report notes that 861 institutions, including 165 federal agencies, had submitted summaries detailing their holdings of unassociated funerary objects, sacred objects, and items of cultural patrimony. Inventories of human remains and associated grave goods had been received from 815 institutions, including 261 federal agencies. Inventories published or scheduled to be published in the *Federal Register* include 27,863 sets of human remains and 564,726 associated funerary objects (including beads and other small objects), 1,185 sacred objects, and 267 items of cultural patrimony as defined by the law. Most of these will eventually be repatriated to federally recognized Indian tribes. Because the law does not require the maintenance of centralized records on completed repatriations, precise information on how much has actually been returned to Native communities is not readily available. The

---

[8]   On federal grants to support repatriation research and activities, see National NAG-PRA, National Park Service, *National NAGPRA FY03 Annual Report*, p. 8. On the law's economic impact on Indian tribes, see Roger Anyon and Russell Thornton, "Implementing Repatriation in the United States: Issues Raised and Lessons Learned," in Cressida Fforde, Jane Hubert, and Paul Turnbull, eds., *The Dead and Their Possessions: Repatriation in Principle, Policy and Practice*, London: Routledge, pp. 190–198. For a list of the 562 federally recognized U.S. Indian tribes as of July 12, 2002, see the *Federal Register* 67 (No. 143), Notices pp. 46327–46333. Approximately 290 tribes are curently awaiting consideration of their intent to petition for federal recognition through the Bureau of Indian Affairs Branch of Acknowledgement and Recognition. Many of these tribes find that their NAGPRA claims are ignored by museums, on the basis of the false presumption that NAGPRA only applies to federally recognized tribes.

[9]   The National Park Service's (NPS's) role as NAGPRA's administrating agency is somewhat awkward because the NPS also controls substantial collections of human remains and other potentially repatriatable items of cultural property. This dual role has occasionally sparked complaints that the NPS's interests are inherently in conflict. For brief discussion, see National Park Service, Minutes of NAGPRA Review Committee, 21st Meeting, May 31–June 2, 2001, p. 24.

cost of completing the process of inventorying, consulting, repatriating, and reburying Native remains has been conservatively estimated by national NAGPRA staff to average $581 per individual burial.[10]

The process of inventorying and identifying Native collections is complicated by the complex manner in which they were accumulated. For decades, networks of professional and amateur archaeologists, historians, and private collectors participated in a nationwide trade in "Indian relics." Native skeletal remains and funerary objects were routinely separated from their original context for sale, trade, or exhibition. Native mortuary practices, spiritual beliefs, tools, and sacred objects were interpreted by using a bewildering array of theories and categorical sorting methods, with no reference to Native points of view. The documentary record of many Native collections is, as a result, woefully inadequate for the task of accurately identifying the source, use, sacredness, and tribal affiliation of Native remains and artifacts.[11]

To facilitate the research and reporting process, national NAGPRA maintains online, keyword-searchable databases of legislation, notices, inventories, and meeting minutes. National NAGPRA staff also provide consulting and training for institutions and tribes. But this process has not always led to more collaborative reporting procedures. Since the passage of the law, some museums have responded to the impending loss, potential illegality, and shifting cultural interpretations of their Native collections by restricting access to information. Exhibits have been pulled from view, valuable items have been placed under lock and key, and consultations have been initiated in an often secretive manner.

Because museums submit their NAGPRA inventories independently of one another, it is possible for different museums, each holding body parts or funerary objects from the same burial site, to assign them different tribal

[10] Data are from National Park Service, *National NAGPRA FY03 Annual Report*, p. 2, and National Park Service, National NAGPRA, "Frequently Asked Questions," updated December 30, 2003, p. 5, www.cr.nps.gov/nagpra/FAQ/ INDEX.HTM (accessed January 15, 2004). On the estimated processing cost per repatriated individual, see C. Timothy McKeown and Sherry Hutt, "In the Smaller Scope of Conscience: The Native American Graves Protection & Repatriation Act Twelve Years After," *UCLA Journal of Environmental Law & Policy* 21 (2), Winter 2003, Vol. 21 Issue 2 pl 53 (60).

[11] This brief summary is part of a longer analysis of how the nature of the collecting process systematically destroyed clear recognition of the original indigenous context. See Margaret Bruchac, "Background History of Regional Collections of Native American Indian Skeletal Remains from the Middle Connecticut River Valley," working report for the Five College Repatriation Committee, December 2004.

affiliations and eventually repatriate them to different tribes. For example, at least five different museums are known to have excavated Native remains from a site in Greenfield, Massachusetts, known as "Cheapside," which is well documented as being located in Pocumtuck Indian territory. Nevertheless, the Robert S. Peabody Museum at Harvard University identifies remains and funerary objects from all sites in Greenfield and nearby Deerfield as "Nipmuc." The Springfield Science Museum identifies them as some unknown combination of "Stockbridge Mohican," "Aquinnah Wampanoag," and "Narragansett." By contrast, four other local institutions (Smith College, Amherst College, the Pocumtuck Valley Memorial Association, and the University of Massachusetts Amherst, the latter now tasked with curating a number of Native remains collected from Cheapside pending their repatriation) have all unequivocally identified these individuals as "Pocumtuck" on the basis of historical documentation, collectors' records, and tribal consultations. The situation would be absurd were it not so tragic.[12]

Unexpected problems of a different sort arise from the recent discovery that many museum objects subject to repatriation under NAGPRA are often dangerously toxic after decades of fumigation in storage facilities. The scant literature on the extent of this contamination conveys alarming results. A recent study of toxic chemicals in seventeen objects repatriated to the Hupa tribe of northern California, for instance, found high levels of mercury, napthalene, and (DDT). Arsenic has been found in high concentrations in objects repatriated elsewhere.[13] This toxicity may be manageable if the objects are destined for display cabinets in tribal museums. But many tribes wish to return religious objects to active use. The goal for sacred masks, for instance, may be to use them in ceremonies until they are worn out and discarded in religiously appropriate ways. This clearly poses a substantial health risk to tribal members and may even pose a risk of groundwater contamination from reburial. Some tribes are contemplating the creation

---

[12] Records in local archives document the shared collecting activities of Amherst College, Harvard College, Smith College, and the Springfield Science Museum, at the most popular Native sites. See *Edward Hitchcock Jr. Papers*, Amherst College Archives, Amherst, MA; *George Sheldon Papers*, Memorial Libraries, Deerfield, MA; *Harris Hawthorne Wilder Papers*, Smith College Archives, Northampton, MA: among others. Also see Harris Hawthorne Wilder and Ralph Wheaton Whipple, "The Position of the Body in Aboriginal Interments in Western Massachusetts," *American Anthropologist* (1917) 19: 372–387.

[13] Peter T. Palmer et al., "Analysis of Pesticide Residues on Museum Objects Repatriated to the Hupa Tribe of California," *Environmental Science and Technology* 37, no. 6 (2003): 1083–1088.

Figure 8.1. The Peace Hat, a Russian-made brass hat commissioned for peace negotiations after battles between Russians and Tlingit Indians in 1802 and 1804, is ceremonially presented to Fred Hope, *left*, leader of the Kiksadi Point House, on July 19, 2003, in Sitka, Alaska. The hat was repatriated by the American Museum of Natural History in response to a NAGPRA claim. AP/Wide World Photos.

of facilities in which repatriated objects can be housed safely while scientists work to develop effective decontamination methods; others have declined to accept poisoned objects.[14] (See Figure 8.1.)

In sum, NAGPRA requires museums and federal agencies to review the attributes and acquisition histories of thousands of items in their care,

[14] The contamination issue was discussed during the public-comment period at a NAG-PRA Review Committee meeting in 2001. Leigh Kuwanwisiuwma of the Hopi Tribe notes that the Hopi had temporarily halted repatriation of items that would otherwise be used by them, pending the implementation of procedures for decontaminating artifacts. See National Park Service, Minutes of NAGPRA Review Committee, 21st Meeting, May 31–June 2, 2001, p. 34. In 2001, the Society for the Preservation of Natural History Collections also focused on the issue of contamination. See "Contaminated Collections: An Overview of the Legal, Ethical and Regulatory Issues" by Rebecca Tsosie, Arizona State University College of Law; "Poisoned Heritage: Curatorial Assessment and Implications of Pesticide Residues in Anthropological Collections" by James D. Nason, Thomas Burke Memorial Washington State Museum and Department of Anthropology, University of Washington; and "Poisoning the Sacred" by G. Peter Jemison, Seneca Nation of Indians, among others. Society for the Preservation of Natural History Collections Collection Forum for Fall 2001, Volume 17, Number 1 & 2, http://www.spnhc.org/documents/CF17-1_2.htm (accessed February 1, 2005).

reconcile records that may be inconsistent or of doubtful accuracy, examine items that may never have been studied in a systematic way, enter into consultation with scores or even hundreds of Indian tribes or Native Hawaiian communities, and ascertain whether repatriatable objects can be safely handled. For their part, Native communities must attempt to gain access to NAGPRA reports created by institutions that are believed to hold related collections, gather information to substantiate repatriation claims, and reach agreements, both internal and external, about the ultimate disposition of objects that qualify for repatriation. It should be clear from this brief sketch that in its ambition and scale repatriation is a formidably complex enterprise, joining what Max Weber identified as the technical expertise and codified rationalism of bureaucratic legal systems, on the one hand, and on the other the most primordial of community sentiments, including a people's feelings about its dead.

IDENTITY, AFFILIATION, AND LEGAL STANDING

At the heart of most repatriation cases is the question of cultural affiliation – that is, whether a community requesting the return of artifacts or human remains can show that it has, in the language of NAGPRA, "a relationship of shared group identity which can be reasonably traced historically or prehistorically between a present day Indian tribe or Native Hawaiian organization and an identifiable earlier group" from which the material was taken.[15] One can immediately see countless possibilities for uncertainty and disagreement. What exactly do we mean by group identity when confronting what James Clifford calls "a living tradition's combined and uneven processes of continuity, rupture, transformation, and revival"?[16]

In principle, affiliation might seem easy to establish. A Native group can assert a close historical connection to materials taken from areas that it now occupies, and that it has occupied for centuries. But even apparently simple cases become difficult as the time depth between object and petitioning group increases. This is an issue contested in the widely discussed "Kennewick Man" case (*Bonnichsen v. US*). In concurring with the federal district court decision denying a request to repatriate the remains to

---

[15] Native American Graves Protection and Repatriation Act, Section 2 (2) of 104 Stat. 3048 Public Law 101–601–Nov. 16, 1990, http://www.cr.nps.gov/nagpra/MANDATES/25USC3001etseq.htm (accessed February 12, 2005).

[16] James Clifford, "Indigenous Articulations," *The Contemporary Pacific* 13, no. 2 (2001): 480.

a consortium of Indian tribes in the Northwest, the Ninth Circuit Court of Appeals held that there is no established affiliation between Kennewick Man and the tribes that claim him – or, beyond that, to any existing Native American group – because the age of the remains apparently makes such connections implausible. If the *Bonnichsen* ruling stands, it is likely to invite additional litigation testing the temporal limits of cultural affiliation. But is the courtroom the proper venue for situating ethnicity and settling questions of human history? Collaboration among archaeologists and Native knowledge bearers may be far more productive than litigation in resolving such issues. Scientific theories and academic practices – the legacy of what Roger Echo-Hawk calls "conquest archaeology" – and indigenous oral traditions all have inherent limitations in constructing our views of ancient human history.[17]

Equally complex is the question of legal standing in repatriation claims. NAGPRA specifically provides for the return of remains and funerary objects to lineal descendants of the deceased. If no direct lineal descendants come forward, the law allows other individuals or groups claiming the same cultural affiliation to pursue repatriation. As Tamara Bray and Lauryn Guttenplan Grant point out in their assessment of an important repatriation case involving the Smithsonian, such a broad definition of standing "potentially expands the scope of this legal principle far beyond its traditional bounds."[18]

In its attempts to define the players, NAGPRA has changed the terminology of indigenous nationhood. In NAGPRA-speak, the term *Native American* encompasses all of the continent's indigenous peoples, but only federally recognized "tribes" can claim to be "culturally affiliated" and "culturally identified" with museum collections. Lineal descendants may make a similar claim, but only if they can produce sufficient documentation to prove it. The remains and artifacts of federally unrecognized tribes and

---

[17] Roger Echo-Hawk, "Forging a New Ancient History for Native America." In Nina Swidler, Kurt E. Dongoske, Roger Anyon, and Alan S. Downer, eds., *Native Americans and Archaeologists: Stepping Stones to Common Ground*, Walnut Creek, CA: AltaMira Press 1997, pp. 88–102. Suzanne J. Crawford, "(Re)Constructing Bodies: Semiotic Sovereignty and the Debate over Kennewick Man." In *Repatriation Reader: Who Owns American Indian Remains*, Devon A. Mihesuah, ed., Lincoln and London: University of Nebraska Press, 2000, pp. 211–236.

[18] Tamara L. Bray and Lauryn Guttenplan Grant, "The Concept of Cultural Affiliation and Its Legal Significance in the Larsen Bay Repatriation." In Tamara L. Bray and Thomas W. Killion, eds., *Reckoning with the Dead: The Larsen Bay Repatriation and the Smithsonian Institution*, Washington, DC: Smithsonian Institution Press, 1994, p. 155.

tribes that are no longer extant as political entities are all categorized as "culturally-unaffiliated" and "culturally-unidentifiable."[19] The terminology of the NAGPRA legislation has had an insidious effect on intertribal discourse regarding sovereignty. Despite an emerging preference for the term *nation* to describe sovereign Native communities, both recognized and unrecognized, the term *tribe*, as used by NAGPRA, now carries more legal weight.

Just as NAGPRA grants a broad right of standing to federally recognized Native tribes, in other words, it explicitly marginalizes tribes that lack this important status.[20] Since unrecognized tribes receive no federal funding for NAGPRA work, their repatriation representatives tend to operate on a shoestring budget. By contrast, federally recognized tribes can apply for NAGPRA funding, including office and travel expenses, above and beyond whatever tribal resources they have at their disposal. Combined with an aggressive approach to initiating consultations, this has given recognized tribes a bigger foot in the door and led many otherwise well-meaning

[19]   The NAGPRA "Final Rule," enacted in 1995, instituted the use of the terms *culturally affiliated* and *culturally identifiable* to apply exclusively to federally recognized tribes. NAGPRA requires institutions to alter their records to identify Native remains as "known" or "unknown," on the basis of not the state of actual knowledge about their identity and history, but the current federal legal status of their descendants. Under Section 10.10 (g), all remains that are not associated with a federally recognized tribe "must be considered culturally unidentifiable" [43 CFR 10.10(g)]. See *Federal Register*, December 4, 1995 (Volume 60, Number 232), Rules and Regulations, Page 62133–62169, posted on the National NAGPRA Web site, http://www.cr.nps.gov/nagpra/MANDATES/43CFR10_12-4-95.htm (accessed February 6, 2005). Also see the new "Culturally Unidentifiable Native American Inventories Pilot Database," http://64.241.25.6/CUI_pilot/index.cfm (accessed February 6, 2005). The NAGPRA Review Committee acknowledges that "there are some cases in which nonfederally recognized tribes may be appropriate claimants." See "Frequently Asked Questions," http://www.cr.nps.gov/nagpra/ FAQ/ INDEX.HTM#Non-Federal (accessed February 6, 2005).

[20]   This misunderstanding seems to arise from ambiguous wording in the NAGPRA legislation enacted on November 16, 1990. Section 2 (3) (D) (7), specifies *Indian tribe* to mean only those federally – recognized Native communities who are "eligible for the special programs and services provided by the United States to Indians." Section 2 (3) (D) (9), however, defines *Native American* to include all of the indigenous peoples of the United States, whether recognized by the federal government or not. See Native American Graves Protection and Repatriation Act [104 STAT.3048 PUBLIC LAW 101–601 – NOV. 16, 1990] posted on the national NAGPRA Web site, http://www.cr.nps.gov/nagpra/MANDATES/ 25USC3001etseq.htm (accessed February 6, 2005).

museums to choose the course of least resistance by working with the first federally recognized tribe who comes calling.

Fortunately, this has not prevented some museums from voluntarily repatriating human remains to unrecognized tribes when compelling evidence of descent or cultural affiliation exists. In some regions, unrecognized tribes have also evoked ancient intertribal relationships to initiate successful partnerships with their neighboring recognized tribes. In 1999, for instance, the NAGPRA Review Committee recommended that the Harvard Peabody Museum of Archaeology and Ethnology repatriate thirty sets of Native skeletal remains from New Hampshire and Vermont directly to the Abenaki Nation of Missisquoi, an unrecognized group. Letters of support were supplied by several of the surrounding federally recognized tribes, including the Mohegan Indian Tribe, the Narragansett Indian Tribe, the Wabanaki Confederacy (composed of the Aroostook Micmac, Passamaquoddy, Penobscot, and Maliseet of Maine), and the Wampanoag Tribe of Gayhead/Aquinnhah, each of whom testified that the territory and the individuals in question were indisputably Abenaki.[21] In another example of indigenous cooperation, the Wampanoag Confederacy consolidated the efforts of three Wampanoag bands, Mashpee, Assonet, and Aquinnah, so that the one recognized tribe among them could be the lead claimant for notices in any of the traditional Wampanoag territories.[22] But many museums, and some federal agencies, fail to review evidence provided by unrecognized Native communities. Federal agencies have little latitude to repatriate items to unrecognized groups, however deserving, because doing so is perceived to be inconsistent with the government-to-government relationship between Indians and Washington. Tragically, this means that some of the Native peoples most devastated by the colonial experience are least likely to benefit from NAGPRA.

Perusal of transcripts of the public meetings of the NAGPRA Review Committee, held approximately twice a year since the law went into effect, suggests how strongly some of the Native Tribal Historic Preservation Officers from federally recognized tribes oppose inclusion of unrecognized groups in the repatriation process. A key reason for this opposition, as the minutes

---

[21] See testimony of Donna Roberts (Moody) in the minutes of the NAGPRA Review Committee, Seventeenth Meeting, May 3–5, 1999, in Silver Spring, Maryland, http://www.cr.nps.gov/nagpra/REVIEW/meetings/RCMIN017.HTM (accessed February 1, 2005).

[22] See testimony of Ramona Peters in the minutes of the NAGPRA Review Committee, Twenty-second Meeting, November 17–19, 2001, Harvard Law School, Cambridge, Massachusetts, http://www.cr.nps.gov/nagpra/REVIEW/meetings/RCMIN022.HTM (accessed February 1, 2005).

of the 1997 NAGPRA Review Committee meeting delicately put it, is "the potential that standing for groups in repatriation issues might extend into other areas not related to NAGPRA." Evidently this point refers to the important role that receiving repatriated items might have in validating a group's authenticity, thus bolstering its case for federal recognition.[23]

After years of debate in NAGPRA Review Committee meetings, procedures for consultation relating to "unaffiliated" remains were formalized in 1999, a move that represented modest progress in the incorporation of non–federally recognized groups into the NAGPRA process.[24] A general prejudice against unrecognized tribes has, however, resulted in troubling repatriations of the remains of Native individuals whose surviving descendants have the misfortune to lack federal recognition. Some of these remains have been assigned new tribal identities, repatriated to recognized tribes, and reburied in territories where they never lived. An emphasis on the speedy reburial of remains, justified by expressed Native concerns about the spirits of the deceased, has sometimes contributed to regrettably hasty determinations of cultural affiliation.[25]

Stepping back from the particulars, we should note that from a legal perspective the most significant feature of NAGPRA may be its high level of conceptual pluralism, far beyond that which is characteristic of American jurisprudence in general. The law declares that cultural affiliation must be substantiated "by a preponderance of the evidence based upon geographical, kinship, biological, archaeological, anthropological, linguistic, folkloric, oral traditional, historical, or other relevant information" (NAGPRA, 7a [4]). This puts folklore on an equal footing with science, with the result,

---

[23]   National Park Service, Minutes, NAGPRA Review Committee 13th Meeting, March 25–27, 1997, p. 9; see also p. 15.

[24]   These principles were primarily drafted by James Bradley, museum appointee to the NAGPRA Review Committee and former Director of the Robert S. Peabody Museum at Phillips Academy. These principles encourage museums to consult with all Native communities, whether federally recognized or not, who might potentially be connected to the remains and artifacts in question. See *"Notice of Draft Principles of Agreement Regarding the Disposition of Culturally Unidentifiable Human Remains"* in the *Federal Register*. June 23, 1999 (Volume 64, Number 120); Notices page 33502–33504 from the *Federal Register Online* via GPO Access, wais.access.gpo.gov

[25]   As Horace Axtell, Nez Perce, has explained it, "When remains are disturbed above the ground, their spirits are at unrest. To put those spirits at ease, the remains must be returned to the ground as soon as possible." See Suzanne J. Crawford, "(Re)Constructing Bodies: Semiotic Sovereignty and the Debate over Kennewick Man." In *Repatriation Reader: Who Owns American Indian Remains?*, Devon A. Mihesuah, ed., Lincoln.: University of Nebraska Press, 2000, p. 213.

as the anthropologist and legal scholar Robert H. McLaughlin observes, that "the repatriation process is thrown open to radically different ways of understanding culture, history, and ownership."[26]

Such dramatic liberalization of evidentiary standards acknowledges the profound differences that exist between cultures. In that sense it is a democratic move. Yet when all kinds of evidence are held to be equally valid, the law risks stumbling into a relativistic quagmire hostile to anything approaching consensual truth. In the face of this broadened spectrum of evidence and logics, how do contending parties establish a common yardstick for reasonableness? How does one weigh competing oral traditions? If intertribal diplomacy fails, and if a museum refuses to consider additional evidence or counterclaims, the only recourse NAGPRA offers is an appeal to the NAGPRA Review Committee.

The records of NAGPRA Review Committee meetings and interviews of museum professionals with considerable repatriation experience provide occasional glimpses of how challenging it can be to reconcile widely divergent perspectives. An attorney who has represented one of the nation's largest museums in repatriation discussions tells of a NAGPRA Review Committee meeting in which a tribal elder cited evidence given to him in a religious vision. "On what basis was I supposed to question the accuracy of his vision?" the attorney asked. At another Review Committee meeting, a spokesperson for an Iowa tribe declared that "no remains are unidentified or unaffiliated" because "Native American people know who they are."[27]

Yet there are limits in how far this conceptual pluralism extends. NAGPRA requires that museums consult Native people, but museums retain sole authority to make the final determination on the cultural affiliation of materials and human remains in their collections. National NAGPRA makes no attempt to reconcile the data in its notices. Instead, it offers the following disclaimer on every notice: "The determinations in this notice are the sole responsibility of the museum, institution, or Federal agency that has control of the Native American human remains [and associated funerary objects]. The National Park Service is not responsible for the determinations in this notice."[28]

---

[26]   Robert H. McLaughlin, "The American Archaeological Record: Authority to Dig, Power to Interpret," *International Journal of Cultural Property* 7, no. 2 (1998): 359.

[27]   Richard Koontz, personal communication to Michael F. Brown; National Park Service, Minutes, NAGPRA Review Committee Thirteenth Meeting, March 25–27, 1997, p. 13.

[28]   See NAGPRA notice templates, http://www.cr.nps.gov/nagpra/NOTICES/INDEX. HTM (accessed February 1, 2005).

NAGPRA places the burden for documentation and reporting squarely on the shoulders of museums, apparently on the assumption that fair and honest consultation with the appropriate tribes will result in the publication of an accurate notice and a satisfactory repatriation. In principle, curators often imagine NAGPRA reporting as a checklist of routine tasks: inventory your collections; sort out Native human remains, funerary objects, sacred objects, and items of cultural patrimony; identify which tribes they belong to; send a list to each of the affiliated tribes; hold a consultation; publish a notice; repatriate. In practice, none of these steps is straightforward, and all must be negotiated in a confusing realm that forces colonial ideologies and Native perspectives into communication, often for the first time.

Museums and curators ill prepared for the task must choose which Native groups to consult with, weigh competing claims, and then assign cultural identities to the remains and artifacts in their collections. Although the legislation suggests that a wide range of evidence be considered, there is no mechanism for compelling museums to examine the documentary record of historical tribal relationships, consider the oral traditions of neighboring tribes, or weigh other crucial sources of information as they make their determinations.

An example of the confusion that may arise from haphazard consultation is provided by a recent repatriation case in Massachusetts. A museum chose to repatriate 84 sets of human remains, 195 associated funerary objects, and 8 pipes, all from sites in the Connecticut River Valley, to a federally recognized tribe, the Stockbridge-Munsee Band of Mohican in Wisconsin. The museum's determination that the material should be repatriated to the Stockbridge-Munsee ignored historically verifiable claims made by two geographically contiguous Native peoples – the Abenaki and Nipmuc, neither federally recognized – as well as the protests of other museums from the same region.[29] The NAGPRA notice filed by the museum also attempted to

---

29   The historic tribes of the middle Connecticut River Valley – the Agawam, Nonotuck, Pocumtuck, Sokoki, Woronoco, and some Quaboag peoples – largely folded into the surrounding populations of Abenaki between 1676 and the 1750s. See Gordon Day, *The Identity of the Saint Francis Indians*, National Museum of Man, Mercury Series Paper No. 71, Ottawa, Canada: National Museums of Canada, 1981. The Mohican people of Stockbridge, Massachusetts, however, originated in the Hudson River Valley of New York and the Housatonic River Valley of Massachusetts. See Shirley W. Dunn, *Mohicans and Their Land: 1609–1730*, Fleishmanns, NY: Purple Mountain Press, 1994. Some of the Wampanoag and Narragansett people, who originated in southeastern New England, did ally with the tribes of the Connecticut River Valley during King

change the long-accepted scholarship on tribal territories by designating the region as being entirely "within the known homeland of the Mohican Indians." A subsequent amendment to that notice extended the claim to include two additional federally recognized tribes, on the basis of oral traditions that make no reference whatsoever to the known indigenous inhabitants of the valley.[30] No effort was made to reconcile this determination with the judgment of other regional museums that hold collections from the same archaeological sites.

The historical evidence regarding tribal affiliation is hardest to reconcile with NAGPRA in those regions of the country that have the fewest numbers of federally recognized tribes. The draft guidelines for consulting on the remains of the unrecognized tribes encourage regional consulting, and there have been instances of fruitful cooperation among recognized and unrecognized tribes as a result. Ideally, honest discussion and collaboration among Native tribes would help to counterbalance implausible claims. But this rarely occurs in the politically charged world of repatriation. Disputes often end up on the docket of the NAGPRA Review Committee, a mix of scientists and Native leaders. The decisions rendered by the Review Committee have generally managed to satisfy cross-cultural standards of common sense – no small accomplishment given its diverse membership – but they also show an inclination to rule in favor of recognized tribes as exclusive claimants.[31]

IMPACT OF REPATRIATION ON NATIVE SOCIETIES

An aspect of NAGPRA that has received surprisingly little attention is its impact on the peoples who are its intended beneficiaries. The handful of articles that have been published on this theme tend, perhaps predictably, to focus on ways that Native communities are uplifted and strengthened

---

Philip's War from 1675 to 1676. This history and these relationships are extensively documented in primary sources, prevailing scholarship, and tribal traditions across New England.

[30] See NAGPRA notices published by the Springfield Science Museum in the *Federal Register* as follows: March 7, 2003, Vol. 68, No. 45 p. 11140; August 20, 2003, Vol. 68, No. 161, pp. 50184–50186; and amended notice September 14, 2004, Vol. 69, No. 177, p. 55460, http://www.cast.uark.edu/other/nps/nagpra/DOCS/nic0781.html (accessed February 1, 2005).

[31] See C. Timothy McKeown and Sherry Hutt, "In the Smaller Scope of Conscience: The Native American Graves Protection & Repatriation Act twelve Years After," *UCLA Journal of Environmental Law and Policy* 21 (2): 53–212.

by the return of ancestral remains. Yet conversations with curators and indigenous professionals close to repatriation cases suggest that the picture is far more complicated. Because the repatriation process has few precedents in the experience of Native communities, it confronts them with difficult questions and sometimes forces changes in the traditions it is ostensibly designed to preserve.[32] (See Figure 8.2.)

Because few indigenous groups have traditional rituals suitable for reburying the remains of their ancestors, some tribes have concluded that repatriation and reburial should not be undertaken at all. The Zuni of New Mexico exemplify this position: after being informed that the Museum of New Mexico was holding human remains and grave goods collected on Zuni lands, the tribe decided that reburial would be deeply troubling to tribal members, who would be uncertain of the clan identities of the deceased and therefore unable to choose appropriate reinterment rituals. The Zuni stated that the materials should remain in the museum as long as they were treated respectfully – meaning, among other things, that they should not be put on public display. Some Oklahoma tribes whose members are predominantly Christian have apparently sought traditional ritual specialists from neighboring tribes to officiate at reburial ceremonies, on the grounds that it would be inappropriate to rebury non-Christian Indian ancestors with a Christian rite.[33]

A handful of ethnographers have begun to document the subtle cultural changes that repatriation can foster. Michael Harkin, for instance, reports that among Indians of the Northwest Coast repatriated objects are seen

---

[32]   See, for example, Edward Halealoha Ayau and Ty Kāwika Tengan. "*Ka Huaka'i O Na 'iwi*: The Journey Home." In *The Dead and Their Possessions: Repatriation in Principle, Policy and Practice*, edited by Cressida Fforde, Jane Hubert, and Paul Turnbull, 171– 189. London: Routledge, 2002; and Connie Hart Yellowman, "'*Naevahoo'ohtseme*' – We Are Going Back Home: The Cheyenne Repatriation of Human Remains – a Woman's Perspective," *St. Thomas Law Review* 9 (Fall 1996): 103–116. In a nuanced and sympathetic assessment of NAGPRA's implementation, Kathleen S. Fine-Dare goes so far as to say that the law "has been nothing less than a nightmare for many of its participants." See her *Grave Injustice: The American Indian Repatriation Movement and NAGPRA*, Lincoln.: University of Nebraska Press, 2002, p. 7. Similar observations about repatriation's power to evoke inter- and intratribal conflict are presented in Orin Starn's moving account of the repatriation of the brain of the Yahi Indian Ishi; see *Ishi's Brain: In Search of America's Last "Wild" Indian*, New York, W. W. Norton, 2004.

[33]   Edmund J. Ladd, "A Zuni Perspective on Repatriation," in Tamara L. Bray, ed., *The Future of the Past: Archaeologists, Native Americans, and Repatriation* (New York: Garland, 2001), p. 113.

Figure 8.2. A procession of 600 Indians accompanies a truck carrying skeletal remains excavated by archaelogists in Pecos, New Mexico, between 1915 and 1929. The remains were repatriated to Jemez Pueblo by Harvard University in May 1999. AP/Wide World Photos.

by younger tribal members as property of the community, whereas older members are more likely to see them as legitimately belonging to specific individuals or family groups. Tribal members who are practicing Christians may also disagree about the propriety of celebrating and displaying powerful religious objects from the tribe's pre-Christian history.[34]

An example drawn from an international repatriation case is provided by Steven Rubenstein, an ethnographer of the Shuar people of the Peruvian and Ecuadorian rain forest. Rubenstein tracked the 1995 repatriation of a dozen *tsantsa* or shrunken heads from the collection of the National Museum of the American Indian (NMAI) to the Shuar Federation of Ecuador, an intercommunity organization that plays a pivotal role in contemporary Shuar politics. The initiative for repatriation was not taken by ordinary Shuar people, who have not taken heads on a regular basis for at least half a century and who traditionally saw the shrunken heads as having little spiritual significance

[34]   Michael E. Harkin, "Privacy, Ownership, and the Repatriation of Cultural Properties: An Ethnographic Perspective from the Northwest Coast," paper presented at the conference Categories, Culture, and Property, Chicago-Kent School of Law, September 28, 2001. See also Sarah Harding, "Cultural Property and the Limitations of Preservation," *Law and Policy* (2003) 25: 17–36.

after the rituals associated with their preparation were completed. Instead, it seems to have been a bilateral process in which curators of the NMAI, committed to purging all human remains from their collections, came into contact with well-traveled Shuar Federation leaders responsive to American Indian insistence that human remains are invariably "sacred." The NMAI offered to return the heads to the Shuar even though it was not legally required to do so. The act of receiving the *tsantsa* under highly charged circumstances imbued them with symbolic capital that the Shuar leaders then used to strengthen their political influence at home. As Rubenstein puts it, "The repatriation of the heads does not merely reverse the Western appropriation of Shuar objects; it effects a Shuar appropriation of Western meanings."[35]

In this and other case studies, then, one sees intriguing evidence that the "recovery of tradition" associated with repatriation may actually destabilize and transform tradition. Some Native communities have had to construct new, often pan-Indian, traditions for the reburial of individuals who were never meant to be disturbed, in hopes of putting their spirits to rest. Federally recognized Native communities may feel spiritually enriched by the return of ancestors and ancestral objects, but the repatriation process may also evoke searching questions over how tradition can be reconciled with contemporary beliefs and practices. The response of unrecognized Native communities to NAGPRA is more ambivalent, since they regularly face the prospect of seeing their ancestors claimed by other Native peoples, their sacred objects put to uses for which they were never intended, and their traditional homelands identified with federally recognized tribes.

REPATRIATION OF THE INTANGIBLE?

One far-reaching effect of NAGPRA has been its power to provide a new vocabulary for disputes over the *intangible* elements of Native cultures – stories, religious beliefs, music, art styles, and biological knowledge. These,

---

[35] Steven L. Rubenstein, "Shuar Shrunken Heads and Problems with Power on the Colonial Frontier," unpublished ms., 2003. I am grateful to Rubenstein for allowing me to quote from his essay. The case raises difficult questions that cannot be explored here. For instance, although the *tsantsa* were probably prepared by the ancestors of the contemporary Shuar, the source of the heads was most likely the neighboring Achuara people. If the *tsantsa* are thought of as artifacts, they were rightly returned to the Shuar. If they are primarily thought of as human remains, though, do not they not belong to the Achuara? For additional information on Shuar attitudes toward shrunken heads, see Rubenstein, "Shuar Migrants and Shrunken Heads Face to Face in a New York Museum," *Anthropology Today* (June 2004) 20: 15–18.

of course, are not directly affected by NAGPRA, but the law's success in reframing relations between Native Americans and museums has made it an obvious model for emulation. Inevitably, then, we have seen the publication of essays and position papers implying that ideas, as can items of cultural patrimony, can be owned and therefore repatriated. This notion is best expressed in a document issued by a consortium of Apache tribes in which Apache leaders lay claim to "all images, texts, ceremonies, music, songs, stories, symbols, beliefs, customs, ideas and other physical and spiritual objects and concepts" relating to the Apache, including any and all representations of Apache people.[36]

For better or for worse, musical and artistic styles or traditional knowledge does not obey the same rules as objects, which by definition can be in only one place at a time. The infinitely replicable quality of information raises two interrelated questions: How does one determine the ultimate origin of ideas, images, musical expressions, and environmental knowledge? And even if we can identify the communities that gave birth to these intangibles, what would be the social and political costs of controlling their movement?[37]

NAGPRA has itself contributed to Native anxiety over the movement of information because the law requires substantiating evidence to support repatriation claims. In a 1997 conference on NAGPRA held in Santa Fe, a Laguna Pueblo official named Paul Pino identified the problem this way. "One of the things that really concerns me," he said, "is again, how much does the government have to know, and how much do the officials have to know with regards to the use and purpose, what these objects are for? Again, we're stuck in that position where disclosure means, you know, losing what safeguards we have with regard to those items."[38] Museum professionals and

---

[36]   *Inter-Apache Summit on Repatriation and the Protection of Apache Cultures*, 1995, ms. in possession of author. Examples of works that use repatriation as a springboard for discussion of intangible cultural property include S. Michelle Rasmus, "Repatriating Words: Local Knowledge in a Global Context," *American Indian Quarterly* (2002) 26: 286–307, and Claire R. Farrer, "Who Owns the Words?: An Anthropological Perspective on Public Law 101–601," *Journal of Arts Management, Law and Society* (1994) 2: 317–326.

[37]   Michael F. Brown, *Who Owns Native Culture?* Cambridge, MA: Harvard University Press, 2003.

[38]   Transcript, *Southwest Tribal Peoples NAGPRA Conference*, October 9–19, 1997, Santa Fe, NM, Museum of Indian Arts and Culture/Laboratory of Anthropology, p. 30. For further discussion of the dilemma of whether to reveal sensitive oral history information in order to preserve it, see Joe E. Watkins, "Beyond the Margins: American Indians, First Nations, and Archaeology in North America," *American Antiquity* 68 (2003): 282.

NAGPRA administrators are working hard to respond to these disclosure concerns, but they face a genuine dilemma: How can they comply with prevailing standards of legal transparency without forcing Native people to reveal information that is sensitive or confidential by indigenous standards? For Natives, one injury potentially becomes two: in order to recover things they believe should always have been theirs, they are asked to give away their religious secrets.

This emerging interest in information marks the next frontier for the global repatriation movement. Advocates for the implementation of legal regimes designed to protect folklore in its many forms celebrate UNESCO's International Convention for the Safeguarding of the Intangible Cultural Heritage, a protocol passed in 2003 and awaiting formal ratification by member states. A key provision of the convention is that each signatory nation must prepare "one or more inventories of the intangible cultural heritage present in its territory." By this the convention mandates formal documentation of every element of intangible culture – the multiple dimensions of language, religion, art, music, dress, technology, folk tales, and local knowledge of the environment – for each social group encompassed by the nation's borders. UNESCO's program is echoed elsewhere, particularly in India, by ambitious campaigns to "digitize heritage" in the expectation that this will help to defend national cultures from transnational corporations determined to profit from local knowledge by taking advantage of global intellectual property conventions.

This is an instance in which formal rationality and substantive rationality are launched on a collision course. In formal terms, the preparation of heritage inventories is a necessary precursor to legal protection. How can we protect something if we have not identified it first? Yet given the zero-sum nature of government budgets, the monumental bureaucratic labor required to prepare these lists is likely to siphon off scarce resources that might otherwise benefit traditional communities in practical ways – education, health care, and so forth. And given the increasing emphasis on secrecy among indigenous peoples worldwide, it is by no means clear that Native communities will be willing to cooperate with state-sponsored documentation efforts that may appear as threatening as the problem they are intended to solve.[39]

From a tactical standpoint, however, the UNESCO convention may have the beneficial effect of convincing the world community to acknowledge that

---

[39] For more extended discussion of these issues, see Michael F. Brown, "Heritage Trouble: Recent Work on the Protection of Intangible Cultural Property," *International Journal of Cultural Property* 12 (2005): 46–61.

the cultural productions of folk communities are vulnerable to alienation. If UNESCO's approach to heritage protection is not entirely convincing, at least it puts the subject on the world's agenda, implicitly challenging the dominance of global media companies, the pharmaceutical industry, and other corporate interests that continue to use intellectual property law as a cover for what critics of economic globalization denounce as legalized theft.

CLOSING THOUGHTS

The return of human remains and sacred objects to indigenous peoples is but one facet of a worldwide movement committed to reconciliation with communities that have suffered historic wrongs, mostly at the hands of European colonial governments. The sociologist John Torpey, a perceptive observer of this movement, suggests that a new focus on undoing the injuries of history – what Torpey calls "reparations politics" – has arisen because our visions of a utopian future have largely exhausted themselves. If we cannot agree about the shape of the future, the movement's logic suggests, we can at least try to repair the past.[40]

As Torpey and others point out, advocates for restitution and reparations almost inevitably find themselves wedded to the racial and ethnic categories that they blame for the injustices of colonialism. In the U.S. context, we frequently hear the demand that unidentified or unaffiliated human remains be "turned over to American Indians, who should determine what happens to them." But which "Indians"? From which "tribes"? Such declarations accept the legitimacy of generic categories that in other contexts have been denounced as fabrications of the European colonial mind. In a similar fashion, ideas about cultural patrimony and tribal identity, as articulated by Native leaders in NAGPRA claims, sometimes seem less grounded in traditional rules of ownership than in romantic European notions of primitive collectivism.

Although NAGPRA surely benefited from the global turn to reparations politics, its effects are more practical and, to our minds at least, more compelling than those of many other proposals for effecting reconciliation with indigenous groups. The dignified treatment of ancestral remains, especially

[40] John Torpey, "'Making Whole What Has Been Smashed': Reflections on Reparations," *Journal of Modern History* 73 (2001): 333–358. See also Elazar Barkan, *The Guilt of Nations: Restitution and Negotiating Historical Injustices*, New York: W. W. Norton, 2000.

those for whom a cultural affiliation is clearly known, is an expression of simple decency that can sometimes help to resolve painful memories. More sensitive policies addressing the disposition of newly discovered human remains have forced archaeologists, scientists, and administrators to acknowledge the moral claims and political authority of Native communities. The return of religious objects may help to revitalize elements of traditional religion. The practical utility of many of the religious objects returned in compliance with NAGPRA is probably the strongest argument against characterizing the law as a narrow expression of what John Henry Merryman has called "retentive cultural nationalism," although there is little doubt that cultural nationalism remains a powerful impetus for the worldwide repatriation movement. It is too early to judge whether NAGPRA has set the stage for broader efforts to return all material culture and folkloric knowledge to their perceived points of emergence.[41]

NAGPRA's effect on the market in Native American art is hard to assess. Experts we have consulted report a mixed impact. Collectors who once might have donated important works to museums may be disinclined to do so now, fearing that their collections will be repatriated against their wishes. Institutions that receive no federal funding – including art auction houses, private dealers, corporations, small museums, and online auction sites such as Ebay – are relatively unconstrained by NAGPRA unless artifacts were obtained by looting archaeological sites, and prices for the most desirable artworks continue to rise steadily. Given increased public sensitivity to the importance of Native American ceremonial objects, however, collectors may find themselves the target of negative publicity. The American Indian Ritual Object Repatriation Foundation has had some success in convincing private owners to donate or share ceremonial objects with federally recognized tribes, using the prospect of tax deductions as an economic incentive.[42]

For anthropology, NAGPRA represents the kind of adversity that some have wisely turned into opportunity. The institutional relationships fostered by the law, including joint stewardship committees and consultation arrangements with regional Native communities, have paved the way for

---

[41]   John Henry Merryman, "Two Ways of Thinking about Cultural Property," *American Journal of International Law* 80 (1986): 831–853.

[42]   Kate Morris, "Strategies and Procedures for the Repatriation of Materials from the Private Sector." In *Mending the Circle, a Native American Repatriation Guide: Understanding and Implementing NAGPRA and the Official Smithsonian and Other Repatriation Policies*, New York: The American Indian Ritual Object Repatriation Foundation, 1996, pp. 64–71, http://www.repatriationfoundation.org (accessed February 6, 2005).

joint research projects of anthropologists and Native peoples. A newsletter published in Tucson, Arizona, for instance, describes a project in which archaeologists have collaborated with knowledgeable members of four Indian tribes to juxtapose oral histories and archaeological data about the San Pedro Valley of southeastern Arizona. In many ways the five versions of prehistory were difficult to reconcile. Yet there were also intriguing commonalities that have led the project archaeologists to rethink their view of the region's past. Among other things, they have begun to consider the possibility that the prevailing genealogical model for the emergence of today's Indian tribes should be replaced by a more "braided" pattern based on the continual exchange of people, technologies, and languages. Many anthropologists are convinced that over the long run collaborations such as the San Pedro Valley project will produce better anthropology than all the thousands of bones and grave goods held by the nation's museums.[43]

A curator at the Smithsonian with considerable experience in repatriation once remarked to one of us that she has been surprised to find that some Indian people were fascinated by the scientific data she and her colleagues gathered before returning bones for reburial. This information often encompasses the individuals' age, sex, and physical condition, and sometimes the cause of death. When taking possession of the bones, these Native people told her that this information "makes the dead seem more like real people." She commented ruefully that if anthropologists had done a better job of communicating this kind of information to Native people and the general public in the past, NAGPRA might not have been needed.

NAGPRA, in other words, is pushing anthropologists and museum professionals to do what we should have been doing all along. As most complex laws do, it falls short of perfection. It encourages museums to part with Native collections but also gives them great latitude to assign tribal affiliations to these materials. It sometimes fosters conflict among Native peoples by forcing recognized and unrecognized tribes to advance competing claims to ancestral remains. It puts in public view sensitive information about religious practices that many Native Americans feel should not circulate beyond the boundaries of their communities. It encourages the misplaced belief that all elements of culture, including intangible ones, can be returned to their original source. Despite its flaws, however, NAGPRA has opened a new chapter in the history of U.S. relations with Native peoples – a chapter based on

---

[43] T. J. Ferguson, Chip Colwell-Chanthaphonh, and Roger Anyon, "One Valley, Many Histories," *Archaeology Southwest* 18 (1)(2004): 13.

collaboration and the search for intercultural understanding whose promising results give us little reason to mourn the abandoned collection policies of the past. That has already provided a deeper understanding of the complexity and vitality of Native societies than could ever have been imagined by the anthropologists convinced that American Indians were destined to vanish from the face of the Earth.

9 FINDERS KEEPERS AND DEEP AMERICAN HISTORY
Some Lessons in Dispute Resolution

David Hurst Thomas

Since the days of Thomas Jefferson – America's first scientific archaeologist – American Indians have been studied as part of the natural world. As were mammoth bones and the fruit trees in Jefferson's own garden, American Indians were "specimens," to be empirically investigated and objectively understood. Following the Jeffersonian model, nineteenth-century anthropologists studied American Indians by digging up their graves and exhibiting Indians in the "ethnographic zoos" that were popular additions to several World Fairs. Sometimes native people became "living fossils" tucked away in the museums of America; when these "museum Indians" died, their bodies were sometimes not buried at all, but rendered into bones, numbered, and stored away as part of America's greater heritage.[1]

By 1900, American Indians seemed to be vanishing as surely as the American bison, and so too were the archaeological vestiges of Indian history. As museum anthropologists hurried to document and collect the last of Indian culture, the United States Congress passed the Antiquities Act of 1906, legislation crafted to preserve America's remote past and to ensure its continued study by a rapidly growing scientific community. The archaeological record was seen as a critical part of America's national identity because it documented its progression from savagery to the most civilized place on Earth, and in 1906 this heritage was formally entrusted to science. Whatever Indians had to say about their past was irrelevant to the American narrative.

But American Indians, of course, refused to vanish. Their numbers bottomed out in the 1890s and have dramatically increased ever since.

---

[1] For more on Jefferson and the early history of American archaeology, see David Hurst Thomas, *Skull Wars: Kennewick Man, Archaeology, and the Battle for Native American Identity* (New York: Basic Books, 2000)

Particularly since the 1960s, Indian people have stepped up their fight to reclaim and reinforce their treaty-guaranteed sovereignty, borrowing strategies and guidelines from the world of international law. Such indigenous ideologies assert an essential native subjectivity, promoting themes of self-worth and cultural preservation, and suggesting that Indian culture could help correct some problems of the modern mainstream.

Achieving power over their own history has tangible payoffs in the everyday life of Indian people, a life still subject to long-conflicted federal policies. Economic development in Indian Country remains integrally connected to politics – intertwined with issues of sovereignty, tribal identity, access to resources, cultural issues, and ideology. By emphasizing histories absent from white-dominated curricula, native people are attempting to build institutional mechanisms to help their communities and reassert their rights. By taking hold of the imagery that still frames negotiations with state and federal governments, they seek to translate historical and cultural identities into tangible political power.

The bottom line is defining which history gets taught and who gets to teach it. In seeking identities independent of non-Indian historians and anthropologists, many Native Americans have begun to resent the appropriation of their ancient artifacts and ancestral bones by "experts" claiming an authority denied to the Indians themselves. As native people across the land try to recapture their own language, culture, and history, they are increasingly concerned with recovering and taking control of tribal heirlooms and human remains.

Congress responded to these sensitivities in 1990 by passing the Native American Graves Protection and Repatriation Act (NAGPRA for short). This legislation marked a significant shift in the federal stance toward the rights of Indian people and a sea change in the perception and practice of American archaeology. As in 1906, the federal government asserted its right to legislate access to the American past. But the 1990 law explicitly acknowledged that Indian pasts are relevant to the American present. This public and visible benchmark reflected a deep-seated shift in thinking, emphasizing America's self-perception as a multifaceted, pluralistic society. The American creed shifted away from the time-honored melting pot to newer perspectives recognizing the merits of a multicultural society.

Such an interpretation of the American character was unimaginable in 1906. The Antiquities Act of 1906, which legally transferred the Indian past to the American public domain, was crafted without Indian involvement and with no suggestion that Indian people might have spiritual affiliations with that past. In 1990, for the first time, native people were empowered to question mainstream American ownership of the Indian past, both literally and metaphorically. No longer were Indian bones found on public lands automatically defined as natural resources, as federal property to be safeguarded in scientific custody. No longer did science have a monopoly on defining the meaning of archaeology; instead, native groups were invited to assign their own spiritual and historical meanings to archaeological sites and their contents. It is hard to overlook the sense of loss among mainstream scientists and historians who see their power and authority eroding as twenty-first-century America experiments with multicultural alternatives to the traditional melting pot imagery.

This chapter will discuss the evolving relationship between the scientific and Native American communities by discussing three important discoveries, each of great significance to science:

- *Kennewick Man*: The nearly complete skeleton of a man who died eight hundred to eighty-five hundred years ago along the banks of the Columbia River
- *The Willamette Meteorite*: The largest meteorite ever found in the Americas, a rock that is older than the Earth itself and may provide clues about the origins of the solar system
- *KDT*: The first well-preserved ancient human body ever recovered from a North American glacier, a frozen man who holds the keys to unlock the secrets of daily life as it existed in America in the decades before the arrival of Columbus

These same three discoveries – known under different names – likewise hold great spiritual significance to Native American people:

- Oyt.pa.ma.na.tit.tite *(The Ancient One)*: The Confederated Tribes of the Umatilla Indian Reservation believe that the remains of their ancestor should be reburied immediately, without scientific study.
- Tomanowos *(The Sky Person)*: The Confederated Tribes of the Grand Ronde believe that the meteorite is rightfully theirs, a sacred object needed for the practice of their traditional religion.
- Kwädạy Dän Ts 'ínchị *(Long Ago Person Found)*: The Champagne and Aishihik First Nations believe that this ancestor has much to tell about their past, but the Coastal Tlingit tribe believes that the frozen man was related to them.

This chapter will use these three examples to explore the shifting relationships between Native North Americans and those non-Indians who wish to study them.

THE CASE OF KENNEWICK MAN/OYT.PA.MA.NA.TIT.TITE
(THE ANCIENT ONE)

The Kennewick saga began in late July 1996, when the coroner of Benton County, Washington, showed the archaeologist James Chatters a skull that had washed out from a Columbia River cutbank in the town of Kennewick, Washington. Chatters accompanied the coroner to the place where the skull had been found by a couple of college students watching a hydroplane race. Although he could find no evidence of a burial pit, he did discover more bones were lying about the riverbank, and he collected them all.

In his preliminary forensic analysis, Chatters concluded that the individual was male, Caucasoid, about forty-five years old at death, and standing about five feet eight inches tall. For his day, the man was probably considered to be healthy, but today, he seems more a survivor, a fellow who had lived a rough life. At the age of five, he had suffered a severe disease (or perhaps malnutrition). He suffered from minor arthritis of the joints. His skull had been fractured, his chest crushed, and a chipped elbow reduced the use of his left arm. Some sort of large projectile – maybe a bullet or piece of shrapnel – had penetrated well into the right side of his hip. The man had survived this injury, and the bone had healed over, sealing the object deep inside.[2] A computed tomography (CT) scan showed that it was a stone spear point, a distinctive leaf-shape "Cascade point," like those used by hunters of the Columbia Plateau between forty-five hundred and nine thousand years ago. "I've got a white guy with a stone point in him," Chatters later told *The New York Times*. "That's pretty exciting. I thought we had a pioneer."[3]

But how was a white settler speared by a stone point perhaps thousands of years old? Chatters decided to resolve the inconsistencies by sending a scrap of hand bone to the radiocarbon laboratory at the University of California (Riverside). The lab called back three weeks later, with news that would change Chatters's life. The bone sample was ninety-four hundred years old, making it one of the most ancient skeletons in the Americas – and perhaps the most complete.[4]

---

2 For a firsthand account of the Kennewick discovery, see James C. Chatters, *Ancient Encounters: Kennewick Man and the First Americans* (New York: Simon & Schuster, 2001); see also Michael F. Brown, *Who Owns Native Culture?* (Cambridge, MA: Harvard University Press, 2003), chapter 7.

3 Chatters quoted by Timothy Egan, "Tribe Stops Study of Bones That Challenge History," *New York Times*, September 30, 1996).

4 Subsequent radiocarbon analysis suggests that Kennewick Man died roughly 8,000–8,500 radiocarbon years before the present. National Park Service Memorandum

Finders Keepers?

So began the saga of Kennewick Man, as Chatters called his find.[5] on the basis of the sketchiest of evidence, archaeologists and journalists alike began framing fresh theories about the earliest Americans. Perhaps several populations crossed the land bridge from Asia to America in distinct waves – white-skinned Caucasoids first, followed by the dusky-skinned Mongoloids of northern Asia. What happened when they met? Was there an ancient American race war? Did the tawny Mongoloids attack Kennewick Man with a stone-tipped spear? Or are modern American Indians descended from a blend of both races – the multicultural product of an original American melting pot? The issue of Indian arrival is critical to Indian people as well, as the Lakota activist Vine Deloria, Jr., pointed out. If Indians had "barely unpacked before Columbus came knocking on the door," will people question Indian claims to the land and its resources?[6]

As theories began to proliferate, archaeologists seemed to agree on just one point: Kennewick is a monumental find that must be studied extensively by specialists. The bones must be analyzed in great detail, additional radiocarbon tests should be run, and ancient deoxyribonucleic acid (DNA) extracted from the bones. To ensure accuracy and eliminate bias, this testing must be conducted in several independent laboratories, supervised by the country's best research scientists.

KENNEWICK MAN AND NAGPRA

As the scientific teams geared up, the already dramatic story of Kennewick Man took an extraordinary turn. Five days after the startling results of the radiocarbon tests were made public, the Army Corps of Engineers announced its intent to repatriate the remains to an alliance of five Northwest tribes: Umatilla, Yakima, Nez Perce, Wanapum, and Colville. The Umatilla tribe of northeastern Oregon took the lead, demanding that Chatters

"Results of radiocarbon dating the Kennewick human skeletal remains," January 13 2000. http://www.cr.nps.gov/aad/kennewick/c14memo.htm.
[5] James C. Chatters, "The Recovery and First Analysis of an Early Holocene Human Skeleton from Kennewick, Washington," *American Antiquity* 65: 291–316 (2000); see also Stuart J. Fiedel, "The Kennewick Follies: 'New' Theories about the Peopling of the Americas," *Journal of Anthropological Research* 60(1): 75–110 (2004) for an update on the scientific implications of Kennewick Man.
[6] Deloria quoted by Jace Weaver, "Indian Presence with No Indians Present: NAGPRA and Its Concontents," *Wicazo Sa Review* 12(2): 13–30; quoted on p. 22.

immediately – and without further study – surrender the bones. Armand Minthorn, a Umatilla leader, said simply: "Our oral history goes back ten thousand years. We know how time began and how Indian people were created. They can say whatever they want, the scientists. They are being disrespectful."[7] Claiming the skeleton as their own, the Umatilla tribe rejected the scientist's name, preferring the name Oyt.pa.ma.na.tit.tite, which translates as "The Ancient One." From the Umatilla perspective, the bones were theirs to name.

The Umatilla explained that the scientific probing and destruction of human bones were offensive, sacrilegious, and illegal under the Native American Graves Protection and Repatriation Act (NAGPRA) of 1990.[8] A significant triumph for Indian people, NAGPRA permitted living Indians to exercise their traditional responsibilities toward the dead. The 1990 legislation covered several basic areas of concern. First, it recognized the importance of tribal consent when dealing with Indian graves on tribal lands and required "consultation" with tribes over remains found on federal lands. NAGPRA also mandated that by November 16, 1993, all museums and universities receiving federal funds (personal collections were not included) send a summary of Native American sacred and ceremonial objects and unassociated funerary items to Indian tribes potentially affiliated with those artifacts. Two years later, on November 16, 1995, these same institutions were required to file an inventory of Native American human remains and associated grave goods with culturally affiliated tribes. Indian tribes culturally affiliated with these artifacts and remains could then request their return. The National Park Service provided museums a listing of 771 tribes, bands, and nations to which the appropriate inventories should be sent. Only federally recognized native groups appear on the list; tribes recognized only by state-level

---

[7] Minthorn in Egan, "Tribe Stops Study," 1996.

[8] Native American Graves Protection and Repatriation Act (NAGPRA) 1990 Pub Law 101–601 (November 16, 1990): 25 United States Code 3001. For a legislative history of NAGPRA, particularly the role of the Society of American Archaeology in crafting the bill, see William A. Lovis, Keith W. Kintigh, Vincas P. Steponaitis, and Lynne G. Goldstein (2004), "Archaeological Perspectives on NAGPRA: Underlying Principles, Legislative History, and Current Issues," in Jennifer R. Richman and Marion P. Forsyth (eds), *Legal Perspectives on Cultural Resources* (Walnut Creek, CA: AltaMira Press, 2004): 165–184; see also Roger C. Echo-Hawk and and Walter R. Echo-Hawk, *Battlefields and Burial Grounds: The Indian Struggle to Protect Ancestral Graves in the United States* (Minneapolis, MN: Lerner Publications, 1994), and Kathleen S. Fine-Dare, *Grave Injustice: The American Indian Repatriation Movement and NAGPRA* (Lincoln: University of Nebraska, 2002).

governments, and those whose federal standing is pending are not covered by the legislation. As a federally recognized tribe, the Umatilla declared that the Kennewick skeleton must be returned to them for immediate reburial.[9]

The Resolution

Scientists across the country screamed foul: If Kennewick Man – one of the oldest, most complete skeletons in the Americas – did not look like an American Indian, how could a modern tribe claim his remains under NAGPRA? Several scientists argued that considerably more study would be required before tribal affinity, if any, could be established. No matter how the study turns out, some argued, the bones are so ancient that they rightfully belong to the American public rather than any special-interest group.

The dilemma landed in the lap of the Army Corps of Engineers, the governmental agency with immediate jurisdiction over the find spot. In September 1996, the Corps confiscated the bones from Chatters and announced plans to turn them over to the Umatilla within thirty days. Although Washington's congressional delegation immediately urged that qualified scientists be allowed to examine the bones, the Corps refused.

The Army Corps refused to allow scientific study because the Umatilla said that such analysis would violate their religious beliefs about the dead. Many archaeologists countered that Kennewick Man could not be adequately affiliated with any living tribe and, most likely, not with Indian people at all. To permit one tribe – or perhaps a single faction within a tribe – to veto scientific study, they claimed, would violate the rights of all other Americans.

In *Bonnichsen et al. v. United States of America*, eight prominent archaeologists and physical anthropologists filed suit to obtain access to the Kennewick bones. The lawsuit questioned whether NAGPRA, a piece of legislation designed to protect Indian graves, could be applied to ninety-four-hundred-year-old remains. Citing a lack of due process, the scientists accused the Army Corps of arbitrary and capricious decision making. Not only does the U.S. Constitution protect freedom of expression, the scientists argued, it safeguards the right to gather and receive information. If the Kennewick skeleton is locked away or reburied, the American public is deprived of potentially irreplaceable information about its own past.

---

[9] The tribal claimants: the Confederated Tribes and Bands of the Yakama Nation, the Nez Perce of Idaho, the Confederated Tribes of the Umatilla Indian Reservation, the Confederated Tribes of the Colville Reservation, and the Wanapum Band (which is not a federal recognized tribe).

The Kennewick lawsuit also reflected the belief that the Corps had violated the Civil Rights Act of 1866. This law, originally written to guarantee non-whites the same legal protection as whites, has recently been read as offering reciprocal protection to whites: If scientists were denied access because of race or ethnicity, then their civil rights were being violated.

In 1997, the Army Corps was prepared to repatriate the Kennewick remains to the tribal coalition. But later that year, the federal court ruled that the Corps had acted inappropriately and instructed the agency to review the matter by using proper procedures. The lawsuit was tabled until this process could be completed.[10] The *Bonnichsen v. US* lawsuit temporarily halted the Army Corps from repatriating Kennewick Man remains to the Umatilla tribe.

Here is a timeline summarizing subsequent legal actions:

- *March 1998*: The Department of the Interior and National Park Service agree to assist the Army Corps of Engineers and commission a series of scientific examinations by eighteen distinguished scientists, who conduct a variety of biological, radiometric, ethnographic, archaeological, and linguistic studies.[11]
- *September 2000*: Bruce Babbitt (Secretary of the Interior) declares that Kennewick Man, by now stored at the Burke Museum of Natural and Cultural History in Seattle, is indeed culturally affiliated with the five Indian tribes and should be returned to them.[12] The secretary's determination precludes further study of the remains. The eight plaintiffs dispute Babbitt's determination and pursue judicial review. Judge John Jelderks, of Oregon's Ninth District Circuit Court, faces uncharted legal waters: Is this eight-thousand- to eighty-five-hundred-year-old man a Native American? And, if so, is he culturally affiliated with the modern tribe claiming him as an ancestor? The legal and scientific answers to these questions promise to condition the direction of American archaeology for decades.
- *August 2002*: Judge Jelderks overturns Secretary Babbitt's decision, concluding that the administrative record from the Department of Interior contains "insufficient evidence to support the conclusion

[10]   *Bonnichsen et al.* v United States et al. 1997 F. Supp. 614, 618 (Dist. OR).
[11]   Available at http://www.cr.nps.gov/aad/Kennewick)
[12]   National Park Service, "Determination That the Kennewick Human Skeleton Remains Are 'Native American' for the Purposes of the Native American Graves Protection and Repatriation Act (NAGPRA)," January 11, 2000. http://www.cr.nps.gov/aad/kennewick/c14memo.htm

that the [Kennewick] remains are related to the present-day tribe, people, or culture that is indigenous to the United States as required by the statute."[13] Judge Jelderks declares that the plaintiffs can study the Kennewick skeleton and the tribal appellants appeal the decision.

- *February 2004*: The Ninth Circuit Court of Appeals upholds the previous district court decision.[14] Writing for the three-judge panel, Judge Ronald M. Gould agrees that because the government had failed to establish Kennewick Man's status as Native American, NAGPRA does not apply. The Joint Tribal Coalition petitions for a rehearing.
- *April 2004*: The Ninth Circuit Court of Appeals denies the tribal appellants' petition, virtually exhausting their legal options.

Before discussing further the implications of the Kennewick court case, we will explore some alternatives for resolving cultural heritage disputes in Native North America.

THE CASE OF THE WILLAMETTE METEORITE/TOMANOWOS (SKY PERSON)

Ten thousand years ago, give or take a millennium, a giant meteorite traveling more than 40,000 miles per hour crashed onto a hillside overlooking the Willamette Valley (near modern West Linn, Oregon). It is the iron core of an ancient planet formed perhaps 4.5 billion years ago and later shattered in a stellar collision. This battered remnant traveled to Earth from an asteroid belt located between Mars and Juniper. Because the meteorite is older than the Earth itself, geochemists believe that it may hold clues about the way the solar system came into being.

The so-called Willamette meteorite is the largest ever found in America. Whereas most meteorites are shapeless lumps, the Willamette meteorite has a starkly powerful, unearthly appearance. It is semicircular – about the size and shape of a Volkwagon Beetle – flattened on the bottom and humped on top, riddled with large, smooth cavities. One photograph from 1911 shows two small children posing *inside* the meteorite itself, surrounded by sixteen tons of nickel-iron ore.[15]

---

[13] *Bonnichsen et al. v United States et al.* 2002 F. Supp. 2d 1116 (Dist. OR).

[14] (*Bonnichsen v. United States* (2004).

[15] Douglas Preston, *Dinosaurs in the Attic* (New York: St. Martin's Press, 1986): 204–206.

Finders Keepers?

The meteorite landed on territory traditionally held by the Clackamas people of Oregon's Upper Willamette Valley. As part of the Treaty of 1855, the tribe ceded this land in exchange for reservation territory in Oregon's Coast Range. The Clackamas survivors joined the Confederated Tribes of the Grand Ronde (established by Executive Order in 1857), which fused nearly two-dozen bands and tribes from western Oregon and northern California (including the Kalapuya, Molalla, Chasta, Umpqua, and Rogue River peoples).[16]

When the Oregon Iron and Steel Company purchased some of the land ceded by the Clackamas, they were totally unaware of the massive meteorite imbedded in the property. In 1902, one Ellis Hughes – a Welsh immigrant who owned an adjoining tract of land – stumbled upon the partially buried iron boulder. A former miner, Hughes immediately recognized the scientific and commercial potential of his find, which he disguised beneath a pile of pine boughs as he concocted a plan to remove the meteorite to his own property.

Assisted only by his teenage son and an aging horse, Hughes jacked and levered the meteorite onto a sturdy log cart, supported by tree trunks connected as wheels and attached by steel cable to a capstan (a vertical log positioned nearby). Working in complete secrecy, Hughes led his horse in endless circles, winding the cable around and around the capstan, inching the cart and meteorite along a wooden plank road toward his land. Three months and three-quarters of a mile later, Hughes announced the discovery of America's biggest meteorite – on his property. He raised a wooden shack over his find and collected twenty-five cents admission to view the meteorite.

The long-term legalities surrounding the Willamette meteorite have proved to be as contorted as its twisted iron surface. One of Hughes's first customers, a lawyer representing Oregon Iron and Steel, backtracked the conspicuous swath leading from Hughes's property and found the original impact crater (located, of course, on his client's land). Although caught red-handed, Hughes refused to surrender the meteorite; the Oregon Iron and Steel Company filed suit to retrieve their property.

---

[16]   In 1901, the Grand Ronde reservation was reduced from the original 59,000 acres to about 33,000 acres, and the remaining land sold to outsiders as "surplus"; see Sylvester L. Lahren, Jr., "Reservations and Reserves" in *Plateau, vol. 12 Handbook of North American Indians*, edited by Deward E. Walker, Jr. (Washington, DC: The Smithsonian Institution Press, 1998): 484–498.

Hughes and his attorney crafted a novel, finders-keepers defense. They called to the witness stand several Native American elders, each of whom declared that the meteorite had long belonged to the Clackamas people. Old Soosap and Sol Clark, two elderly Wasco Indians, recounted (under oath and before a court recorder) their conversations with long-deceased Clackamas elders, including Chief Wochimo.[17] Using the term Tomanowos (meaning Sky Person in the Chinook language), the Indians explained the Clackamas belief that the meteorite had journeyed from the Moon as a representative of the Sky People. Resting in its new home, Tomanowos collected rainwater in its bowl-shaped cavities, thereby symbolizing the unique union of sky, Earth, and water.

When the Clackamas owned the land immediately surrounding Tomanowos, tribal members had collected water from the rock's cavities for medicinal use. Hunters, seeking courage in war and good fortune in the hunt, dipped their arrowheads in the sacred water. Even after ceding the land, those seeking strength and children at puberty made spirit quests to the meteorite, but in the 1870s, the Clackamas people bowed to government pressure directed at suppressing traditional Native American religious practices. Although they stopped making pilgrimages to the meteorite, the tribe maintained a spiritual link with Tomanowos through ceremonies, songs, and oral tradition.[18]

The lawyer defending Hughes argued three points: (1) Although the Clackamas tribe had originally owned the meteorite, (2) they had abandoned the giant "artifact" when they relocated to the Grand Ronde reservation; (3) thus, it was perfectly legal for Mr. Hughes to claim the cast-off meteorite as his own. Was this not just like picking up an ancient stone arrowhead in the woods? Finders keepers, right?[19]

The judge dismissed Hughes's claim as "irrelevant" and ruled in favor of the plaintiff. During a flurry of appeals, injunctions, and additional lawsuits,

[17] The Willamette Meteorite. http: www.usgennet.org/alhnorus/ahorclak/Wilamette-Meteorite.

[18] June Olson, "Cultural Resource Protection Submits Claim to Ancient Meteorite," *Smoke Signals* [a publication of the Grand Ronde Tribe], November 15, 1999; Diedtra Henderson, "Meteorite Custody Case," *Archaeology online news* (February 25, 2000).

[19] As a further legal backstop, Hughes's lawyer attempted to cloud the issue of "ownership" by suggesting that perhaps the meteorite had originally fallen someplace else and subsequently been transported to Oregon Iron and Steel Company land by glaciers. If so, who was the actual "owner"? Or, perhaps, the Indians had moved the meteorite themselves. Given the tangled web of custody, Hughes's attorney argued that only Mr. Hughes had clear title; see Preston, *Dinosaurs in the Attic*, 205–206.

Oregon Iron and Steel Company posted on around-the-clock guard – who sat atop the meteorite, loaded gun at the ready – until a team of horses could finally remove the meteorite from the Hughes property.

On final appeal, the Supreme Court of the State of Oregon ruled on July 17, 1905, that "meteorites, though not embedded in the earth, are real estate and consequently belong to the owner of the land on which they are found." Later that year, the Oregon Iron and Steel Company displayed its meteorite at the Lewis and Clark Exposition in Portland, where the governor proudly announced that America's largest meteorite would stay in Oregon forever.

But Oregon Iron and Steel had other plans, and a year later, they sold the Willamette meteorite to Elizabeth E. Dodge II of New York City, for the sum of $20,600. Mrs. Dodge immediately donated her meteorite to the American Museum of Natural History, where the meteorite has remained on display ever since.[20] Neil deGrasse Tyson, astrophysicist and current director of the Hayden Planetarium, estimates that 40–50 million people have now seen the Willamette meteorite, including "untold numbers of visitors who were turned on to science because of their encounter with this meteorite. . . . It's not simply an artifact on display."[21]

Tomanowos and NAGPRA

As were many smaller tribes, the Confederated Tribes of the Grand Ronde were officially "terminated" during the Eisenhower administration, a time when Indian policy emphasized the total assimilation of Indian people into the American mainstream. After years of intense lobbying, the Grand Ronde (and several other tribes) were "restored" in 1983, and five years later, Congress added ninety-eight hundred acres of land to their reservation, which is still headquartered in the Willamette Valley (about sixty miles southwest of Portland). The forty-five hundred tribal members own and operate the Spirit Mountain Casino, the most successful gaming operation in the Pacific Northwest. Since 1997, the Spirit Mountain Community Fund has donated more than $25 million to nonprofit organizations, making it one of Oregon's largest charitable foundations.[22]

---

[20] At the time, this was highest price paid for any single specimen in the museum's collection.

[21] Robert D. McFadden, "Meteorite Dispute Greets Opening of Planetarium," *New York Times,* February 19, 2000.

[22] "Spirit Mountain Community Fund, Tribal Council Working Together," *Smoke Signals,* May 15, 2004.

As part of the NAGPRA-mandated consultations between tribes and museums, a delegation from the Grand Ronde visited New York City in the fall of 1999, specifically to examine objects in the collections of the American Museum of Natural History for potential repatriation. During this consultation, they learned that Tomanowos was slated to become the centerpiece of the new Cullman Hall of the Universe, the lower exhibition space in the museum's ambitious Rose Center for Earth and Space, which was scheduled to open in a few weeks as part of Millennial Celebration of January 1, 2000. Visiting the hard-hat construction area, the Grand Ronde delegation saw for themselves that the gleaming glass-and-steel Rose Center was literally being constructed around the massive meteorite.[23] "To be close to it," marveled June Olson (the tribe's cultural resource manager), "to be able to know my ancestors stood in the presence of this stone was a real moving experience for me."[24]

So moving, in fact, that the Confederated Tribes of the Grand Ronde soon declared their intent to claim Tomanowos as a "sacred object"[25] as defined in the Native American Grave Protection and Repatriation Act of 1990 – the very same piece of legislation under which the five tribal claimants had claimed Kennewick Man three years before.[26] "It's an extremely important sacred object to us," explained Olson. "It is a link from our tribal people today to our ancestors in traditional beliefs. It's a connection that we're all kind of looking for, and there isn't a lot of them left." To bolster their case, staff members of the Grand Ronde Cultural Resource program began

---

[23]   McFadden, "Meteorite Dispute Greets Opening of Planetarium," *New York Times*, February 19, 2000.

[24]   Diedtra Henderson, "Meteorite Case Update" *Archaeology* 53(3).

[25]   According to NAGPRA " 'sacred objects' ... shall mean specific ceremonial objects which are needed by traditional Native American religious leaders for the practice of traditional Native American religions by their present day adherents"; Section 2 (3B).

[26]   The Grand Ronde are not the first Oregonians to attempt a retrieval of a mete-orite. In the late 1980s, a group of schoolchildren from Lake Oswego persuaded the Oregon senate, former U.S. Senator Bob Packwood, and former U.S. Repre-sentative. Les AuCoin to champion the cause to return the meteorite to Oregon. They convinced the Oregon Museum of Science and Industry to make a suitable home for the meteorite, should it return home. The schoolchildren also appeared on *The Tonight Show* with Johnny Carson. But citing scientific protocols and con-cern over shipping the meteorite across country, the museum declined to return the meteorite. Geneva Cobb Iijima, "Who Owns a meteorite?" *Odyssey* 4(2) (1995), http://www.usgennet.org/alhnorus/ahorclak/MeteorWhose.

interviewing elders and other knowledgeable persons, to formalize the oral tradition surrounding Tomanowos. "So much of Indian culture has been lost. Our people were discouraged, even forbidden to practice their religion," said Tracy Dugan, a tribal spokewoman. "We want the meteorite back, and not some settlement."[27]

Under the provisions of NAGPRA, any tribe requesting a cultural repatriation must prove three key points: (1) the tribe must have legal standing, (2) the object must fit into a NAGPRA category ("funerary object," "sacred object," or item of "cultural patrimony"), and (3) "cultural affiliation" must be demonstrated between the claimant and the object being sought.[28] Museums have ninety days to respond to a repatriation claim, in this case meaning that a formal response was required from the American Museum no later than February 29, 2000.

But rather than addressing the NAGPRA claim (which is administered by the National Park Service and the Department of the Interior), the American Museum pursued a second legal option by suing the Confederated Tribes of the Grand Ronde in Manhattan federal court. The lawsuit, filed only a week after the long-awaited opening of the Rose Center, argued that the meteorite is not the kind of "sacred object" covered by NAGPRA; it is, rather, "a natural feature of the landscape, [not] a specific ceremonial object." The museum contended that the meteorite "has never been marked or altered. There's no indication that it was ever moved by the tribe. No custody or control was taken over it."[29] Alleging that the tribe's claim "potentially impairs the museum's ability to share this exceptional scientific specimen with the public," the museum sought a court ruling specifying (1) that the museum is the rightful owner of the meteorite and (2) that the museum is not required to repatriate the extraterrestrial object being claimed by the Grand Ronde.[30]

A spokesman for the Grand Ronde expressed disappointment in the lawsuit ruling and suggested that "the museum should do the right thing and resolve this dispute now, directly with our tribe, instead of marching off to court behind a squadron of attorneys. . . . We intend to gather our thoughts, communicate with our tribal members and, then, take the steps necessary to

[27] McFadden, "Meteorite Dispute . . ."
[28] According to Tim McKeown, a National Park Service official charged with overseeing NAGPRA claims, quoted in Henderson, "Meteorite Case Update."
[29] Henderson, "Meteorite Case Update."
[30] Benjamin Weiser, "Museum Sues to Keep Meteorite Sought by Indian Group," *New York Times*, February 29, 2000.

regain what is rightfully ours."[31] The tribe added that, if successful in their repatriation claim, they wished to take Tomawonos to the Grand Ronde reservation, perhaps making it available to view by tribal members and the public in an open-air indoor garden. "I know the stone is important to non-tribal people, to Oregonians, and people around the world," said Olson. "We are aware of the need to provide access to these folks as well."[32] The "Return the Rock" movement quickly gained momentum in Oregon as a states' rights issue and became a familiar theme in the pages of Portland's *The Oregonian:* "If we had our way," one editorial read, "it would be heading back on the next westbound freight train."[33]

Archaeologists and Native Americans across the country closely monitored the escalating custody battle over the Willamette/Tomanomos meteorite, eager to see whether a law that had mandated the return of thousands of artifacts and hundreds of human skeletons could be broadened to apply to unmodified artifacts of nature.[34] Whereas the Kennewick case promised to provide a legal review of protocols for extending the definition of cultural affiliation back into distant time, the meteorite dispute carried with it a potential for significantly broadening the definition of "sacred object." After all, if an eight-thousand-year-old skeleton could be "culturally affiliated" with a modern Indian tribe, could an object on the landscape – or maybe even the landscape itself – be repatriated as a "sacred object" under NAGPRA?

There were also major financial concerns because, should the courts grant custody of the meteorite to the Grand Ronde, the costs to the American Museum would be staggering. The gleaming new $210 million Rose Center for Earth and Space had literally been constructed around the sixteen-ton meteorite.[35] A year before, contractors had sunk three deep steel pilings into bedrock, then hoisted the meteorite into place with a crane, then firmly secured it in a permanent exhibition hall. The ninety-five-foot high glass and steel "cube" that comprises the Rose Center – itself the largest suspended glass curtain wall in the United States – would literally have to be disassembled piece by piece to remove the meteorite from the exhibition hall.

31 Henderson, "Meteorite Case Update."
32 Courtnay Thompson, "Tribes Claim Willamette Meteorite," *The Oregonian* November 17, 1999.
33 Cited in Gersh Kuntzman, *Newseek Web Exclusive* http://gershkuntzman.homestead.com
34 *New York Times*, February 29, 2000; Henderson, "Meteorite Case Update."
35 McFadden, "Meteorite Dispute"

The Resolution

As both parties marshaled their courtroom arguments, they also insti-
gated a series of private, off-the-record discussions aimed at heading off
a Kennewick-like standoff. On June 22, 2000, the American Museum of
Natural History and the Confederated Tribes of the Grand Ronde Community of Oregon jointly announced a "historic" out-of-court settlement that
(1) maintained the presence of the meteorite at the museum (for scientific
and educational purposes) (2) while ensuring access for religious, historical,
and cultural purposes to the tribe.[36] The tribe agreed to drop its repatriation
claim for the meteorite and not contest the museum's ownership of it, but
the agreement also stipulated that the meteorite would be conveyed to the
tribe should the museum fail to display it publicly (excepting during temporary periods for preservation, safety, construction, and reasons beyond
the museum's direct control). The agreement "reflects mutual recognition
of and respect for the traditions of both the Tribe and the Museum."[37]

Both parties breathed deep sighs of relief. "I can't begin to tell you how
much this means to us," said Kathryn Harrison, Tribal Council Chair of
the Grand Ronde. "Since the termination of our tribe by the federal government in 1954, we have worked hard to gather our people together to
share our unique and important past. This agreement goes even further
because it looks towards our future. I consider it one of the outstanding
milestones we've reached for our tribal members." Ellen V. Futter, President
of the American Museum of Natural History, noted that "this constructive resolution demonstrates the Tribe's and the Museum's enlightened and
progressive approach to discovering the opportunities that lie within our
traditions. Our agreement reflects mutual respect and understanding and
signals new possibilities for an ongoing and fruitful relationship."

---

[36] "The American Museum of Natural History and the Confederated Tribes of
the Grand Ronde Community of Oregon Sign Historic Agreement Maintaining
Willamette Meteorite at Museum, Recognizing the Tribe's Spiritual Relationship
to the Meteorite," June 22, 2000, http://www.amnh.org/rose/meteorite_agreement.
html.

[37] Growing out of these discussions – but separate from the formal agreement – the
tribe and the museum agreed to establish an internship program for Native American young people to foster Native Americans' sharing a deeper understanding and
appreciation of their customs, traditions, and history with the museum community and the general public; to share with Native Americans information from the
museum collection; to share museum expertise in archaeology and anthropology;
and to cultivate scientific knowledge and appreciation of modern Native American
tribes.

The Grand Ronde began making plans for a new pilgrimage – this time to New York City – to reestablish their ties to Tomanowos. Several tribal members expressed skepticism about visiting New York, but others felt strongly that a personal reunion was long overdue. On May 16, 2001, when a delegation from Grand Ronde arrived at the museum, "everyone . . . wondered if the rock still had power." The Cullman Hall of the Universe was temporarily closed to the public to allow F. Travis Benoist (Cheyenne River Sioux) and the Grand Ronde tribal member CeCe Kneeland to conduct a private blessing of the meteorite. The ceremony and the talking circle that followed proved to be emotional moments for many in the group.[38] According to Kathryn Harrison, if they listened intently, Tomanowos spoke to the visitors. "Why did it take you so long?" she heard it say; "I've been waiting a long time to see you."[39]

Today, the meteorite sports two silver labels. One oval plaque explains the geophysical specifics of the Willamette meteorite ("Billions of years ago, an early planet orbiting the sun was shattered, perhaps in a collision with another protoplanet.) A second plaque describes the special significance of this meteorite to the Clackamas and their descendants, explaining that Tomanowos has "has healed and empowered the people of the valley since the beginning of time."

Every June, on their annual pilgrimage to visit and bless Tomanowos, the Grand Ronde delegation also drops off two teenage interns and a tribal staff chaperone, to participate in the Inside View program at the American Museum. They join dozens of high school-age New Yorkers, each of whom is assigned to work on special projects with a mentor or one of the museum scientists.[40] Cristina Lara, one of the first of the Grand Ronde interns, was assigned to work in the museum's Discovery Room, a section for kids that featured fossils, bones, and a model excavation site. Lara said the fit was good because it renewed her interest in history, which she decided to study in college: "It has given me some direction, that's for sure."[41] Teresa Henry, another Grand Ronde intern, was assigned to the Communications Office, researching press releases and working in the IMAX theater. Subsequent interns have studied the geology of New York City and answered questions

[38]   Brent Merrill, " 'Tomanowos' Meteorite – Star Power," *Smoke Signals*, June 1, 2001.
[39]   Brent Merrill, "Tribal Members Reunited with Tomanowos in New York City," *Smoke Signals*, June 15, 2003.
[40]   May 1, 2001, "Tribe to Visit Willamette Meteorite in New York," http://www.grandronde.org/PR
[41]   Chris Mercier, "Tribal Members in New York," *Smoke Signals*, September 1, 2001.

about the tribe for visitors and museum patrons. "A lot of people don't know about Indians," said Richard Sohappy. "Or what they do know is from movies. So it was good for them to break down those barriers and perceptions. It was cool."[42] The interns also spent some private time with Tomanowos meteorite. "I touched it," said Cristina Lara. "It was a trip. I mean this thing is from outer space." But Teresa Henry had some misgivings after returning home. "There kids crawling over it. I didn't understand. It felt awkward. It was out of place. It should be here."[43]

Smoke Signals, the tribal newspaper of the Grand Ronde, tracks each New York pilgrimage and publishes accounts of the adventures of the tribal interns. The writers generally speak of the experience in positive terms, although an occasional dissenting voice suggests that one day, Tomanowos might still return home. To Kathryn Harrison, the threatened legal actions and amicable settlement demonstrate beyond doubt that "Tomanowas still has power.... Look what it's done. Whoever thought it would be the center of this new museum?"[44]

THE CASE OF KWÄDAY DÄN TS'ÍNCHI (LONG AGO PERSON FOUND)

On August 14, 1999, three hunters stalked Dall's sheep in the remote St. Elias Mountains of northwestern British Columbia, not far from the Yukon/Alaska boundary. As they were traversing the remote and roadless landscape of the Tatshenshini Alsek Park, one of them, squinting through binoculars, saw a curious "smudge" on the faraway blue snow. "It looked like the National Geographic pictures we'd been seeing for years," recalled Warren Ward. "I could see a lot of tattered bucked leather, and pieces of fringe."[45]

Finders Keepers?

The hunters were soon staring down at a headless frozen corpse, lying on its side near the edge of the ice. Not far away were a wooden throwing dart, an extraordinarily fine hat woven of cedar roots, and a decomposing fur robe. Knowing that this man had died long ago, the hunters immediately

[42] Peta Tinda, "Tribal Youth Experience the Big Apple," Smoke Signals, August 15, 2002.

[43] Chris Mercier, "Great Story," Smoke Signals, September 1, 2001.

[44] Larry McShane (AP) "Oregon Tribes Agree to Share Sacred Meteorite with NYC Museum," June 22, 2000.

[45] Quoted in James Brooke, "Ancient Man Uncovered in Canadian Ice," New York Times, August 25, 1999.

grasped the importance of their find. They retrieved the hat and part of a fur garment, headed out across the raw landscape, and arrived two days later at the Beringia Centre at Whitehorse (the Yukon capital) to report their find.

Tatshenshini Alsek Park is located in the British Columbia portion of the traditional territory of the Champagne and Aishihik First Nations (CAFN). These are Tutchone Indians, traditionally a highly mobile people who once subsisted by hunting and fishing. Their aboriginal language is Southern Tutchone (one of several Athapascan dialects spoken in the area). Over the past two centuries, the Tutchone people have adjusted to the impact of the fur trade, the Klondike gold rush, and the building of the Alaskan highway. In recent years, several Southern Tutchone leaders have been active in negotiating land settlement claims with both federal and territorial governments, and the CAFN has been active in attempting to preserve certain aspects of their traditional lifeway.[46] The Southern Tutchone have long traded with the Tlingit, their coastal neighbors in Alaska. Intermarriage between the two groups has been so pervasive that the Southern Tutchone have adopted features of the Tlingit clan system, and many speak the Tlingit language.

When heritage officials in Whitehorse notified the CAFN elders of the new find, many recalled haunting stories about the mystical, ethereal world of the glaciers, where unseen chasms can swallow up the unsuspecting. Owls sometimes emerged from their sleep beneath the ice to consume the unwary. According to one well-known legend, a coastal trader was left for dead after a fall into an ice chasm in the southern Yukon. Entombed, he listened to mourners miles away, wailing at his funeral potlatch. But this legendary traveler was eventually saved by a dogged search party who refused to give up. Both the CAFN and the Tlingit maintained stories about travelers who had vanished on the ice, and many Tlingit felt that perhaps the frozen man was one of their own. But because the body had clearly been found in Southern Tutchone territory, the CAFN assumed legal authority over the find.[47]

[46] For more on the history and ethnography of the Tutchone people, see Catharine McClellan, "Tutchone," in June Helm (ed), *Subarctic, volume 6 of the Handbook of North American Indians* (Washington, DC: Smithsonian Institution Press, 1981): 493–505. The rights of the CAFN to the Yukon portion of their traditional lands and resources were confirmed in a land claims agreement in 1993. Their claims to the corresponding land in the British Columbia portion of the park remain disputed, but in 1996, the province and CAFN signed an agreement to comanage Tatshenshini-Alsek Park. The First Nations has had a formal Heritage Program since 1993.

[47] This meant that Canadian heritage laws would govern the disposition of the new find.

When they first learned of the new find, several CAFN elders had expressed the concern that "this man has not had a burial. You can't leave him there," said Gaunt, a heritage planner for the Yukon First Nations. "Bring him down and try to find who he was and how long he'd been there."[48] And so they did.

Nine days after the initial find (on August 22 and 23, 1999), a recovery team flew by helicopter to the find site. The team leader was Owen Beattie (University of Alberta), a well-known physical anthropologist with previous research experience with frozen remains from the Arctic. He was accompanied by archaeologists, a glaciologist, and First Nations representatives.

Wearing Tyvek biohazard suits and sterile latex gloves, the recovery team approached the remains from the downwind side, to minimize contamination. After locating the frozen remains lodged in an east-west ridge feature, they found that the body had been severed in two by slow glacial movement. The head and right arm had disappeared entirely (perhaps carved away by rushing torrents of meltwater or scavengers), but the surviving remains were astonishingly well preserved. His flesh still showed goose pimples and strands of his neatly trimmed black hair lay in the nearby ice. They gingerly lifted the remains by hand, immediately shrouding the body parts in two layers of sterile hospital wraps and an outer layer of sterile clear plastic sheeting. These bundles were stored in rigid plastic containers, which were temporarily housed in a nearby snowbank as the team scoured the area for additional human remains and artifacts. A pressing cold front forced the recovery team to cut their trip short, and the remains were taken to Whitehorse.

The Iceman and Cultural Heritage Law

A round of meetings was held in Whitehorse, and diverse opinions were expressed about the proper way to proceed. Recovering the remains caused some concern because among the Champagne and Aishihik people two clans – the Wolf and the Crow – are charged with supervising all mortuary functions, and neither clan felt comfortable in claiming the frozen body as a clansman. Some were even unsure whether he was really a tribesman at all. Some CAFN members, perhaps influenced by evangelical Christian theology, attributed a series of local accidents to the fact the frozen body

---

[48] Quoted in Heather Pringle, "Out of the Ice. Who Was This Ancient Traveler Discovered in an Alpine Glacier?" *Canadian Geographic* July/August 2002: 56–64.

remained unburied; they urged immediate cremation of the remains and all of his possessions.

Several members of the Coastal Tlingit tribe also traveled to discuss the matter with their Interior relatives and representatives of other Canadian Indians. Each group expressed the belief that the frozen man might be one of their tribal members. Coastal Tlingit people recalled a song about one of their tribal members who was injured on a glacier on a return trip form the Interior, and they argued for continued studies of both the remains and the cultural artifacts.

The Resolution

Three weeks after the recovery, the research team and First Nations representatives held a press conference to announce their find to the world. The frozen man was to be called Kwädąy Dän Ts'ínchį (pronounced KwuhDAY Dun Sinchee), which means "long-ago person found" in the Southern Tutchone language; the name has since been commonly abbreviated as *KDT*. In assigning this name, Kwädąy Dän Ts'ínchį, CAFN leaders assured the Tlingit that they were not asserting a tribal affiliation. CAFN was simply assuming responsibility for his care because he was found on their lands.[49]

In light of the comanagement agreement that governs the Tatshenshini-Alsek Park, the CAFN and the Province of British Columbia formed a collaborative partnership that emphasized two key points: (1) the need for respectful treatment of the newly discovered human remains and artifacts and (2) the desire for state-of-the-art scientific study of the find, including contextual studies involving ethnography and oral history. From the outset, the decision regarding final disposition of the human remains and artifacts was assigned to CAFN, effective December 31, 2000. This compromise position thus allowed for scientific studies to be conducted within a specific period, after which the remains would be cremated, and the artifacts retained for additional study.

On August 25, 1999, the *Yukon News* quoted the CAFN leader Bob Charlie:

The Elders have indicated that we should use this situation, what appears to be an ancient tragedy, to learn more about this person, when he lived and how his clothes were made and how he died. This person has much to tell us, to help us understand

---

49   According to Rosita Worl (a Tlingit leader involved in the process), the Tlingit "came to the conclusion that he was instead claiming us all" (personal communication, 2004).

our past, and the history of our homeland. We wish to see these human remains treated with dignity and respect and to see the most positive outcome of this long-ago event. . . . In fact, the band sees the find as more than a cultural boon. It's already planning to tap into the research grants that will help pay its members to study the remains"[50]

Members of CAFN also recognized the importance of the new find in reinforcing pending land claims with the Canadian government. According to Diane Strand (the tribe's Heritage Resource Officer), "Stories recorded by our elders, [say] we have been here since time immemorial, since when animals could speak to people."[51] At the initial press conference, the CAFN spokesman Ron Chambers emphasized the delicate political situation surrounding his people and stated that since the find proved the long-term aboriginal use of the landscape, it thereby strengthened the First Nations claim on the land.[52]

With the blessing of the Yukon's First Nations, two dozen researchers from Canada, England, Scotland, Australia, and the United States were recruited to apply the most advanced high-tech forensic and palaeobiological techniques to the remains of Kwädąy Dän Ts'ínchi.[53] The frozen body had been were temporarily stored at a Yukon Heritage Branch facility at minus seventeen degrees Celsius, while an agreement was negotiated between CAFN and the British Columbia Archaeology Branch. Seeking to establish the most stable environment for the remains, the conservation team also consulted a number of experts in the field and ultimately elected to follow the protocols established to preserve Ötzi, the famous "iceman," who had died fifty-three hundred years ago in the area of the Oetzal Alps, found in 1991 along the Austrian-Italian border.[54]

The entire freezer was flown to Victoria in the constant company of the conservator and representatives of the British Columbia Archaeology Branch and CAFN. At the Royal British Columbia Museum (in Victoria),

---

[50]   Murray Lundberg (2001) "Kwaday Dan Sinche, the Yukon Iceman," *Explore North*, (http://www.explorenorth.com/ (accessed July 24, 2001).

[51]   Quoted in Brooke, "Ancient Man Uncovered," 1999.

[52]   Murray Lundberg, "Kwaday Dan Sinche," 2001.

[53]   The specialties include miochondrial and microbial DNA, parasitology, entomology, pathology, palaeoradiology, paleobotany, palaeodiet, skeletal biology, low-temperature preservation, glaciology, taphonomy, trace elements, and additional radiocarbon dating.

[54]   O. Gaber, O. K. H. Küunzel, H. Haurer, and W. Platzer, "Konservierung and Lagerung der Gletschermumie," in *Der Mann Im Eis, Band 1*. Edited by F. Höpfel, W. Platzer, and K. Spindler (Insbruck: Eigenverlag der Universität Insbruck, 1992): 92–99.

the human remains were housed in a large sterile freezer that simulated the glacier's high humidity and subzero temperature. Most of the artifacts were taken to the Yukon Heritage Branch, which maintains an agreement with CAFN to assist in the care and management of such materials. The fur garment and some of the smaller artifacts were subsequently transferred to the Royal British Columbia Museum for conservation and analysis.

Kwädạy Dän Ts'ínchị was the first well preserved ancient human body ever recovered from a North American glacier, and his remains took on special significance to the research team. Unlike most frozen burials – including those of the Inuit, the sacrificed Andean children, or the Siberian Pazyryks – KDT had died accidentally, taking with him only everyday items; no elaborate funerary items had been added by grieving kinsmen. This meant that KDT held the keys to unlock the secrets of his daily life, and the research team framed several basic questions: How old was Kwädạy Dän Ts'ínchị when he died? What did he look like? What did he eat? Was he healthy? Where had he traveled? Did KDT belong to a coastal people, such as the Tlingits, or an interior, Athapascan-speaking group (such as the Champagne and Aishihik First Nations), in whose traditional territory the body was found?

Answers to the questions emerged slowly as the scientific examination proceeded.[55] A series of radiocarbon dates determined that the hat and robe had been made sometime between A.D. 1415 and 1445. This meant Kwädạy Dän Ts'ínchị had likely died a few decades before Columbus waded ashore in the Caribbean (and a full three centuries before European vessels appeared off the coast of British Columbia).

The palaeoautopsy, conducted by forensic specialists, disclosed that KDT had died in his late teens (or possibly early twenties). He was in excellent health before he died alone in the bitterly cold Canadian northland. His neatly combed and trimmed hair was worn loose and unbraided. His clothing was clearly aboriginal, a conclusion confirmed by DNA analysis (which revealed that KDT was clearly a Native American, likely from the local area). His broad-brimmed hat had been constructed from roots of cedar (or maybe spruce), so tightly woven that it still repels rain.

His robe was made from the skins of ninety-five Arctic ground squirrels, each one pierced by tiny holes, then sewn with a very fine, two-ply animal sinew – "almost as fine as button thread." The collar was made of moose

[55] A preliminary analysis of the scientific finds is reported by Owen Beattie, Brian Apland, Erik W. Blake, James A. Cosgrove, Sarah Gaunt, Sheila Greer, Alexander P. Mackie, Kjerstin E. Mackie, Dan Straathof, Valerie Thorp, and Peter M. Troffe, "The Kwädạy Dän Ts'ínchị Discovery from a Glacier in British Columbia," *Journal Canadien d'Archeologie* 24: 129–147 (2000).

(deer or caribou?) hide, and fringes were added to prevent rainwater from penetrating; a mix of grease and red ocher sealed the seams from the inside. An admiring conservator at the Royal British Columbia Museum marveled, "I'm pretty sure that some granny or mother made this for him to keep him warm."[56]

Kwäday Dän Ts'ínchi carried a small wooden hand tool, housed in a leather sheath and encrusted with a curious rust stain. If KDT died decades before Columbus arrived in the Americas – as the radiocarbon evidence clearly indicated – then how did he acquire an iron-tipped tool? Although the iron might have originated from a meteoritic source, the more likely source would be an (unknown) pre-Columbian shipwreck, perhaps blown off course from a distant Asiatic coastline.

KDT also carried a small hide bag or pouch that the First Nations researchers immediately identified as a personal medicine bag concealing the man's sacred objects. Because of the cultural significance and private nature of such medicine pouches, they asked the scientists refrain from opening, studying, or documenting the artifacts. Although curious about the contents of the sealed bad, all scientists involved in the TDK research complied with the request and the medicine bag was kept in its frozen state and stored with the human remains.

KDT's clothing thus posed a problem: his exquisite robe of Arctic ground squirrel pelts is an interior-type garment, once a common mode of dress for the Tutchone people. But the Coastal Tlingit immediately recognized the woven hat as their own, and they even commissioned a skilled weaver to study and replicate the piece at her home village of Klukwan. So where was home to Kwäday Dän Ts'ínchi?

One clue is from the small pieces of fish and scales found adhering to the fur robe. This four-year-old chum salmon had been caught just as it entered its spawning run. Unlike other salmon species, chum salmon are unusual in that they spawn only in the lower reaches of the rivers; this evidence seems to suggest that KDT may have lived near a riverbank along the coast. But, of course, if the fish had been smoked, he could also have traded for it from elsewhere.

Seeking more clues, scientists conducted both electronic and light microscopic studies of remains in the intact alimentary canal (i.e., stomach and intestinal contents, plus fecal material). These results indicate the meals consumed during the last few days before death and can be compared with long-term evidence available from stable isotopic study (conducted on collagen extracts from tissue). KDT's digestive tract contained pollen from glasswort

---

[56]   Quoted in Pringle, "Out of the Ice," 62.

(today restricted to intertidal marshes and inland salt flats) and pieces of a marine crustacean (likely a marine crab from the shores of the Pacific Northwest coast). The coastal connection is further reinforced by the fruit of a flowering plant (mountain sweet-cicely) and a needle of a coniferous tree (mountain hemlock) found adhered to his robe. Stable isotope analysis of bone and tissue samples further confirmed that 90 percent of KDT's diet derived from marine sources. James Dickson and his colleagues concluded that "this individual had strong coastal connections during his life, and had been on the coast shortly before he died."[57]

Isotopic studies were also conducted on KDT's hair. Because human hair is known to grow about one centimeter each month, incremental isotope studies can indicate something about short-term diet as well. A distinct "terrestrial" isotope signature characterizes the most recent hair fragments, indicating that KDT spent his last days (perhaps even a few months) in an inland environment.

To sum up, KDT was found buried within a glacier about eighty-five kilometers inland from the nearest point along the strongly indented Alaskan coastline. He likely lived along this Alaskan coastline for most of his life and moved inland shortly before he perished. Ethnography and oral history from both Tlingit and Southern Athapascan people amply document the well-used trade routes that connected the coastal fjords with the interior Tutchone homeland. The combined paleobotanical evidence thus suggests that his homeland was most likely somewhere between the Chilkoot/Chilkat Inlets and the Yakutat.[58]

Kwädąy Dän Ts'ínchį was probably caught in a freak summer snowstorm as the young traveler headed home from a trading trip – maybe swapping lynx, wolverine, moose, skins, and bighorn sheep horns from the interior for sea resources. Overtaken by hypothermia, he lapsed into a final lethal sleep, and his body was quickly buried in snow, and quickly frozen before decay set in.

A friendly rivalry continues between Coastal and Interior groups, both eager to establish direct tribal affiliation with Kwädąy Dän Ts'ínchį. Some recalled the story of Cheddar Man, a nine-thousand-year-old skeleton whose

---

[57]   James H. Dickson, Michael P. Richards, Richard J. Hebda, Peta J. Mudie, Owen Beattie, Susan Ramsay, Nancy J. Turner, Bruce J. Leighton, John M. Webster, Niki R. Hobischak, Gail S. Anderson, Peter M. Troffe, and Rebecca J. Wigan (n.d.), "Reconstructing the Last Days of Kwädąy Dän Ts'ínchį by Intestinal and Biomolecular analysis" (in press).

[58]   James H. Dickson, personal communication.

bones were discovered in 1903 inside Gough's Cave, about 130 miles west of London. In 1997, scientists at Oxford University's Institute of Molecular Medicine studied mitochrondial DNA extracted from one of Cheddar Man's molars. Wondering whether any descendants could still be living in the area, scientists collected DNA samples from a number of local schoolchildren and adults at their school. The genetic fit between Cheddar Man and Adrian Targett (a history teacher at the school) was almost exact, immediately establishing the world's oldest family tree. Mr. Targett is thrilled with his Ice Age genealogy, and scientists have used this evidence to argue that modern-day Britons descended from early hunter-gatherers who later farmed the area.

More than one hundred Coastal and Interior Tlingit have contributed their DNA study (conducted in June 2001). Harryet Rappier, of Juneau, said she was curious to learn about her northern relatives, especially since her mother was born in 1903 in Klukshu, Yukon. "I can't get enough information from that part of the world."[59] Loretta Marvin, one of the more than one hundred Coastal and Interior Tlingits participating in the DNA testing, agrees. "This is pretty interesting, very fascinating, to be able to find out and check back what it is, 500 years, and there is maybe a possibility I could be a relative." Says Rosita Worl, "We Tlingit have a concept 'haa Shagoon' which ties simultaneously to our ancestors and future generations. In the instance of Long Ago Person Found . . . our traditional leaders said that our ancestors are offering us and our future children knowledge. They were also especially gleeful since they [the Tlingit] said now these finds confirm that 'We have been here since time immemorial.'"[60] At the present writing, financial problems plague this intriguing project, and the study has yet to be completed.

After extensive consultation, Champagne and Aishihik leaders cremated the human remains and medicine bundle in July 2001, returning the ashes to the glacier where he was found. Says Diane Strand, the ceremony was "very emotional. It was as though you were burying your loved one. It was an extremely uplifting and moving thing to do."[61]

CONCLUSION: LITIGATION OR NEGOTIATION?

We have presented three case studies, each illustrating a rather different approach to the issue of cultural patrimony in Native America. We began

[59] CBS News, "The Iceman Cousin Cometh?" June 6, 2001.
[60] Rosita Worl, personal communication.
[61] Quoted in Brooke, "Ancient Man Uncovered," 1999.

with the multicultural tug-of-war over Kennewick Man, which raises deep
questions about how the past can serve the diverse purposes of the present,
Indian as well as white.

The Kennewick conflict has often been portrayed as a face-off between
science and religion, a reprise of the famous Scopes trial of the 1920s – except
that Red Creationists have now assumed the role of Christian fundamentalists. But the facts of the case indicate otherwise.

At the heart of the matter, the Kennewick dispute boils down to issues
of power and control. Who controls ancient American history – governmental agencies, the academic community, or modern Indian people? To
understand the deeply political nature of the Kennewick conflict, one must
remember the long-term interactions between Euroamerican and Indian
populations. Over more than five centuries, several distinct American Indian
histories have developed, of which three are especially critical: a larger
national narrative that glorifies assimilation into the great American melting
pot, an academic discourse written by anthropologists and historians who
view Indians as subjects of scholarly inquiry, and an indigenous "insider's"
perspective long maintained in the oral traditions of Indian people themselves. Although sometimes overlapping, these distinct histories often paint
quite different visions of America, past and present. Proponents of each
strongly believe that "their" history is the correct one, the version that
should be published in textbooks, protected by law, and defended in the
courtroom.

The Kennewick case also challenges us to define when ancient bones stop
being tribal and become simply human. If Indian people lose the fight to
retain and rebury their ancestors' bones, will they also lose other treaty-
guaranteed rights that define their unique, sovereign status under United
States law? If archaeologists surrender the right to study ancient human
bones and artifacts, will the scientific community have to fear continual
censure by the religious beliefs of a few? Should this happen, then mainstream archaeology's views on American origins would no longer carry the
clout of authority. From whatever perspective, Kennewick became a very
public fight that neither side felt it could afford to lose.[62]

But in a real sense, all sides lost. Many Native Americans are, of course,
deeply disappointed in the outcome of the Kennewick case. One tribal
spokesman termed the Gould decision "a staggering blow to the tribes'

---

[62] Patty Gerstenblith, "Cultural Significance and the Kennewick Skeleton: Some
Thoughts on the Resolution of Cultural Heritage Disputes," pp. 162–200.

ability to protect their cultural properties."[63] The Umatilla had opposed
the destructive DNA and radiocarbon testing conducted to prepare the
court case and protested the National Park Service decision to send fragments of the Kennewick skeleton to laboratories in Arizona, California,
Florida, Michigan, and Connecticut. The tribe claimed that "these studies
are not being done to prove cultural affiliation. They are being done to
appease the scientists and the court."[64] And amazingly, when Douglas W.
Owsley, one of the *Bonnichsen* scientist plaintiffs, inventoried the Kennewick
remains in October 1998, he found that some of the bones had been stolen.
Although the Department of Justice launched an investigation, nobody has
been charged.[65] In other words, even had the tribes ultimately won custody
of the bones, tribal officials fumed, the remains had already been treated in
a destructive and disrespectful manner.

The Gould ruling also casts doubt on the status of oral history in subsequent court cases. A key provision of NAGPRA stipulates that "cultural
affiliation" is established by "a preponderance of the evidence based upon
geographical, kinship, biological, archaeological, anthropological, linguistic, folkloric, oral traditional, historical, or other relevant information or
expert opinion."[66] In so doing, NAGPRA implicitly recognized that differing histories had evolved for ancient Native America. One was written in
books, taught in schools, and exhibited in museums – this is mainstream
history reflecting the perspective of the outsider, the conqueror of con-
tinents. An entirely different history existed in Indian Country, a history
handed down by Indian people from elder to child as tribal tradition, language, spirituality, ritual, and ceremonies – even in jewelry and personal
ornamentation.

Archaeology and oral tradition differ, of course, in the ways observations
are made and interpreted. Western science relies on discrete observational

---

[63] Associated Press, "Scientists Win Another Battle over Kennewick Man," April 20,
2004.

[64] Confederated Tribes of the Umatilla Indian Reservation, "Tribe Opposed to DNA
Testing of Ancient One," 2000, http://www.umatilla.nsn.us/kman5.html

[65] Douglas W. Owsley and Richard L. Jantz, "Kennewick Man – a Kin? Too Distant,"
in Alazar Barkan and Ronald Bush, *Claiming the Stones/Naming the Bones: Issues:
Cultural Property and the Negotiation of National and Ethnic Identity*. Los Angeles,
CA: Getty Research Institute, 2002): 141–161 (citing p. 153).

[66] NAGPRA 1990, Sec. 2(3)B; see also Roger C. Echo-Hawk, "Ancient History in the
New World: Integrating Oral Traditions and the Archaeological Record," *American
Antiquity* 65: 267–290 (2000); Peter M. Whiteley, "Archaeology and Oral Tradition:
The Scientific Importance of Dialogue," *American Antiquity* 67: 405–418, (2002).

units and measurable variables that can be analytically combined and/or held constant. Native observations arise from people who view themselves within a holistic environment and societal framework. These are separate ways of knowing the past, but they tend to converge in a broad sense because certain important issues tend to dominate both realms – migrations, warfare, land use, ethnicity, and so forth. Because different standards apply to the ways relevant information is collected, evaluated, and used, however, the two ways of knowing will never completely coincide.

But Judge Gould's decision states, in part, that "because oral accounts have been inevitably changed in context of transmission, because the traditions include myths that cannot be considered as if factual histories, because the value of such accounts is limited by concerns of authenticity, reliability, and accuracy, and because the record as a whole does not show where historical fact ends and mythic tale begins, we do not think that the oral traditions ... were adequate to show the required significant relationship of the Kennewick Man's remains to the Tribal Claimants."[67] Thus, not only have the tribes (apparently) lost the battle over the bones, the February 2004 ruling may undermine the role of oral tradition in establishing cultural affiliation in future repatriation cases.

The archaeologist Robson Bonnichsen, one of the eight scientist plaintiffs, calls the recent court decisions "fantastic news. We've been waiting so long, and it's been so immensely frustrating."[68] But the Kennewick case has extracted a dear price from the scientific perspective as well. For one thing, the actual site of the Kennewick discovery has been destroyed. Although permitting a preliminary geological study of the Kennewick site, the Corps defied the will of Congress and in April 1998 covered the Kennewick Man site with six hundred tons of boulders, gravel, logs, and backdirt and planted thousands of closely spaced cottonwood, dogwood, and willow trees on top of the fill. In this $160,000 cover-up, the Army Corps had not only made the site inaccessible to scientists and tourists; they had destroyed any undiscovered evidence beyond recovery. In his August 2002 ruling, Judge Jelderks ruled that the Army Corps had violated the National Historic Preservation Act by burying the discovery site.

At its legal core, *Bonnichsen et al. v. United States of America* was a lawsuit against a federal agency for lack of compliance with existing laws, and the

---

[67] *Bonnichsen et al. v United States et al*, 2004 Ninth Circuit Court of Appeals, No. 02-35996, 2004 U.S. App.; *Bonnichsen v US* 2004: 1607.

[68] Quoted in Hill 2004.

costs involved are staggering.[69] To date, the federal government has spent at least $1.1 million (and perhaps as much as $3 million) on this case, and these expenses continue to mount, for storage fees (to conservators, time and travel by government personnel) for the skeleton at the Burke Museum. According to Alan Schneider, lead attorney for the plaintiffs, "Despite all the time and money invested by the federal government in the Kennewick Man affair, little has been accomplished other than to provide an expensive example of poor decision making."[70]

Further, although some important information was generated in the course of presenting the court case, many are critical of the various scientific and contextual studies commissioned by the National Park Service. The geological study was quite incomplete, leaving numerous questions that should have been answered (but may never be because of the heavy-handed approach of the Corps in burying the site). Some believe that excessive samples of bone were sacrificed for radiocarbon dating, destroying fifty grams of the Kennewick skeleton (as opposed to the four grams requested by the *Bonnichsen* plaintiffs). Excessive use of X rays may also have damaged any residual DNA in the Kennewick bones.[71]

Finally, many observers had hoped that the high-profile Kennewick lawsuit would generate, for the first time, an adequate judicial review of the circumstances under which NAGPRA would (or would not) permit the scientific study of human remains.[72] Despite the twenty-two thousand pages of documented testimony, this considered review did not take place. In a lone footnote, Judge Jelderks noted that because Kennewick Man was not a Native American under the law, the provisions of NAGPRA for scientific

---

[69]   Owsley and Jantz, "Kennewick Man," 155.
[70]   Alan L. Schneider, "Kennewick Man: The Three-Million Dollar Man, in Richman, Jennifer R., and Marion P. Forsyth (eds), *Legal Perspectives on Cultural Resources* (Walnut Creek, CA: AltaMira Press, 2004): 202–215; quoting p. 202.
[71]   Schneider, "Kennewick Man," 208.
[72]   Douglas W. Ackerman, "Kennewick Man: The Meaning of 'Cultural Affiliation' and 'Major Scientific Benefit' in the Native American Graves Protection and Repatriation Act," *Tulsa Law Journal* 33: 359–383 (1997); Robert W. Lannan, "Anthropology and Restless Spirits: The Native American Graves Protection and Repatriation Act, and the Unresolved Issues of Prehistoric Human Remains," *Harvard Environmental Law Review* 22: 369–439 (1998); Rebecca Tsosie, "Privileging Claims to the Past: Ancient Human Remains and Contemporary Cultural Values,"*Arizona State Law Journal* 31: 583–677 (1999); Michael J. Kelly, "A Skeleton in the Legal Closet: The Discovery of 'Kennewick Man' Crystallizes the Debate over Federal Law Governing Disposal of Ancient Human Remains," *University of Hawai'i Law Review* 21(1): 42–72 (1999).

study were irrelevant. Furthermore, the 1990 statute had clearly established independent criteria for determining whether remains are "Native American" and, if so, whether they are "culturally affiliated" with a modern tribe or Native Hawaiian organization.[73] The Jelderks and Gould decisions seem to muddy the waters by collapsing the two lines of inquiry and conflating the terms in a way that Congress certainly did not intend.[74]

The Kennewick controversy clearly highlights the difficulties in asking the court system to resolve disputes involving cultural heritage and intellectual property rights. To be sure, the eight scientists who filed the Kennewick Man lawsuit felt a sense of urgency, even desperation. But as the argument over Kennewick Man came to be viewed in terms of "winners" and "losers," it overshadowed the search for a relationship based on mutual respect and consensus.

The dispute over the Willamette meteorite (Tomanowas) was resolved because parties explicitly recognized the downside of a Kennewick-style court battle. In the early rounds, the Confederated Tribes of the Grand Ronde argued that NAGPRA required the return of Tomanowas because it qualified as a "sacred object." The American Museum of Natural History countered by asserting its right of possession and arguing that the meteorite was a natural feature of the landscape (and hence immune to NAGPRA). But rather than proceeding with the threatened litigation, both parties worked behind the scene to find channels for mediating their differences. That is, instead of framing their differences in the finders-keepers, winners-losers mentality that characterized the Kennewick Man case, representatives of the Grand

---

[73] Common sense, of course, would seem to suggest that any eight-thousand year-old skeleton found within the United States was indeed Native American. In fact, Secretary of the Interior Babbitt decided that Kennewick is Native American largely because he predates A.D. 1492, the generally accepted beginning of European colonization of the New World. In overturning this view, Judge Jelderks insisted that legal determination of whether human remains are "Native American" requires a closer reading of NAGPRA's definition of *Native American*: "of, or relating to, a tribe, people, or culture that is indigenous to the United States." Emphasizing that age does not figure in this definition, Jelderks ruled that Kennewick is Native American *merely* because he predates A.D. 1492.

[74] It likewise remains unclear whether NAGPRA could withstand a constitutional challenge; see Jennifer R. Richman, "NAGPRA: Constitutionally Adequate?" in Jennifer R. Richman and Marion P. Forsyth (eds), *Legal Perspectives on Cultural Resources* (Walnut Creek, CA: AltaMira Press, 2004): 216–231; Christopher A. Amato, "Using the Courts to Enforce Repatriation Rights: A Case Study under NAGPRA," in Jennifer R. Richman and Marion P. Forsyth (eds), *Legal Perspectives on Cultural Resources* (Walnut Creek, CA: AltaMira Press, 2004): 232–251.

Ronde and American Museum explored alternatives in an atmosphere of mutual respect and common interest.

Because Kwäday Dän Ts'ínchi was found in British Columbia, the NAGPRA legislation was not directly involved. Canadian law dealing with cultural heritage, repatriation, and reburial had been in place long before the NAGPRA legislation was passed in the United States. Because the First Nations' authority had been established by previous protocols, a spirit of cooperation and respect permeated the discussions about KDT.

There were some compromises, to be sure. The consulting scientists worked within the constraints set out by the CAFN. Museum officials, for instance, agreed not to release any photographic images publicly without permission of the CAFN.[75] Although the scientific team would have vastly preferred that the remains be curated for further studies, they respected the CAFN decision to cremate and reinter the ashes. Archaeologists would, of course, have wished to study the associated medicine bundle and its contents, but they too abided by tribal wishes for privacy. Many of the scientists involved in the project had previously studied the remains of Ötzi, the famous fifty-three-hundred-year-old "iceman" from the Austrian-Italian Alps; to them, it seemed natural to draw parallels to the New World "iceman," but responding to the wishes of CAFN, the scientists agreed that the term *iceman* will never appear in the scientific literature discussing Kwäday Dän Ts'ínchi.[76] "We are lucky in that we have a long-standing tradition of cooperation between archaeologists in the Yukon and British Columbia and Elders of the Champagne and Aishihik First Nations," asserts Paige MacFarlane, an official with the Canadian government in British Columbia. "Because of this relationship, we have been permitted to go ahead with an in-depth analysis of the remains."[77] Grant Hughes, head of the research project at Royal British Columbia Museum, agrees, suggesting that the case of Kwäday Dän

[75] Kim Lunman, "Iceman Provides Clues to Life before Columbus" (2000), http-www.shopyank.com/docs/gmarticle.html

[76] James H. Dickson (personal communication). The power to name has been the single most enduring theme throughout the centuries of Indian-Euroamerican interaction because the names ultimately reflect the power to conquer and control. Naming is central to the writing of history, and history is a primary way we define ourselves. By explicitly recognizing the importance of native names and by acknowledging previous difficulties in the lasting legacy of the finders-keepers strategy, scientists have been able to pursue their studies in a more respectful, more sensitive manner; see also Thomas, *Skull Wars*, chapter 1.

[77] Angela M. H. Schuster (1999), "Who's Buried in the Ice?" *Archaeology Online News*, September 15, 1999.

Ts'ínchį is "a model of cooperation between a First Nation and a museum to allow for respectful research. We have this balance between the needs of the scientific community and the cultural sensitivities to the aboriginal community. This is a project where we're respecting both."[78]

Robert McLaughlin speaks of "a more introspective" brand of museum anthropology that is being practiced during the NAGPRA era.[79] Although the Willamette meteorite and KDT cases did not generate the headlines associated with Kennewick Man, they may well indicate future directions for resolving disputes over cultural heritage and reburial issues.

Archaeologists and Native Americans increasingly agree on certain key issues: The past is important – we should attempt to understand it and preserve whatever remains of it. As we saw in the case of Kwädąy Dän Ts'ínchį, the archaeological evidence may support CAFN land claims over disputed territory. Some tribes have used their own archaeology to promote tribal sovereignty, a critical social and political issue throughout Indian Country. Many tribes and First Nations today maintain large and effective archaeology programs that employ both Indian and non-Indian archaeologists. Some native groups are conducting archaeology to encourage tourism, to inform educational programs, and to preserve sacred sites on their own land. Several tribes sponsor their own museums that display archaeological materials. The Society for American Archaeology (SAA) sponsors a Native American Scholarship Fund – named after Arthur S. Parker, an American Indian who served as the SAA's first president – encouraging Indian people to train as professional archaeologists and funded, in part, from royalties earned on books written by archaeologists about the Native American past. Throughout Native North America, Indian people are increasingly involved in archaeological meetings and publications – not merely as "informants," but as participants and collaborators.

Perhaps the lasting legacy of the Kennewick Man dispute is that of negative role model. Litigation and legislation appear to be increasingly unattractive ways to settle conflicts over cultural patrimony and intellectual property rights. Over the past decade, we can document literally dozens (and dozens) of cases in which American Indian and scientific interests have elected to work together to resolve their differences amicably, in a process that the ethnologist Michael Brown characterizes as "thoughtful people

[78] Kim Lunman, "Iceman Provides Clues to Life" (2000).
[79] Robert H. McLaughlin, "NAGPRA, Dialogue, and the Politics of Historical Authority," in Jennifer R. Richman and Marion P. Forsyth (eds), *Legal Perspectives on Cultural Resources* (Walnut Creek, CA, AltaMira Press, 2004): 185–201.

coming together to negotiate workable solutions, however provisional and inelegant."[80] Perhaps the Kennewick case will be viewed as a worst-case scenario – quite literally, a court of last resort – for resolving disputes between American Indians and the non-Indians who wish to study them.

Belittling the *Unum* to Glorify the *Pluribus?*

I conclude with a couple of comments intended to situate my discussion within the larger issues addressed in this volume: Specifically, what does NAGPRA tell us about the potential return of the great artworks, acquired in a bygone age of imperialism, that now reside in the great museums of the first world?

There are, to be sure, some obvious parallels among repatriation efforts around the globe. With respect to Native American heritage issues, I emphasize how "finders keepers" and "the name game" have established the agenda under which the rest of the European encounter would be played out. After discovering a patch of "unclaimed" land, the conqueror would wade ashore and plant his royal banner. He proclaimed that these newly discovered lands were now his patron's domain and laid claim to the new-found riches, the natural resources, and the things living and inanimate – all of which was simply wilderness before being "discovered" and defined by Europeans. During the Golden Age of Discovery, European colonial powers competed in a high-stakes game of finders keepers. The power to name reflected an underlying power to control the land, its indigenous people, its history, and its cultural items.

Similar processes, of course, phrase the discussion over the return, or not, of the great works: Were the "Elgin Marbles" rescued from certain destruction? Or were the "Parthenon Marbles," the "Athenian Marbles," or even the "Phidian Marbles" spirited away in defiance of their deeper ties to ancient and modern Greek culture? Clearly, the nuancing of names will always be an issue in framing the repatriation debates.

More broadly, I must admit that my own anthropological bias comes into play here. As Clemency Coggins, an archaeologist with extensive experience in Latin America, has aptly noted, "Anthropologists who work with the indigenous cultures of America like to emphasize that history is continuous," whereas "historians and guardians of the ancient heritage tend to compartmentalize history for the sake of explanation, and seldom make

---

[80] Michael F. Brown, "*Who Owns Native Culture?*," 9; see also Thomas, "Skull Wars," 254–267.

a convincing connection with the present."[81] As an anthropologist, then, I tend to privilege a "longer view" of historical processes than do my colleagues in the fields of art history and international law.

This dynamic shifts somewhat the focus of the repatriation debate. In the past, European explorers invented the American Indian, and American colonists incorporated this Indian imagery into mainstream history as part of the nation-building process. The resulting narrative lionizes national heroes and emphasizes the most dramatic events of the exploration, settlement, and development of new territory. Histories that minority people tell about themselves – Irish history, black history, Armenian history, and Indian tribal history – become invisible and irrelevant to this national American epic. Courts have long given preference to the testimony of non-Indian historians and anthropologists over the authority of tribal elders. Legal authorities have long discounted tribal perspectives, yet they commonly accept at face value the firsthand written observations of European colonists.

The 1990 NAGPRA legislation explicitly acknowledges that Indian pasts are relevant to the American present. This public and quite visible benchmark reflects a deep-seated shifting in thinking, one that emphasizes America's self-perception as a multifaceted, pluralistic society. NAGPRA, in effect, is monitoring the shift away from an American creed grounded in the time-honored melting pot to newer perspectives recognizing the merits of a multicultural society.

The backlash, of course, has been heard as well. Many mainstream Americans still believe that the "real, authentic" Indians did indeed vanish a century ago. There is great concern that revisionist myth making and a lack of objectivity may reflect a pandering to a political correctness of the moment, by both Congress and Indian people. With the melting pot metaphor under attack, critics such as Arthur Schlesinger worry about an America "giving ground to the celebration of ethnicity. . . . The multiethnic dogma abandons historic purposes, replacing assimilation by fragmentation, integration by separatism. It belittles *unum* and glorifies *pluribus*."[82]

This is why I am uncomfortable in viewing international repatriation strictly through the lens of "postcolonial" thought. Rather than emphasizing

[81]   Clemency Coggins, 2002. "Latin America, Native America, and the Politics of Culture," in *Claiming the Stones, Naming the Bones: Cultural Property and the Negotiation of National and Ethnic Identity*, edited by Elazar Barkan and Ronald Bush, Los Angeles, CA: The Getty Research Institute, 2002, pp. 97–115.

[82]   Arthur M. Schlesinger, Jr., *The Disuniting of America: Reflections on a Multicultural Society* (New York: W. W. Norton and Company, 1992), page 18.

decisions over imperial plunder acquired in a bygone age, NAGPRA forces us to recognize that new archaeological finds – such as Kennewick Man and Person Long Ago Found – will continue to crop up in the twenty-first century, and their disposition will always reflect an intense political undercurrent. At least in the New World, the repatriation dialogue must be balanced, therefore, between adjudicating heritage claims from the past and establishing a workable mechanism for resolving disputes that will continue to arise in the here-and-now.

Made in the USA
Lexington, KY
31 July 2014